VERY FAR FROM NORMAL

the real journals of a wife betrayed

By

Josie Allen

Cottage Porch
Press

Cottage Porch Press

PO Box 7646

Clearwater, FL 33758

cottageporchpress@gmail.com

www.cottageporchpress.com

Paperback ISBN 978-0-578-86126-5

Cover design by Keith Conforti

Book design by Barbara Aronica-Buck

Manufactured in the US

They say it takes a village, and this author is so thankful for the village that held her broken parts together, even when she could not.

With tremendous amounts of love and gratitude for Jason, Krista, Catherine, Mike, Jhodessa, Miki, Johannah, Sadie, Noah, Patty, Sara, Joe, Eddie, Rindy, Amanda, Lena, my family, who held me up to the light. Thank you to my wonderful team: Sue Maxwell Rasmussen, my editor, Keith Conforti, whose cover artwork is jaw dropping, and Barbara Aronica-Buck, who made beauty look so easy. Thank you to Daisy—you're beautiful. Thank you to Kent who believed in me and helped me find a way, and to Sue, who led me to Steve, who led me to you.

"One day you will tell your story of how you overcame what you went through, and it will be someone else's survival guide."

–Brené Brown

This book is dedicated to my heroes, Joh, Jemily, Buddy and Lulu. I love you to pieces.

This is my story. It is in turn mundane, fascinating, and frightening. It is also true.

This is not a self-help book. I am not a doctor, nor am I a therapist. I took just one psychology class in college. I am not a writer although, for the last ten years, I've had a story rolling around in my head, driving me crazy—a romantic story—historical fiction. I even began to research it. Then my life changed. This is definitely not that story.

This is my story. Mine and Sam's. I am telling it because when it happened, when my life came crashing to a halt, I felt entirely alone. I felt like no one could ever possibly understand what was going on in my head or in my life. Hell, I couldn't even understand it. My shame was a palpable thing. It gripped me like a vice, and I felt myself suffocating under the weight of it. As I began to heal, as we began to heal, I thought if I could just reach one person whose life is in tatters, let one person know that they are not alone, then maybe I would begin to understand how and why it all happened. Maybe, after feeling like I was shredded into a mass of bloody ribbon, I could put the pieces back together and make a difference for someone, somewhere. So, this is my story, but it could be yours too.

I once wrote a short story that won a prize. But then, in my incredibly vulnerable high school years, I was led to believe that I was not, and probably never would be, a writer. Since writing made me feel exposed, I avoided it at all costs. I went to college in a small coastal New England town. While there, I chose every alternative project that I could in order to avoid writing papers. I have never, until that horrible January, kept a journal. When my marriage abruptly ceased to exist, I began to write everything down. For me it was an act of survival, an alternative to crawling into bed and never getting up. I wrote every day for a year, four books full. That is what I have to offer—companionship, an end to the isolation. It is intended to be a support for anyone who is undertaking the same struggle. It will not provide answers, but you will know you are not alone. And as the information superhighway makes it easier for those wishing to live a secret life, our ranks will continue to grow.

In order to understand what happened, it is important to start at the beginning. Sam and I met as I was graduating from college. I moved to The City by the Sea where I was hired to be part of a summer theater company. He was the director; I was an actress and the costumer for this small band of players. Fifteen years my senior, he was a journalist at the local paper. He was handsome, articulate, warm, and attentive. We found lots to talk about, to laugh about. Our friendship grew quickly. He was married to a dancer who was dramatic, flamboyant, and waif-like. They had two of the most adorable little girls, blonde and curly haired. What I didn't know at first was just how unhappy his marriage was. She would breeze in to bring him lunch, keeping a watchful eye on all the girls in the company. What he never let on was that she was actually checking up on him. As the summer passed, something happened. We began to fall in love.

We dated all through his very long, ugly, drawn-out divorce. My friends didn't understand the attraction and I'm not sure I did either. I came from a broken home and, since visits with my father were sporadic, I had never really had the attention of a man in my life. I was searching for someone to love and Sam stepped in. He made me feel beautiful and intelligent and wanted and loved.

I moved to New York to pursue my acting career. I was hoping he would call me home to him. But he was working hard to sort out his life. We continued like this, from a distance. I worked for an off-Broadway theater and a professional ballet company; he continued his life in The City by the Sea. Four years later, after long distance dating, much discussion and decision making, we came back together. I moved back to The City by the Sea and we moved in together. We found a lovely apartment in an old mansion. It had brick walls and built-in bookcases. We began to make a home for us and for his girls.

I had never known a more loving, generous person. Christmas was magical! My stocking was filled with lingerie, jewelry, and makeup. There were clothes, shoes, boots and purses, books, music, all unique and well thought out. I felt like a princess. We surrounded ourselves with books, music, laughter, and amazing lovemaking. I blossomed in the glow of his love. He was a wonderful father. I was building a strong relationship with his beautifully vibrant daughters, Becca and Rachel, and we were happy. We had each other and it seemed like that was all we would ever need.

After we had been together for just over a year, his ex-wife remarried and decided to move fifteen hundred miles away to Iowa. Panic set in. His girls were with us every other day. He was definitely not an "every other weekend" dad. We spent the next eight months trying to keep his children from being uprooted and dragged from the only home they'd ever known, a quaint, mansard-roof Victorian in The City by the Sea. It was an incredibly costly battle, both financially and emotionally. There was constant underlying tension. Becca was six, and Rachel was twelve. They were feeling caught in the middle. We tried hard to take the high ground, but the children still struggled and so did Sam. After eight grueling months, we lost the court battle and four days later they were gone. I was afraid he would never recover. The love of my life, this beautifully spiritual, incredibly loving man was completely torn apart. I felt helpless.

But life continued, as it does, and we moved on. In order to pay our legal fees, we gave up our sweet little apartment and moved in with his parents. He visited his girls in Iowa as often as we could afford it. They came to us a few times a year, but never without a great deal of drama from their mother and new stepfather. The first summer, they arrived for five weeks with empty suitcases. I got a job at a retail store that sold children's clothing so I could clothe them. It was hard on us and hard on them. It was not the picture we had painted for ourselves, but it was what we had, and we were determined to make the best of it.

I opened a business, a preschool, with a wonderful woman I'd met at my job. It took off faster than any of us anticipated. A year later, Sam and I bought an old colonial home with wide pine floors and fireplaces in all the rooms. A house we could live in forever, raise our family in, and one day entertain our grandchildren. And then seven years after we met, Sam and I got married, in our flower-filled backyard in The City by the Sea, with our families and children there to share the day. It was a magical time.

Sam and I would walk through the cobbled streets and dream. We'd talk of our life and our plans. We'd go to church, window shop and just spend hours being together, quietly in our old house in The City by the Sea. We were so excited when I became pregnant. We found out we were having a boy and Sam was walking on air. I was thrilled. In the meantime, his ex-wife had had two more daughters with her new husband. Rachel was the oldest, but now there was another oldest for the new husband and another baby. I wanted Becca to still be someone's baby girl. She was really struggling with the move and her new life. She was a sweet girl, but when they would arrive for a visit, it would take several days of her swearing like a sailor until she could calm down and just be a kid.

Our son Caleb was fittingly born on Thanksgiving Day. Both girls loved their baby brother. He was blonde and blue-eyed and the happiest child I'd ever seen. He had a huge toothless grin that could bring tears to my eyes. I never knew I could love someone as much as I loved my baby boy. He grew to be bright and articulate and incredibly engaging. We were so happy, Sam, Caleb, and me. With the success of my preschool and Sam's income, we were doing great financially, and his girls told us they wanted to move home and live with us. But there was more drama and heartache from Iowa and that idea was squashed.

In many ways, our life looked like a Norman Rockwell painting. We were deeply in love. We did everything together. He was a well-respected journalist, and I ran a school so in demand that our registration days took on the quality of a Macy's handbag sale. Our home was cozy and so was our life. I baked cookies and we ate dinner by candlelight. We had created a life that would be forever.

Then my business lost its home and we scrambled to find a new location. It was a time of stress, but we were still feeling like we were connected and on solid ground. When Caleb was three and a half, I became pregnant again. I was almost thirty-five and Sam was a day away from fifty. I gave him baby booties for his birthday. I was thrilled; Sam was terrified–something he didn't let on, but it came out later in lots of little miserable ways. We sold our beautiful old house to buy a big Victorian home where we would live above my preschool.

Sam had been a journalist with the local paper for twenty years. My school was flourishing. When sweet baby Faye was born, it looked like we had put our lives back on track. Then, six weeks later, Sam was abruptly fired from his job. They said he was falsifying his timecards–something he vehemently denied. I believed him. I mean, why wouldn't I? He loved me, I adored him, and he'd never been anything but honest with me, right?

I've always been a problem solver, so as scary as it was, I looked at it like a blessing in disguise. He would stay home with baby Faye instead of sending her to childcare. I cut my maternity leave short by two months and I went back to work, and we learned to live with much less. The problem was that Sam was not a stay-at-home dad. He was a babysitter. Because of that, I stepped on a crazy treadmill and could never seem to get off. We were not making ends meet so we both went to work at The Theatre, the local dinner theater company–seven to nine shows a week on top of the forty hours I was putting in at the preschool. I kept this job for years. When Caleb was four and a half and Faye was five months old, my schedule looked something like this:

5:30 a.m.

   Get up

   Make coffee

   Nurse Faye

   Wake Caleb

   Make breakfast

   Pack lunch

   Shower and dress

7:00 a.m.

   Wake Sam

   Get Caleb and Sam out the door to school

   Fold Laundry

7:30 a.m.

   Get to work (job #1)

9:30 a.m.

   Come home and nurse Faye then back to work

1:00 p.m.

   Do it again

3:30 p.m.

   Go home

   Play with both kids

   Start homework for Caleb

4:00 p.m.

   Start dinner and laundry

5:00 p.m.

   Feed and bathe kids

6:30 p.m.

   Leave for the theater (job#2)

11:30 p.m.

    Come home and switch laundry

    Cleanup the house and pack the school bags for tomorrow

12:30 a.m.

    Nurse Faye one more time and climb into bed

Where was Sam? Reading. Drinking wine, "taking care of Faye" during the day. He couldn't see me drowning. Or, now looking back, maybe he could. When I had a post-delivery follow-up with the doctor, Sam told me to ask him what was wrong with my libido. I was shocked.

"What?" I asked.

"You don't initiate sex anymore. Find out what's wrong."

I was so embarrassed, but I did it. My doctor looked at me for a minute and said, "Your husband told you to ask that, didn't he?" I nodded.

"You tell him if he wants more sex, he needs to do more around the house."

I thought this would be a turning point! I went home and told Sam. He responded, "He can't just give you a pill?"

I didn't put it together. You must be thinking I'm incredibly blind or a special kind of stupid, but this was my husband! The man who loved me. It was bound to turn around. I was not a disposable marriage kind of person. When I said, "Till death do us part," I meant it, and I knew he did too.

Now as I said, I'm a problem solver by nature. I read an article somewhere; it may have even been in the doctor's office that day, about how to keep the flame burning even when you're not really feeling it. I determined to work sex into my already crazy schedule. Every other night, I made sure that we had sex before I fell into an exhausted sleep.

It did get better. A little bit. Things seemed to find their own rhythm and we moved on, but the pace of my life never let up. A year and a half later, Sam's father died. He was a wonderful man, engaging and loving, but he'd been suffering with Alzheimer's disease for several years by then. Sam's mother had cared for him, even though she was legally blind from Macular Degeneration. They were so in love. It really warmed my heart watching them walk down the aisle in church on Sundays, always holding hands. None of us thought she'd last long without him. After she moved in with Sam's sister and her husband, she asked us to move into her now empty house. Although his sister was mean and miserable, it would be a good move for us, so we left The City by the Sea and moved one town over. It was a great area with better schools. The only thing that didn't get better was my life on the treadmill.

By this time, Sam was working in a group home with developmentally disabled adults, a job I found for him in the local paper. He was working for a fraction of his old income. We were always strapped financially, and he never could seem to feel motivated to make things better for his family. My sister-in-law used to sneer that we had "the deal of the century," living in her parents' house, and she wasn't wrong. We just didn't have anything else.

She was an interesting person. She could be nice one minute and then completely flip and become someone else entirely. She was verbally abusive to her mother. The whole neighborhood could hear her when the windows were open in the summer. My brother-in-law used to come talk with me where our gardens met. I had planted a little garden with Caleb and Faye. We would go out to weed and water, and my brother-in-law would come out to work in his garden. He would tell me how bad things were in his house and beg me to take Sam's mother in. I finally did. She was eighty-eight. Now I added elderly caregiver to my list of jobs.

As time went by, something else that became a struggle for me was Sam's developing obsession with porn. He collected it. There was a big box full of it in the upstairs closet. There was a big garbage bag full of it under his side of the bed. We'd fight over it. I'd throw it away and more would appear. He always said it was given to him. I was too tired to argue or think otherwise. Caleb found it once when he was about seven or eight. I walked into my bedroom and my son was on the floor, on Sam's side of the bed, looking at the covers of the videos that Sam kept there. My heart broke. I threw it out. More showed up. I tried to be diligent, but Sam just kept calling me uptight and a prude. I began to think he was right. Maybe he just needed something to boost his self-esteem.

A friend was selling her store in a beautiful wharf area back in The City by the Sea. It was a tiny store, a venue for artists, mostly local. Sam loved art and was an outgoing, engaging man who loved to share his knowledge about the city. In a city that saw a lot of tourists, it seemed like the perfect opportunity, so I encouraged Sam to buy it. I thought it would be just what he would need to bolster his self-confidence. I was wrong. After a while it began to look unkempt, just like Sam. In a couple of years, he had run it and our finances into the ground. We were on the edge of bankruptcy. We were more broke than we had ever been. He needed to close the store. I played it up as a great thing with our children, now eight and twelve. Dad was going to be home more. We could do things all together instead of just them and me. I was constantly trying to find the positive, because when you love someone, your gut may be telling you something, but your love and commitment creates a blind spot that works against it.

I thought this was my life. Since I had never been married before, I thought this was what marriage must be and it would be like this always. Sam was struggling. I was unhappy. And then it stopped. Just like that.

BOOK ONE

If I were to make this into a movie, it would be dismissed as implausible and over the top.

Sunday, January 20

All thoughts of writing a book were gone now. The silly, romantic story that had been plaguing me had evaporated into thin air. There was an entirely different story now and I felt if I could write the story down, it would hurt less. It didn't work.

It all started with a snow day. It was January 13th and we had just returned from spending the weekend with my father and step-mother in Maine. My aunt Bitsy was there as well as my sister Hannah and her boys. We celebrated a late Christmas together. It was wonderful to have Sam there for the first time in a long time. The kids were amazingly happy and well behaved.

It was Monday and, although it didn't snow much, it was enough so that the schools were closed. I was relieved to have the day to tackle the mountain of laundry that had built up, and our bedroom was a Christmas disaster. After putting away the last of the Christmas things, I thought I would help relieve some of the pressure Sam was feeling over finances. He had recently received loan consolidation paperwork from a local company, and I thought I would read through it. I remembered that he had left it on his nightstand, but when it wasn't there, I looked in his briefcase. I didn't find the loan papers. What I did find was a pink canvas case. Curious, I unzipped it and found that it contained a vibrator as well as another sex toy that I couldn't even name. I felt numb. It was as if I were watching myself in slow motion as I looked through the bag. I found several condoms and a feathered sex toy I had seen before.

The only words I have to describe how I felt as I waited for him to come home would be "basket case." I asked him outright if he was having an affair. He paused and looked at me for a moment and then said, "Of course not. Who would I be having an affair with?"

I showed him what I had found in his briefcase. He began to pace around our bedroom, his words tumbling out, and told me he had bought the feathered thing in London for us. I knew that. He said the condoms were ancient. That was also probably true. Then my husband, the man I loved, while avoiding my eyes, said he had found the vibrator in the store when he had been cleaning it out. I asked him where he had found it. He paused. "Upstairs." I pointed out that I was the one to clean upstairs and that it had definitely not been there. I asked him why it had batteries in it from an open pack in his drawer, a store brand. Another pause. "What?"

He frantically began to explain that first he had found the vibrator upstairs in his store. Then he moved it and put it downstairs under the counter. After that he brought it home because he thought we might use it. I felt like throwing up. I pressed him again about the batteries and his story changed. Now he said he had brought it home and put batteries in it to see if it worked. I didn't believe him. I told him to "get that thing the fuck out of my house!" He didn't say anything more. He got up and threw away the vibrator and the condoms and put the feathered thing on his bureau.

That night, when he was kissing the kids goodnight, I went through his phone. There were the usual numbers, some I recognized and some I didn't. There was a number marked ET. I should have written it down. I should have known it would come up later. He slept in our bed and I slept on the couch. Actually, I slept very little.

The next day he kept insisting that he had done nothing wrong, but everything felt wrong. This was not my husband, not my marriage, not my life.

When I came home from work, I began to search in earnest. I was on the computer checking email and decided to pull up the history. There was a website with a very high number of hits. It was www.ALT.com and he had been on it nearly every day. I pulled it up and was literally sick at what I found. ALT.com is a website for alternative lifestyles, S&M, and bondage and domination. He had not only registered but had also been looking up people in our area who were interested in "active participation."

I was paralyzed by fear. I had no idea what to do. I am rarely at a loss when it comes to jumping in to fix things, but this time, I didn't even know what to think, let alone what to do. I called my friend Shawn. Shaking uncontrollably, I told him everything. Shawn never acted surprised. His voice was soothing and calm, settling me down. He told me to go in and register to see if I could find Sam. I had no idea how to even go about it. There were more than twelve thousand members in my area alone. For all I knew, he had had sex with all of them. I felt absolutely exhausted.

That night, he came home from work early. It made me

wonder if he actually worked until 11:00 p.m. after all. I confronted him about ALT.com. I tried to keep calm, but he kept lying to me. He said he found the site in a weekly newspaper and only went on for a laugh to see if there was anybody he knew. I told him I didn't believe him, and I didn't trust him either. At that point, I asked him to simply tell me the truth—lay it all out on the table—but he assured me there was nothing more to tell.

After a long silence, he stunned me again when he tried turning the whole thing on me. He asked me why I looked up an old friend from high school the year before. I couldn't believe it. I told him that I look up a lot of people from my past—old friends and colleagues, old boyfriends and roommates, his ex-wife—and that in no way could my searches compare to what he was doing. Then things really began to escalate.

I completely lost my cool and threw my wedding rings at him, yelling something about keeping it in his pants. Right then, Caleb walked in the room. Poor kid. He was naturally upset. He began to feel ill the next day and ended up missing two days of school. I was ashamed of the behavior he observed. No child should ever witness that kind of ugliness between his parents. That night I slept no better on the couch.

The following day, I talked with my best friend, Sophie. *She moved to The City by the Sea at the same time I did. She is a school counselor and therapist who had just gone through a divorce herself. She is the sister I would choose.* So calming and rational, she was just what I needed when life seemed increasingly insane.

Things were strained but calm over the next couple of days until Friday when my life, as I knew it, blew completely apart.

When I got home from work, Sam went out to run a couple of errands. While he was gone, I went back on the computer to see if he had been back on ALT.com. He hadn't. What I did see that I hadn't noticed before was a Gmail account that was being checked frequently. Now things were beginning to make more sense to me. When I had registered myself on ALT.com, they emailed me a password. When I had asked Sam what email account he had used to get his password, he told me it was our joint email account. I knew that wasn't true. It was time for us to talk again.

After everyone was in bed, I sat down to talk with my husband of nearly fifteen years. I asked him about the Gmail account. He ignored the question and just kept insisting that there was nothing going on, just some innocent looking. When I told him I was not going to let him sidestep the question, He admitted to having the account. He told me that when Becca had come home for Christmas, he was asking about her account and so she helped him set up his own.

"Why do you need it? Who emails you?" I asked.

"Well, you're not going to be happy about this." He gave a long, drawn-out sigh and said, "My friend Bonnie from Vermont."

Years ago, I had found inappropriately suggestive emails going back and forth between Sam and Bonnie. I thought I had put a stop to it then but apparently not. They had been an item before Sam and I got together.

"How long has this been going on?" I asked. "Apparently you think I'm stupid."

I told him to log in to his email account. There it was, in his inbox, an email from Bonnie. I was starting to feel sick but then

I opened up his trash folder and thought, *oh my God*. There is nothing in your life that can possibly prepare you for something like what I found. There were seventy-seven emails from Bonnie, ALT.com, correspondence from people he had been trying to hook up with on Craigslist, and still other people responding to his MySpace page. That was yet another shock—he listed himself as forty-nine and single. Then there was ET. Emily Ty.

"Who is she?" I asked.

"Someone who wants to have an affair with me."

"Bullshit. I know you better than that."

The bottom fell out of my world and I could barely breathe. This man, whom I had known and loved for twenty-two years, was having at least one affair, and was soliciting sex from nameless, faceless people. Not just sex. Emily wanted him to buy a riding crop and he had been searching online for one. Then came the most devastating line when I read, "I really want to direct "The Country Wife" and put you in it." It was more than just sex. No wonder he wouldn't discuss any kind of theater project with me. Sam and I had dreamed for years about opening a local theater. It was a big part of our bond but, as time went on, he wanted to talk less and less about it, and I didn't understand why.

Monday, January 21

I had to get out of the house. I couldn't be near him or else I would vomit. I got in my car and called Sophie. She could barely understand me. I sat in her living room, in my pajamas and big winter boots, a birthday present from Sam, and talked and cried for over two hours. She helped me find a little clarity end cautioned me not to jump to rash decisions. I told her I thought I screamed the word "divorce" at Sam before I left. I couldn't even say it without a fresh flood of tears. Sophie helped me focus on the kids and concentrate on getting through each day one minute at a time.

When I returned home at 2:00 a.m., I found Sam in the family room. As I sat down on the couch, I couldn't remember a time I had felt so exhausted. I told him I wanted him to move out for a week. I couldn't even look at him and think straight. I saw the man that I loved, the man that had fathered my children and shared my hopes and dreams. I had to come to terms with the man that shit all over that love and trust. I was so hurt. I was angrier than I had ever been. I felt as if every nerve was exposed and bleeding. I slept, though not really, in Caleb's bed. He was at a sleepover, thank God. I fell asleep crying and woke up crying.

The next morning, Sam looked like shit, pale and unkempt. I think he wanted me to feel sorry for him but there was no way. He had utterly betrayed me. He had lied and manipulated me for God knows how long.

He talked to his mother and then to the kids. It was awful and I wanted him to go. His mother was confused and judgmental and the kids were anxious and angry. I had no idea how I would ever get through this. I began to clean. It was as if I thought scouring the refrigerator would somehow remove the filth that had settled on my life. I couldn't eat; my stomach hurt. And yet, I was worried about Sam.

Before he left, Sam placed a call to our old therapist, Dan, and left a message. *When Caleb was struggling socially in school, we started seeing Dan as a family. We had been to see him both*

individually and also in a group, on and off for several years. I
called Dan, too, and finally reached him in the afternoon. I could
barely choke out the words as I told him what was going on. I felt
so humiliated. Dan called me back later to tell me he and Sam had
made an appointment. He said Sam would be staying at his late
uncle's house. I was just thankful he wasn't in his car; it was only
eight degrees outside. Then Dan said he didn't think Sam was
suicidal. I started crying again.

Later, it hit me. I realized that when I went to my next OB/
GYN appointment, I would have to tell my doctor that I needed
to be tested for STD's and HIV. I was terrified and overwhelmed
with the shame of it all.

After a dinner that I couldn't eat, I spent the entire evening on
the computer checking everything. I saw some email addresses I
knew and some I'd never seen before. Then, there were the personal ads he had answered on Craigslist. He had been cruising for
W4M and T4M. I wasn't entirely sure what those meant. I also
found a map to a house three towns over. I wondered if it led to
one of the people on Craigslist. Man or woman? He had already
closed his MySpace account and deleted his email.

One thing I did discover, while searching online for support,
was that my husband was the poster child for sexual addiction.
For some people, sex can be as addictive as a narcotic and, over
time, the addict needs more and more to stay stimulated. How
on earth could I not have seen this? I used to laugh, thinking that
sex addicts were cartoonish women, crazy nymphomaniacs that
hopped from one bed to the next. Somehow, it wasn't so funny
anymore. He exhibited all the symptoms:

Excessive masturbation
Excessive ownership of porn
Cruising the web for porn
Inappropriate comments and finding sexual innuendo
everywhere
Casual and anonymous sex
Affairs

The websites I found on sexual addiction also talked about my role as codependent. Did I really know? I wondered, was my whole marriage a lie? Had he been unfaithful since the beginning? God, it made me feel so stupid.

When he talked to his girls, Becca and Rachel, I was afraid he would present it to them the same way as he did when he talked with his mother. He said that we were overwhelmed by the issues in our lives, particularly financial, and we needed some time apart. I knew they would think I threw him out of the house because he didn't make enough money and they would hate me. He didn't seem to care how many people were going to suffer because of what he had done.

At this point, I absolutely hated him. I saw him as nothing more than a cowardly, lying piece of shit. Angry thoughts swirled around in my head. *This must be why he doesn't have a job. This is why he can't support his family. This is probably why his store failed. He was locking the door and using it as a place to have little private fuck fests.* I felt sick to my stomach. I had to get out of the house—his mother's house. I felt trapped, angry, and alone.

Tuesday, January 22

I still was unable to get a handle on all of this. I felt like I had to repeat the same thoughts over and over in my head, like a child writing lines on the blackboard. "I will not talk in class. I will not talk in class."

My husband is a liar.

My husband is unfaithful.

My husband is untrustworthy.

My husband is having an affair.

My husband is soliciting sex.

My husband has a secret life.

My husband is probably into things I can't even guess.

It was surreal and absurd. Unfortunately, it was also true.

Wednesday, January 23

It was a rough day and I'm still not sure how I made it through, but I did. I went to see my OB/GYN in the morning. He came into the room with a big smile and asked about the surgery I recently had. That felt like another lifetime ago, but it had only been just under three weeks. I told him everything seemed fine—there weren't any more leaks from my bladder. Then I took a deep breath and told him I had a problem. My body, betraying me completely, began to tremble from deep within. Before I completely lost my nerve, I told him I needed to be tested for all STDs. I'm not sure what kind of reaction I expected, but he was phenomenal. He was calm and never even gave a mild look of surprise. After examining me, he said I looked clear for gonorrhea and chlamydia but would need a blood test for syphilis and HIV. I didn't even know how to spell those diseases. I wanted to try and go in the next morning for blood work, but I also had to take my mother-in-law to her accountant. I would feel better once I knew, one way or another.

I had to go home to pick something up and Sam was there. I felt absolutely nothing. I talked to my landlord at the school about staying at his house while he was away. It would give me a little bit of power and choice, and I wouldn't feel quite so trapped.

Gabriel called me from The Theatre in the afternoon. He wanted to see how I was doing but I didn't want to talk to him. *Being an actor requires a certain amount of vulnerability onstage. Barriers come down and, without even realizing it, lines can be crossed. It was that way with Gabriel. We had been friends for years and, after a while, I began to care about him more than I should. One night, backstage, we shared an intimate moment and a kiss. He was still married at the time, although separated, and also involved with someone, and I wasn't looking for more. I just loved the way he made me feel. The way Sam used to.*

My friend Faith called. *She's a redhead, warm, outspoken, and fiercely loyal. Sam can't stand her.* On the way to school in the carpool, Caleb had confided in her husband, Jasper. He immediately called Faith who then called me, very worried. I didn't tell her anything other than the fact that Sam and I had separated.

I only talked to Sophie because she doesn't judge. She really was the voice of reason. I simply refused to get into a husband-bashing game with anyone, even if it came from Faith's big heart. My husband was sick. That was the only explanation I had.

There was a part of me that, despite what he had done, wanted to protect him from what people were going to think and say when they found out. Maybe that was how I enabled him. Maybe that was my codependency showing.

I managed to eat dinner with the kids without getting sick. That was progress.

Thursday, January 24

One step forward and two steps back. I was on the verge of tears all day long. I went to the hospital for my blood work and managed to hold it together, despite the feelings of intense shame. My head was pounding, and my stomach was in knots. As I was leaving the hospital, I started to cry. I just wanted to wake up to see that it was all some outrageous nightmare.

I went to the bookstore to get the book that Sophie recommended, *Should I Stay or Should I Go?*[1] It was out of stock and I had to order it. Another bout of tears. On the way home, I realized I had forgotten to buy milk. I stopped at a local convenience store and Sam was there with Caleb. He was buying milk. I cried all the way home and then again when I had to actually speak to him. It was brief, awkward, and painful, as he was leaving.

Sam and I needed to sit down and talk, really talk. A lot of where we went from there would depend on how honest he was with me. How would I believe him anyway? I came to the realization that I had spent exactly half of my life, my entire adult life, loving him. Twenty-two years. I was twenty-two when we met, and

---

[1] Lundy Bancroft and Jac Patrissi, *Should I Stay, or Should I Go? A Guide to Knowing if Your Relationship Can – and Should – be Saved* (Berkeley: Penguin, 2011)

now I am forty-four. No wonder I feel so sick.

I thought about my meeting with Caroline the following day. *She is the therapist that Dan highly recommended. Dan decided he would not be able to treat both Sam and me and gave me Caroline's name.* I wondered If I would even be able to choke out the whole story.

Friday, January 25

Sam came to take Caleb to the carpool for school that morning. *Caleb went to a private school, recommended by Gabriel's wife, and was a full year younger than his classmates. He had been bullied in public school and absolutely loved Saint Andrews.* Faye wanted to ride to the carpool, too, and when he dropped her off at home afterwards, she came into the kitchen, her nose all red from the cold. She was trying to keep a brave face on and was so close to me, she was actually leaning on me. I wrapped my arms around her and told her it was perfectly all right to cry. Then I held my beautiful little girl while she sobbed and told me how much she missed her daddy. How could he do this to her? And to Caleb?

The meeting with Carolyn was liberating. For the first time, I was able to talk completely unguarded. I told her the entire sordid story—my nearly unbearable hurt and my terrible fear for the future and my children. I had no home of my own, no income, no resources other than my business, and the tremendous debt load. She suggested it would be best if I stayed put for the time being and keep my children in their home. It sounded like divorce-speak already.

In my shame, I told her I could put this together from an

intellectual point of view. I understood what had happened but emotionally I felt raw and bleeding. She looked at me with clear intelligent eyes and said, "Of course. You're hemorrhaging." I stopped and just stared at her and thought, *yes, I really am, and if I don't do something, I will bleed to death.* Caroline completely validated my emotions and assured me that, in spite of what I was feeling right then, I would be able to survive. How Caleb and Faye would come through the ordeal would depend entirely on the choices Sam and I made as the waters cleared and we began to deal with this mess.

As I was thinking later, I realized a big component of the difficulty I was experiencing was that Sam and I had been intertwined on so many levels for so many years. He was my husband, my lover, and the father of my children. Beyond that, he was also a colleague in the theater and my absolute very best friend. As I untangled the various levels of hurt and betrayal, I had to identify which of these relationships had been affected and which, if any, could be healed. A large part of that would hinge on his ability to face and take responsibility for what he had done.

Saturday, January 26

I was sure Becca and Rachel thought I threw their father out because he didn't make enough money. I hadn't heard from them lately. That saddened my heart even more if that was possible.

I had a good day, relatively speaking. I needed to get out of the house so that Sam could come over and help Caleb with his application for high school. Sophie invited me to go over to the university to see some architectural miniatures that had been in the attic of a local mansion. Faye and I trooped off with Sophie and her girls. The doll houses were exquisite. It was a relief to focus on something out of the ordinary, and it was nice to watch Faye relax and enjoy the day with her friends.

It was a win-win situation. Caleb got to spend some time with his dad, and I was able to get away from the house for a while. Sometimes it felt like a prison. I couldn't leave except to go to work because of my mother-in-law. We couldn't just go to a movie or spontaneously go out to dinner or meet up with friends. As if that weren't bad enough, I had no idea who he had brought into my home and what they had done and where. It made me feel trapped.

When I got home, Caleb asked me if Sam and I could switch places for a week. I couldn't tell him that there was no way his father was capable of caring for him right then. He wouldn't even be able to feed them for a week. I also couldn't tell him that I didn't trust Sam.

I had been thinking about what I would do if Sam didn't come clean. How would I react if he tried to introduce crop-wielding Emily into the lives of my vulnerable children? Just thinking about it made my stomach ache, something it hadn't done all day.

I checked the computer each day to see where he'd been. I noticed he was logging into his credit card accounts every day. I wondered why. What was he charging that he had to check on a daily basis? I had not been able to even remotely interest him in our household finances for the last five years. What was so interesting on those credit cards?

Sunday, January 27

Oh, dear God, what an awful day. I cried and grieved and had been angry and cried some more. My face hurt. My body hurt. My head hurt. My heart hurt. The kids both cried tonight after calling Sam to say goodnight. I did what I could to comfort them, but I couldn't give them any answers. I didn't want them to know what their father had done. My eyes burned and I felt tired and lost. It was probably a good thing I had my mother-in-law to take care of. I stayed up and wrote in my journal only because she needed medication between ten and eleven at night. Otherwise, I would have just gotten into bed when the kids did and slipped into an even deeper depression.

I was done mothering my husband. I had to concentrate on what I needed. I couldn't continue to let him come in the house looking like he had lost his best friend and to make me feel guilty. He was the liar! He was the betrayer! I told him he'd better pray to God that I didn't have an STD! Hell hath no fury . . .

Monday, January 28

The kids were in better spirits and that made it easier to get through the day. It broke my heart when they were sad. The natural parental instinct to shield them from ever feeling pain and loss had kicked into overdrive. Unrealistic but instinctual. That was what made me so angry with Sam. I could deal with divorce just fine. Well, not fine, but better than hurting his children. After a divorce, he could go out with his little girlfriends and his casual sex buddies and have as much fun as he wanted. I'm a big girl. I knew I could get over it, but Caleb and Faye were just children. They were innocent, vulnerable, and fragile, far more fragile than he understood.

I still had not heard from Becca or Rachel. I felt loss and anger over that too. The great relationship he enjoys with them is due in large part to my efforts, influence, and support. They were all so quick to dump me. What is wrong with this family?

What I needed from him right then was for him to lose the "oh poor me" look he was wearing around. The time for my pity was long over. He had a chance to have it and he threw it away, just like he threw away my love, my support, my friendship, our marriage, and our children. I hoped, for his sake, that it was all worth it.

I wondered if I would ever be able to trust anyone enough to be intimate again. Had I had sex for the last time?

Caroline told me at our first meeting that she was amazed that I was able to go to work. She said there are people who can't even get out of bed. I completely understood. I had been wandering through my days. I was functioning on a basic level but that was all. Putting an outfit together was beyond me. I wore the same black pants and gray turtleneck. I wasn't sure how I would get through the show at The Theatre when it reopened. *The Theatre closed for four weeks in January. When they reopened, they opened with the show that played in December. So, the play I was expected to open was a show I had already performed for five weeks. It was a cute little comedy about a couple that grows apart and she creates an imaginary lover. And Sam had not yet seen it.* I was not looking forward to it. I couldn't think about that now. It was making my head hurt.

Tuesday, January 29

I had my staff holiday party tonight. It was nice to have all the girls here for dinner. A welcome distraction and very different from last year.

It was another rough day. I had to call Sam about the electric bill. At over two thousand dollars, they were ready to turn it off. I had been asking Sam to deal with it for months. Apparently, he was too busy. We talked a little for the first time. He wanted to know when we could sit down and talk for real. I told him I didn't know, that I couldn't even look at him without crying. He said he cries all the time. I wanted to scream at him, "Big fucking deal! This is all your fault!" But what good would that have done? It would only have torn him down and made me petty, neither of which would be helpful. I told him that he would not get my pity. That the time for that was long over. I could hear him breathing as if each breath was a struggle for control. He declared how important I was to him. I couldn't believe him, and I told him so. He explained that he had been doing a lot of work with Dan, excruciatingly painful work. Honesty was the issue, I told him, and I was certain that neither Dan nor I knew even half of the story. He didn't deny it. There was a long silence. My heart felt as if it would tear right out of my chest. I finally told him about leaving messages for both Becca and Rachel, and my disappointment at not hearing from either of my stepchildren. He explained that Rachel was arriving tomorrow and that he would have to be completely honest with her. At that point he was crying so hard he had to hang up. I stood there, in my classroom, with my phone in my hand trying desperately to hold myself together. Only two of my staff knew what was going on. I wanted nobody's pity. That phone conversation was the first time that I had seen or heard Sam upset like that since this whole sordid business came out. How could I tell if he was truly upset over his behavior or because he got caught?

I picked Caleb up from school. He was very quiet in the car on the way home. I encouraged him to talk about how he was feeling. He said he was just so sad, and he felt like he had awful mood swings. I tried to reassure him that his feelings were normal given the circumstances. I hoped he could keep talking. I didn't want those toxic feelings to sit and fester. I had mixed thoughts about telling him about Rachel's visit. If she didn't make an effort to see him, he would feel doubly abandoned. So would Faye.

At the party tonight, I told my staff that Sam and I had separated. It was awkward, but not as bad as I feared. Toward the end of the party, we began to watch baby videos. I watched as Sam lay on the bed, a very chubby three-month-old Faye on his belly, cooing and trying to get her to talk. I found myself thinking, "Was it then? Is that when you decided to cross the line?"

I hadn't heard from the OB/GYN. That made me nervous.

Wednesday, January 30

I cried at the grocery store. I felt like an ass. There I was, wandering around, carrying my little basket with tears streaming down my face.

I also had a long talk with Caleb's guidance counselor, Ann. She met with Caleb. He was so sensitive and vulnerable. I was very worried about him. Ann told me what everybody tells me—that I'm so strong—I've held this family together for so long, blah, blah, blah.

Newsflash! I didn't want to be strong! I was scared and sick all the time! Sophie told me that I looked like crap. I knew I did. I was pale and drawn and there were dark circles under my eyes.

Sam needed to tell me about Ginny. *When Faye was eighteen months old, I got an anonymous note in the mail. It said, "We love you and don't want to see you hurt anymore. You need to ask Sam about Ginny. And don't let him lie." Of course I asked. I had my office manager, a good friend, drive me to a coffee shop where he had taken Faye for breakfast. Shaking, I handed him the note. There was not a flicker of recognition on his face. My friend, who was watching him closely, agreed that the note had been a hurtful lie. Hmm . . . hindsight?* I also needed to know who he brought home. A couple of years ago there was a small bottle of lubricating gel in the desk drawer downstairs in the playroom. Caleb and my mother, of all people, found it. Who did he bring into this house? I knew he'd say nobody. How would I believe him? Would it be true or just another of his lies?

Was this really how I was destined to live the rest of my life? Not believing anything he said. Always wondering where he was. Was he really at work? Or the grocery store? How could I live like that?

I was going to see Caroline tomorrow. Maybe she would help me make sense of it.

Thursday, January 31

And now, to add injury to insult, I was sick. I had no voice, a hacking cough and thick yuck down the back of my throat. I needed sleep.

I met with Caroline. I know she was just doing her job, but she made me feel so good about myself. She said I was thinking clearly and was in a place it usually takes people months to get to. I just needed to wait for clarity.

I didn't want to make a decision that I would regret later. I would decide based on what was right for me first, for the kids second. As painful as Sam's journey would be, he'd have to make it alone. The mother in me (or was it the enabler?) wanted to protect him. The wife and lover was still seething with rage at his betrayal. But I needed to focus on me and let him work through whatever it was he needed to work through. Who knew where it would come out in the end? One thing was for certain. I was not making any decisions until I got some truthful answers.

I needed to contact my attorney regarding my rights. I needed to set up my own bank account so that I would never find myself in this vulnerable financial position again.

I got a call tonight about Caleb's tuition. We owed January, February, and March. Three thousand dollars. I made a plan to call them in the morning. My mantra became:

I can get through this.
I am strong.
I am good.
I am worth loving

I installed a program called NetNanny on the computer. It blocks certain types of sites and logs activity. I set it to block pornography, chat sites, and any place I thought he could try and hook up.

Friday, February 1

Rachel came.

A new month. A rotten day at school. Were the kids picking up on my vibe?

Faye and I went bowling tonight. I really needed the laugh. After we got home, Sam returned from dinner with His mother, Rachel, and Caleb. Rachel came to me as I stood in the kitchen not knowing what to say or where to look. She put her arms around me and held on tight. She asked if she could call me tomorrow night when she got back to New York. I didn't realize until just that moment how much the girls' silence hurt.

Sam and I talked some. Calmly, with great effort to contain the emotion. I could feel my muscles straining to hold me together. He was a wreck, and I couldn't bring myself to feel sorry for him. I tried to explain what Caroline and I talked about—the intertwined different aspects of our relationship, wife, lover, colleague, friend, and how each one had been betrayed on some level. I tried to explain how I needed to identify the betrayals to each relationship to decide which, if any, could be salvaged. I told him that what hurt more than anything was his "Country Wife" connection with Emily. I think because it was completely nonsexual. It made me realize that this was about more than just sex, even though he claims he never loved her.

He wanted to come back into the house. I couldn't stay here with him. What should I do? Where would I go? I was not going to his late uncle's house, where he had been staying. I seriously did not think that Sam was capable of caring for Caleb, Faye, and his mother on any kind of level. I also didn't trust that he wouldn't have someone over, or cruise online again, this time exposing the kids.

I found myself wishing he would just leave. He said he wanted to hug me but knew I didn't want to be hugged. I used to love the fact that we held hands a lot. Tonight, I didn't want him to touch me. After he was gone, Faye and I both cried for a long time. Mother and child, comforting one another.

Last night, I woke up at 1:15 and couldn't get back to sleep until after 4:00. Of course, my mind was racing. I came to the realization that because this infidelity, for lack of a better word, had been going on so long, I didn't know if the man I loved all these years even existed. Or, worse, if he ever did. For more than half of our married life he had been unfaithful. Was the man I thought I loved truly a figment of my imagination? And if so, how could any mere mortal ever live up to that?

I had finally begun, with the gift of this journal, to write the story that had been tapping on my head for the last ten years begging to get out. I began with the middle names of my family as the main characters, Ruth, Elizabeth, Abraham. My hero was Edward, my heroine, Emily. Now the story would never be written. It died inside me like so many other things.

I needed to sleep. Faye was in bed with me tonight. She was too sad to sleep in her own bed. Maybe her warm little body would help me relax, bring me some peace. Mother and child, comforting one another again.

Saturday, February 2

I just got off the phone with Rachel. We talked for a long time.

I more than understood the shock that she was feeling. I hoped I had given her some sense of peace. I was glad that Sam was honest with her. I was also completely aware of the fact that he told her only what I had already discovered. I was sure there was so much more that I didn't know. I was very worried that she would now take this burden on as her own. I saw her do it with her mother and now I feared she would feel obligated to do the same with her father. As needy as he was, he just might turn to her. I hoped not. She deserved her own life. I asked her to stay involved with Caleb and Faye. They needed to feel like they were still connected.

Caleb said to me tonight that he feels badly. That maybe he should have been nicer, kinder to his dad. My heart sank. I didn't want him to feel responsible for any of this. I knew he already felt guilty because of finances and the cost of his tuition. How could I keep him talking? Once again, I ended my day with sore eyes, a stomachache, and a headache.

Tonight, we went to a birthday dinner for Faith and Jasper's daughter. There were several families there. They were all smiling and celebrating. I just wanted to scream, "STOP IT! DON'T YOU KNOW MY LIFE WILL NEVER BE THE SAME?" Needless to say, I just kept up the small talk and got through the evening. Then I began to mark time until I could go to bed, and sleep, and stop thinking.

Sunday, February 3

What an awful day. I don't think I have cried this hard since Sam first left. Caleb was so angry. All he could see was his father's "oh, poor me" face and my inability to meet Sam's eye. Self-preservation on my part. I couldn't look at Sam without crying and feeling utter anguish.

When I told Caleb that his father and I were working on things, grown-up issues, he accused me of lying. He yelled and screamed at me and told me he wanted me to change places with Sam. And I fell apart.

I called my sister Hannah. I told her that I was just so unprepared to deal with all of this. She assured me that Caleb would come and apologize. I didn't believe her. But she was right, and he did. He hugged me and wouldn't let go, like a drowning man clinging to a life preserver. My heart was breaking for him, for me, for Faye. Even the dogs seemed a little lost.

I put dinner on the table and ran to the grocery store. I called Sam and told him to turn off the wounded-animal look. It was just making it harder on Caleb. He apologized over and over. I finally had to tell him to stop. It was pathetic.

I was so angry this afternoon. Sam fucked us all over. He put his family last, and the kids and I were paying for his choices. He went off to rebuild himself, God knew he needed it, and I was left to pick up the pieces. I couldn't even write this without crying.

> God, grant me the serenity to
> Accept the things I cannot change
> Courage to change the things I can
> And wisdom to know the difference.
> Amen.

Monday, February 4

So here I was, sitting at Barnes and Noble eating a grilled cheese sandwich while Sam was at home with the kids, a fire in the fireplace and lasagna (that I made) hot out of the oven. And I felt angry that he was home and I was out. I felt angry that my children blamed me and that is how it would have to be for now. I felt angry that we were even here in this position at all. I felt beaten up. I wanted to cry. I wanted to run away.

I bought the book Sophie recommended, *Should I Stay or Should I Go?* I also picked up a book about sexual addiction that Sam had been reading called *Out of the Shadows*[2]. I felt sad and sick. I was terrified about finances and how I was going to make it all work. I was afraid that His mother was going to die when I was alone with her. I was afraid all the time. I feared that the good and loving part of me was dead. I was afraid that I would never stop crying. I was afraid that, although all my blood work came back normal, in six months I would develop HIV. I struggled to understand how people lived through this. I began to take sleep medication at night, so I was sleeping a little but still tired all the time.

Sam left his journal in the car for me to read and I did. It was full of pain and self-loathing. Part of me wanted to hold and comfort him and part of me wanted to see him suffer the way he made the rest of us suffer.

Conflict. Betrayal. Agony. Lies. Adultery. Betrayal. Lies. Lies! LIES!

---

[2] Patrick Carnes, PhD., *Out of The Shadows; Understanding Sexual Addiction* (Hazeldon: Simon and Schuster, 2001)

Tuesday, February 5

I began to read "*Out of the Shadows* and *Should I Stay or Should I Go?* Both were very eye opening. As I read about sex addiction, there were so many things that came to mind.

Sam crossing the line from fantasy to reality with our friend.

The need for constant talk during sex, "Tell me about you and _____"

The insistence on anal penetration despite the severe pain it caused me.

The inability to remain aroused during sex.

Feeling that sex with him was last on my list. The constant pressure to "put out."

The growing lack of any other intimacy, hugging, kissing, holding. It was sex or nothing. No romance, just sex.

I decided that I would never be a victim again. I would stand on my own feet in my own space. I would protect my children as best I could from developing this same sexual addiction or looking for it in a partner.

I often expressed concern over his mother, whenever we had company, coming out of her room exposing herself in some way. It was, of course, particularly embarrassing to Caleb when he had friends over. Sam always brushed it off as old age. Is that what it was or was it something more sinister? Did it happen to him? Did she do this in front of him and his friends when he was growing up? She often alluded to some very difficult and trying times in her marriage and how forgiving she was. Did Sam learn this from his father? Did his father also lead a secret life full of lies and adultery?

I went to see a house. It was perfect for me. It was pink. There were so many signs that it should be mine:

A garden gate at the kitchen door just like my school.

Faye's fairies on the dining room wall.

Harry Potter mural painted on the back patio.

I realized that at this time I had no money for anything. I tried hard not to despair. Panic is not productive, and I needed to be able to think and act clearly if I was going to change the life of my family for the better.

Wednesday, February 6

I actually had a good day until after dinner. I laughed at the kids for the first time in weeks. I met with Caroline and was able to talk freely, intelligently without tears. I told her about the house, about the book on sex addiction, and how I found the whole thing fascinating. If it weren't for the insane fact that it was my family, my life.

We talked a lot about Sam's parents, his attachment issues from his premature birth and his father and mother's possible lack of clear boundaries. All contributing factors to his addiction.

When I got home the kids and I had a picnic on the rug and watched a movie. A really good day. Then the bottom fell out.

Caleb collapsed into anger and was verbally combative, if not abusive. He didn't understand. He felt lied to, betrayed, and totally abandoned. He was right. I couldn't tell him about Sam. First, he was not old enough to hear it. Second, it would destroy the love he feels for his father and add to his feeling of abandonment. I spoke to Sam on the phone. I felt bad telling him, but he needed to understand just how great the destruction was that he left behind. Afterward Caleb felt terrible. Now we added more guilt to his plate.

I decided to do everything in my power to get that house. We needed a fresh start out of this toxic environment filled with sad memories that threaten to overshadow all the happy ones.

Thursday, February 7

It was just after midnight and Sam just left. We were talking since just before 10:00. Sad, frustrated, angry, grieving, so many emotions. I couldn't write. I couldn't think straight. I felt like I was cold on the inside and afraid I wouldn't be warm ever again. I needed to stop.

The thought of reopening the show at the theater tomorrow night was making me sick.

Friday, February 8

The show went amazingly well. I was dreading going on. Gabriel really pulled through. I was so stressed out all day that I gave myself a massive headache.

When I came home, Sam was there. I have been so used to his accusatory remarks that I read anger into everything he said. I felt myself panicking when I returned to the dressing room after the show, my cell phone reading 10:58. I was sure he was going to give me a pissy attitude and be accusing. "Why are you so late?" He even did it to me after rehearsal last night. I wouldn't mind if he were genuinely interested, but he projects that the time spent away from him is not allowed, or needs to be monitored, or granted permission for.

I found myself getting very angry at him tonight. He and Caleb got into a fight. Caleb blew up at him. Sam was obviously very upset. I knew how terrible it felt to fight with Caleb, but I just wanted to say to Sam, "Good. Now you know how I feel."

Then he told me how hurt he was and how he had so much to work on. It was like he needed to keep saying it to somehow make it real to us, so we would all join him in his pity party. I sometimes wanted to kick him and scream, "You stupid fuck! Why do you think we are all in this position? Look at what you did to us!"

And he told me he wanted to come home. I wouldn't live under the same roof with him. I couldn't get sucked down again. He would stop working so hard. He would get comfortable and slip right back into what was easy. But this was his house, his mother's house. I needed a plan.

The girl who worked the box office at the theater told me that she was all done there as of Friday. I asked Gabriel if I could work some of her hours. It paid twelve dollars an hour. If I could pick up fifteen to twenty hours per week, I could put it all away to help with a house. I could work when Sam had the kids so I wouldn't miss any time with them.

So, in my desperate need to rescue my family, it had become impossible to sever my ties to The Theatre.

Saturday, February 9

Now what should I do? He went cruising online again last night at sexsearch.com. I also found a lot of photos on the computer that I didn't find before. I was sick over it. He talked incessantly of all his hard work, how hard he had been trying and how much he had had to face. When would I learn? He had done nothing but lie.

When I found the pink house for sale, I had visions of making a home that would welcome him as a whole, healed person. He was pushing me toward divorce, a place I never wanted to be.

I hated him for what he did and how he lied. I hated myself for believing him.

Sunday, February 10

Was I destined to be in a state of confusion and helplessness forever? Sam said, "Read the book. Just read the book." Now I have read the book and re-read some of the book. I understood that he had been operating under a warped sense of self and was engulfed in pain. That did nothing to alleviate the pain of his betrayal. There was a part of me that loved him, wanted to hold his hand through all the pain, and assure him that he would come out whole on the other side. Then there was the other part of me that had been ripped and was bleeding from his betrayal. That part needed to keep my distance, nurse my own wounds and those of my children, and begin to figure out my own wants and needs. Maybe he would be a part of it in the end. I just didn't know.

He swore that he did not go onto those sites. "It was an accident," he said. I didn't believe him. Those accidents seemed to happen only to him. NetNanny had a log. 8:00 and 8:11. He was blocked.

He said that part of his recovery was to do simple tasks to contribute to the day-to-day running of the house, i.e., laundry, dishes. He had been really good at keeping them up. When I came home last night, the counter and sink were full of dishes and the laundry had not been touched. Typical pattern for him, to put his addiction first.

He never mentioned "accidentally" ending up on those websites until I brought it up. Caught again. He was a liar. I knew he was trying to be honest, but I think that he believed that his lies and half-truths would be less painful to me. Oh, so wrong. I just wished we could put it all out on the table and deal with it.

Back to housing. It had become a priority, here or somewhere else. I needed to figure it out. Maybe he and I could do it together.

Monday, February 11

Faye was sick with a fever. We were up all night. Now she was finally sleeping. I thought about the last day I stayed home from work. It was the snow day when my old life ended. Wow! What a difference a month had made. I could sit now and write without having the exhaustion of the end of the day pressing down upon me.

I was thinking back over our marriage and wondering how we ended up here. I could only think that the loss of Sam's job, when Faye was six weeks old, was where it all began to free fall. I remember having lunch with a friend, talking about new jobs for him. I said, "I have to get him a new computer." She said, "Oh, my God! Listen to you! *You* don't have to do anything. *He* needs to pull it together and go out and support his family." I should have listened to her. I loved him so much and I wanted so badly to take away his pain and shield him from rejection. All I did was feed his low self-esteem, allowing him to withdraw more.

Up until that point we had always worked as a team. I considered myself to be one of the luckiest women alive. As the years went on and we became more and more distant, I kept trying to convince myself that I had a great marriage with a loving, giving, intelligent man. Was I trying to recapture what we once had? Or maybe it was never there at all, except in my own mind.

We used to do things for fun. We'd go out on long drives and look at houses, window shop, and talk about our dreams. When did we stop that?

It seemed that when he lost his job, after twenty years, he lost his identity. I tried to help him reinvent himself. I found his new job. I encouraged him to buy an inn and start again. I found the store for him. All I succeeded in doing was making him lose his money, and I gave him a place where his addiction could flourish, ensuring his failure.

Maybe he was right to say, "Get away from me."

I looked at the list for co-addicts in "Out of the Shadows" and I tried to be honest with myself. It was difficult to look at this list, knowing what I now knew, and try to remember what I didn't know before. Most of these things I could check off due not just to sex, but also his job.

- **Protecting the addict from consequences of behavior.**
    Job loss—I wanted so badly to protect him
- **Denial of the obvious—Was it obvious?**
    After I got the anonymous letter I should have known. I believed him.

An actress at the theater complained that he was making unwelcome advances. He brushed it off.

I asked him last year if there was someone else. I really didn't think there was, but I knew something was wrong. He denied it.

Collection of porn.

Excessive masturbation.

Surfing websites years ago. He said it was just for fun and I was uptight.

The economy was bad.

The newspaper destroyed his self-esteem.

He was headed for a depression.

- **Feelings of responsibility for the addict's behavior.**

He kept telling me he wasn't getting enough sex. Was it my fault?

- **Efforts to confront the addict with his problem.**

Talked to him about the porn, repeatedly.

Left him notes when I found it because talking got me nowhere. Tried to shame him into stopping.

- **Belief that if the addict changed, all problems would disappear.**

If he could just make a living, then we could go back to how we were.

- **Attempts to catch or trap the addict.**

Only after I began to find stuff.

- **Ongoing list of resentments.**

Over time, when I couldn't connect with him at all, the resentment began to grow.

- **Feelings of depression and remorse.**

    This was my life. I tried to come to terms with the fact that I was destined to struggle forever with a husband who didn't care how much I hurt.

- **Loss of friendships.**

    He didn't want me to have any friends. They took away my focus from him. He was always finding fault with people who befriended me.

- **Deterioration of family pride.**

    We didn't have a family for a long time. I feel as if I had been a single parent for years. It had been me and the kids.

- **Growing self-doubt and fear.**

    Having him lose his erection in the middle of sex = I am undesirable.

    I couldn't motivate him to try and reconnect with his family or want to care for them.

- **Efforts to control family expenditures with increasing inability to do so.**

    After a while he just stopped paying the bills, so I took over the checkbook, something I really didn't want to do.

    More and more money went out, much of it to his store. More and more credit card debt. Most of it, I was not involved in at all. My name was on credit cards I had never seen.

- **Take over the duties and responsibilities of the addict in order to keep the family life normal.**

    As he withdrew more and more, I took on more and more.

I earned the majority of the money
paid the bills
cleaned the house
did the shopping
clothed the kids
did the laundry
did all the cooking
was the contact for the schools

- **Overextension or overinvolvement in work or outside activities.**

    People always say, "I don't know how you do it all!" In some ways, the workload I was carrying was a source of pride. In other ways I wanted someone to "please take this burden before it kills me!"

Looking this over I was afraid. Afraid of who and what I had become. Afraid that we were way too unhealthy to ever make this work.

I decided I was not going to take on an extra job in the box office. ENOUGH! I needed to talk to Sam about a "controlled separation." We most likely would need to share an apartment as well as this house. He wanted to come home. He missed the kids and the stability (what a laugh) that he felt here. He said the kids needed him and so did his mother. He didn't say he misses me. I didn't think he thought of me at all as an individual who loved and wanted to be with him. He never called me. I seemed to be just this invisible part of his family. Maybe I would ask him to stay for dinner. Maybe we could talk practically tonight about how we go on from here. Maybe not.

It was difficult to look at what I had checked off on the list from "Out of the Shadows" and not feel like I caused Sam's addiction. Truth be told, I felt like he had forced me into most of these behaviors. Self and family preservation.

So, we talked. We ate dinner and we talked some more. It was very confusing. In some ways, it seemed so normal. But I needed to keep in mind that we were very far from normal. After we were done talking, we hugged. I wanted him to know that he was not alone. But I didn't know if I would ever trust him enough to be intimate again. Would I ever trust anyone? Where did we go from here? Next week, school vacation, he suggested that Faye and I go to visit my sister Thea. Caleb was still in school. Sam and Caleb could use some quality time alone. After that we would re-evaluate.

I was fairly certain I was not ready to live under the same roof with him. Tonight's dinner proved that. It would have been too easy to just slip back in, and before we knew it, we would be right back where we were before.

I needed to make some changes for me. I needed to know that I could do more than just survive. I could thrive. And then there were the kids. If we were living under the same roof again and we came to a place where we needed to part, what would that do to Caleb and Faye?

No matter what happened in the end, we would still parent together. I would like us, at the very least to still be friends. Could that happen?

Tuesday, February 12

I felt like I was always taking one step forward and two steps back. When I hugged Sam tonight, I think he took that to mean that we are going to put this all back together. I just didn't know. I still had not gotten any facts or answered questions. And he deleted the history on the computer. Why? If he had nothing to hide, then why delete it?

I decided to take Faye to my sister's in Maine next week. We really needed time away. I simply didn't know what to do. I did know that until I had some answers, I just wanted to get out of here. His mother was making me crazy. Four days in the house with her and I was ready to jump off the bridge. She was such a passive-aggressive woman. I was beginning to hate her for what she had done to the man I loved. She was a major contributing factor to where we found ourselves.

I came to the realization that I had been unhappy for a long time. I had not been free to state my needs and feelings without being made to feel like I was unreasonable or a nag. My self-confidence was slowly whittled down to such a low level that I believed my needs didn't matter and that I was being selfish and demanding. When I voiced my concerns over the years about excessive porn, excessive masturbation, and excessive drinking, it was met consistently with anger and disdain. There must have been something wrong with me.

This separation was good for me in that I was forced to re-evaluate my needs. Rethinking the farce that my marriage had become, I was enjoying the solitude and reflection. I did not want to live under the same roof right now. I needed space and time.

And Sam needed help and the ability to work without the temptation of leaning on me.

Wednesday, February 13

I talked with Sam for a long time. He was at work and for the first time in a long time he called me. It was "awkward as ass," to quote Daniel Cleaver. I felt so torn. On one hand, I felt very badly for him. I knew he was missing me and the kids. We missed him too. But on the other hand, when he had me and he had the kids, he chose to piss all over that.

I've kept getting "How are you feeling?" and "I feel badly that I haven't seen your show," and "I miss . . . blah, blah, blah"

Well, honestly, I'd been feeling like I was run over by a truck. He *should* have felt badly that he hadn't seen my show. It already ran for five weeks and he chose not to support me. And it was his own fault if he missed us. He should have thought of that.

He accused me of not thinking he was trying. God, I hope I hadn't been projecting that, but maybe I had. I found that I was not in a position to reward his work. It felt like it was too little too late. I realized how hard this was for him. But I had been operating in survival mode, self-preservation. Our checking account had fourteen dollars. I had to feed two children and find a place to live. I refused to live with him until I was ready. I still had gotten no answers. He was still lying by avoiding:

The anonymous letter
Bonnie—he thinks I still believe it was all before we got married

Emily

Craigslist

Prostitutes—London, New York

Wedding Ring—how exactly did he lose it?

Sam went to trade shows in New York for his store. He also went to London with the intent to open a store there. After one trip to NYC, he came home without his wedding ring. He said he had taken it off his ring finger because it was bothering him and he put it on his pinky. He said it fell off and he didn't notice until it was too late. He said.

Who and what else? Maybe I was going crazy. That was how I felt sometimes.

Thursday, February 14

I couldn't help thinking about the year I was living in Maine and Sam was living here. The valentines from him began to arrive in early January and continued almost daily until Valentine's Day. It was so romantic and so much fun. It made me feel loved and incredibly special. Last year I did the same for him. I began sending him valentines in early January and kept it up until Valentine's Day. Did it make him feel good? And loved? And special? He never said.

He told me tonight that he was so afraid of being hurt and abandoned that he did what he did to avoid letting anyone (me) get close. Didn't he realize that I stuck with him when he was fired from the newspaper? Through all the court fights with his ex-wife? How could he possibly have thought that I would abandon him? And how could he so readily have abandoned me?

I had my period. It was my second period since he had been gone. I found the vibrator one month ago yesterday. I have marked time in our relationship by before or after the girls left, not when I started my school or when we got married or when we bought the house. Why did I use painful times as a marker? What did that say about me?

Sam said he doesn't ever want to go through this again. I know I couldn't. God, it would probably kill me. I looked like I'd aged ten years in the last month. Believe it or not, he looked better now than he had in a long while. Maybe seeing his therapist had given him some peace. I truly hoped so. *Dan determined that Sam required a therapist with expertise in sexual addiction. Dan would treat Sam for marriage issues, but he sent Sam to Josh for his infidelity and addiction.*

Friday, February 15

I was beginning to enjoy our talks. For the first time in a long time, I felt like we were dealing with some degree of honesty. God, I hoped so. It was difficult sometimes to tell him what I felt. I didn't want to keep hammering away at him, but I needed to be truthful. True to myself. It was and continues to be exhausting.

It was nice to come home to a warm, snuggly kid in my bed. I loved my children so much my heart could burst.

Saturday, February 16

I came home so tired from The Theatre. We had two shows. It was interesting how my relationship with Gabriel had completely changed. There had been absolutely no flirting, no underlying sexual tension, just friendship. It was nice. Another actor, an old friend, told me the other night to give his love to Sam. I forgot to pass the message on to Sam. I felt badly because I kept forgetting. Sam and I have been having these long talks and I knew he would have liked to know that there were people, friends, in his life that had genuine affection for him. I needed to remember.

Sam was a wreck tonight. He said he felt all day like he would fail. I didn't know how to support him. I had never felt so helpless in my life. Would all these awful feelings ever end?

Sunday, February 17

What a shitty day! It started with Sam and me fighting in the morning over my friends, or lack of, and my perception of his dislike of them. He seemed to think that I had a misconception regarding his dislike of my friends.

Then I went to church. I cried all the way through. I just felt so abandoned and alone. I have tried to do what God asked of me. I have tried to be loving and kind, building people up, and all it has gotten me is a kick in the stomach.

I had two shows again. During the first one, I felt a little out to lunch, but it wasn't a bad show. I went home and tried to rest a little. It was depressing. I have never felt so undesirable or unlovable in my entire life.

The show tonight, our closing night, sucked. The lights were screwed up. That threw Gabriel and it threw the audience. I feel like we never really got our rhythm back. When we were done, someone slipped and told me that Sam had been there. They all knew but nobody told me. It was probably better that way. I would have been a nervous wreck. I just started to cry. Gabriel held me, the tattletale felt like an ass, and I felt awful. Why didn't Sam tell me? I thought he was supposed to be working.

After the shock wore off, I started to second guess everything. If all of this crap hadn't come out, would he have come to support me? Probably not. Did he come to be supportive or because he felt he had to make it look good? I hated this. Was there an ulterior motive to everything?

I struggled through cabaret. He was not there. After I packed up my backstage station, I took all my stuff to the car. There was a note on my seat.

"Very, very good show. You were adorable."

I just didn't know what to think or feel. I wanted to give him credit for trying but I was too afraid.

The night before, he said to me," Don't expect me not to have setbacks or slip ups." What was that supposed that mean? That he would probably have sex with someone else? I would be done for. How do people move on from this? I couldn't even get past the shock of what he did.

I had a splitting headache and I needed sleep. I was afraid I would have another one of those bizarre scary dreams. I still struggled with what my life had become. I just couldn't believe it. God, I was pathetic.

Monday, February 18—His mother's 92nd birthday

Faye and I arrived in Maine and I was looking forward to my first full night's sleep without his mother calling me in the middle of the night. I told Sam that I was constantly confused. I didn't know what to think or feel—ever. Sometimes I missed him terribly, and sometimes I wanted to take the kids and drive away and never see him again.

He went to his first twelve-step meeting tonight. He was scared, so I called him to see how it went. He said it felt good to know that there were other people out there struggling with the same inner issues. The stories were different, but the issues were the same.

I wondered if I would ever know the whole story. Did I want to? I thought I needed to.

I was glad he went and I truly hoped it helped him. I hoped he and Caleb would use the week to reconnect. Right then, I was ready to snuggle up to Faye and get the sleep I desperately needed.

Tuesday, February 19

I slept all night, thanks to the sleep meds, but still felt tired and sluggish in the morning. Faye and I met up with Aunt Bitsy. While we were out, I bought a new journal. I was afraid of running out of room to write. There have been times when I felt the writing was the only thing keeping me sane if, in fact, I really was sane. It took a long time for me to choose which one to buy. I kept going back to one that had a bold black-and-white-patterned cover. I didn't know why the choice of journal was so important. I suppose that the words, written on any page, would be the same. But, for some reason, the book itself was very important to me. I finally put the black and white journal down. I feared seeing the world in black and white, either all good or all bad. Instead, I opted for a book with more muted tones, with leaves and a peacock feather. It may sound trivial and stupid, but it seemed important at the time.

I never kept a journal until all of this happened. When Sam gave me the first one for Christmas, he explained that he had not known it was a journal. I'm not sure what he thought it was or why. I was thrilled. I thought it would be a great way for me to finally work on my book. I made myself a promise to do so, and I actually started. Then the bottom completely dropped out of my world and it became my only connection to sanity. How ironic.

I decided to read another chapter of "Out of the Shadows." This one was about 'Looking for Mr. Goodbar' and how, in the throes of her addiction, Theresa would not sleep with whom she had just had sex. I thought back to when Sam and I were dating. Sam and I first had sex in his car. We continued our relationship for a year while I finished school and then moved to New York. It wasn't until he came down to stay the next summer that he stayed all night. Was I already part of his addictive behavior? We were intimate for a year before he slept over. So, if I was part of that crazy cycle, or at least started out that way, I wondered what our relationship had really been based on?

When we were in court, fighting to hang on to his girls, I found out he had been having a sexual relationship with the mother of Rachel's best friend, while I was living in New York. This all happened when he was seeing me. Why didn't my alarms go off?

Even though Sam was not a bad person, he had done so many really bad things. I worried that the fundamental building blocks of our relationship had all been lies. I began to believe that at no time was our relationship ever built on honesty. That was a painful thing to admit. It was hard to look at this situation and not say,

"God, Josie, you stupid broad! How could you be so naïve and gullible?" My only response would have been, "I am not stupid. I loved him. I trusted him. I believed that he would never hurt me." Wow. Live and learn.

Wednesday, February 20

I just got off the phone with Sam. So painful. We talked a little about women in our past. His recollection of these experiences and mine were very different. Maybe a large part of the problem was that our definitions of "committed relationship" vary greatly.

I felt his pain. I really did. But my own pain was so overwhelming, it threatened to engulf me. I told him that I didn't feel safe with him. That's true. I didn't feel safe physically or emotionally. I wondered how I could overcome that. If he wasn't going to keep me safe, I would have to do it myself.

I didn't sleep that night and I had diarrhea. Would this ever get any better?

The next day I had lunch with my sister Katie. We had never been particularly close. She wasn't close with any of her siblings. During this, however, she was very supportive. She cried for me. I never knew that she thought I was such a good person or that she envied my happiness and commitment to Sam. She encouraged me to really take my time and find my own heart.

My sister Thea was different. I don't think she had any idea what to do or say, so she fed me. At first, I was afraid to tell my sisters. And although they didn't know the whole story, they turned out to be a tremendous source of support for me and, hopefully, for all of us.

I went to Borders with Aunt Bitsy, my Guardian Angel. I bought *Don't Call It Love*[3] and found it a fascinating read. I just wished it wasn't my family, wasn't my life. I felt sick again.

A real estate friend offered to find us an apartment to share. Please God, let this work.

Thursday, February 21

What a beautiful day. My sister Thea and I took Faye sledding in the field out back. I had forgotten so much of my childhood. How good it felt to tramp through the snow and experience the joy and wonder of discovering fresh deer tracks and the exhilaration of riding a sled to the bottom of the hill, only to be dumped out at the end. The way Faye squealed and giggled with sheer enjoyment. The cold metallic smell of snow. It was so much fun and brought me such joy and even a little peace.

Now as I snuggled up to Faye in the bed, the cat on my other side, I began to feel sad. I just wanted to go home. I didn't have a home anymore. Not really. I supposed that was the task I set for myself over the next few weeks—to make a home. I just wanted to cry again.

God, grant me the serenity to
Accept the things I cannot change
Courage to change the things I can
And wisdom to know the difference.
Amen

---

[3] Patrick Carnes, PhD., *Don't Call it Love: Recovery From Sexual Addiction* (Random House: Bantam Books 1991)

I would try very hard to stop feeling sorry for myself, to move forward and to heal.

Friday, February 22

I read that the time period after you find out about your loved one's addiction and infidelity is called "the blackout." It is like being in loved and familiar surroundings when the lights go completely out. At that point, everything that is familiar and known takes on new characteristics. It becomes unfamiliar and frightening.

I took a big step and called S-Anon. I actually made it through the entire phone call, shaking, but not crying. There was a meeting on Monday night, two hours away. That was also Sam's Sexaholics Anonymous (SA) meeting night, so I had to figure out a babysitter.

Okay, so if I was a co-addict, I needed to take a serious look at my own behavior. First of all, I *did not* cause this in Sam. He was like this long before I met him. I suspected he was acting out when he was married to his ex-wife—hard to know—and that was how he found me. I felt like a great deal of the co-addictive behavior I had was a direct consequence of Sam's behavior but nonetheless, I needed to examine it and STOP!

I made my first attempt to stop the madness. I knew that this was the day we were scheduled to pick up the boys for the carpool. Normally I would have called Sam to remind him. I didn't call him at all. It was on the calendar and I told him about it before I left. He was a capable adult, and he would sink or swim of his own accord.

He was researching debt solutions. He had buried us in nearly two hundred thousand dollars of debt. When we separate, he will need to take care of that. I would provide for myself and the kids, but he would need to cover his own financial problems.

Oh, for the love of God! I had diarrhea again.

I decided that one of the most difficult behaviors for me to stop would be checking up. I never did that until all this exploded. I didn't know how I would ever have any way to trust him, or even if I cared to, but for now I had to stop. That behavior made me feel crazy.

Bonnie—Emily—ALT.com—Craigslist—MySpace—Gmail—ENOUGH!

I would try to discover what my likes and dislikes are so that I could make honest healthy choices.

I would not wear Chanel No. 5. I discovered that this is the perfume his mother wore; sick.

I would choose my bras based on comfort and not based on what he liked, or thought was sexy.

I wouldn't have sex out of obligation or guilt when I was too tired, not feeling well, or just not in the mood.

I would wear shoes I liked. If they were painful, I would not wear them, even those that he finds sexy.

I would wear clothing that was appropriate for my age and style; I would not try to look like I was twenty-five again.

I would cut my hair if I chose.

I would wear my nails short and unpolished if I wanted.

I would let no one cause me pain during sex. That included anal penetration, which caused me to tear and bleed.

I would not take on all the jobs in the house. When I needed help, I would ask. If help was not freely given, I would deal with that and not just assume responsibility.

I would love my children unconditionally. I would provide them with a healthy example and celebrate them, not only for what they do, but more importantly, for who they are.

I would not assume full financial responsibility for my family. I would contribute what I could, but I would not work myself into the ground to keep my family afloat.

I would not feel inadequate, undesirable, or less than I am, based on someone else's assessment of me.

It was a beginning. I called my priest to sit down and talk. I felt abandoned by God; maybe he could help.

Saturday, February 23

I was afraid for Caleb. The more I read the more afraid I was. He already struggled with his feelings and his actions. How did I help keep him from developing this addiction?

We arrived home. Part of me was glad to be here but part of me felt empty. I ate dinner with Faye and now I felt sick again. I found out tonight that his sister made dinner for Sam, Caleb, and his mother three nights this week. That was a positive thing only if he didn't use her as a crutch the way he had used me all these years.

I read a letter tonight that Sam had started to write to me on the computer. It detailed his infidelity. He tied me to so much of it. It was funny how we could both be present for the same thing and see it so differently. Dan was right all along. Reality is totally subjective.

Years ago, when Sam dumped me for Carol, I was lost. I knew

nothing of Carol. All I knew was that we had made plans to go to London together and at the last minute he changed his mind and broke it off. I didn't even know Carol existed.

Then there was Adele, our mutual friend that he solicited a threesome with and sealed the deal with a blowjob. He says that it was "our" fantasy, something we had discussed. Yes. In bed. I never thought that he would cross the line and try to make it a reality. If I had ever been on board with it, why would I have fallen apart when he told me?

Then there was Edward. Yes, I broke up with Sam to date Edward, a total loser who was verbally abusive. I couldn't get a commitment from Sam. We dated for four years and we were no closer to a permanent commitment than we were when we started. We were apart for five weeks.

There was Joe when I lived in New Jersey, kissing in the van. One night. That was it. We never dated. We never had sex. He was married, unhappily, and I didn't want to get into that situation again.

And let's not forget about Gabriel, kissing and touching in the dark, backstage at the theater. It was something that still brought a blush of shame to my face.

So, since meeting Sam, twenty-two years ago, I had kissed three other men and had sex with one. The one that I slept with was when Sam and I were broken up. That was three years before we got married. I never slept with anyone else when we were together. All this in twenty-two years.

He says we were very sexual. Yes, we certainly were. It was wonderful. Then it began to shift and change, very subtly at first.

He needed stories of me and other men to stay aroused, so I made them up. Did he really believe I did all those things? I told him they were made up. Sam always wanted anal penetration and if I refused, he would always ask "why"? Could he not remember from one night to the next that I told him how much it hurt or that I was bleeding? Every time I got my period he would say, "Oh well, I guess we can't fool around tonight." Like the functions of my body interfered with his physical pleasure.

After Faye was born, I was exhausted. I was working two jobs and nursing full time as well as taking care of Caleb who was four, cooking, cleaning, and doing laundry.

Then he started to collect the porn and visit websites. We used to watch porn together occasionally and it was fun. But this was different. This had nothing to do with me. When I told him this, he told me I was uptight and said I was just like all women. Once I got what I wanted, a wedding ring, I was cold and indifferent to meeting his needs. I tried to prove him wrong. I wanted him to know that he was attractive and desirable to me, so I added sex every other night to my already ridiculous schedule. It became another job. I was exhausted, but he was needy and demanding.

Finally, my wants and needs just went away. He shut down and withdrew. I was lonely, frustrated, and becoming miserable. I loved him so much and I just couldn't understand how he could be so uninterested in me—in us.

I began to think, "*Well, he's fifteen years older than I am and he refuses to take care of himself. I suppose he will die first and then I will be free.*"

God, it made me feel horrible to admit that, but that is where

I was and had been for a while. No wonder I felt sick all the time.

Sunday, February 24

I read at church and I think I did pretty well. I was still having a hard time praying. I told my priest I would call him tomorrow. It was time to sort it out.

Sam and I talked for a while in the evening. My realtor friend found us a cute, tiny studio apartment. I thought we could share it, alternating nights, and work on a controlled separation. *I thought if we got an apartment together, then the kids could stay in the house while Sam and I went back and forth to the apartment. That way, the kids are not jostled about.* Sam was very angry. He said he was ready to try and come home. I was nowhere near ready to have him there. We were still all contradictions and confusion and mistaken meanings. I had not forgiven him for what I didn't even know about. And I wasn't sure I ever would.

We ended up talking for two and a half hours. It was exhausting. I knew it was good to have these kinds of talks, but it was so emotional. Sometimes I just wanted to go to sleep and never wake up. Thank God for Caleb and Faye. They kept me grounded and somewhat sane.

Monday, February 25

A mixed day. I did so much better when I was at school. I had people who depended on my guidance and I had problems to solve. I may not have been operating up to standard but at least I was not wallowing.

I was angry this morning. My eyes were swollen and painful. I came to the realization that my talk last night with Sam made me more resentful than ever. He was using this whole situation to say, "Okay, now I know what I want and it's you. So, let's get going and put this back together." The difficult and infuriating part of this whole scenario was that his moment of clarity was my moment of unbearable devastation and he expected me to just get on with it. I was getting very tired of his use of the word "we." *We* had some issues, and *we* developed some bad habits. I felt like he was using me as a scapegoat and trying to make this catastrophe a fifty-fifty affair. Bullshit. I told him so.

I spoke with my priest. I know that priests have heard and seen it all, but it was almost as if I could feel his shock over the phone. Maybe I was just projecting that. I told him my feelings of abandonment by God, my inability to pray and my fear that I am somehow less of a person, or at least not "the good wife," because I couldn't seem to get over this. He said something that gave me great peace. He said that even when actions are controlled by addiction, that doesn't mean they are without consequence. Most importantly he gave me a sense of hope that I would make the right decision for myself and the kids. He used the word "divorce" without instilling fear, dread, or panic in me. He made me feel supported and loved and even more, said he would pray for me.

I opened my own bank account with money from The Theatre and from my sister Katie. I had taken a step toward never being this financially vulnerable again.

Emotional Extortion—an interesting term Sam picked up at his SA meeting.

Tuesday, February 26

What the fuck!?!

I had a good day. A really good day. I had a little panic over the apartment situation but then I looked at the S-Anon pamphlet which read "decide to be happy." And, wow, it worked.

Then all of a sudden, I was crying, feeling like the world's worst parent and an even worse person.

Caleb went off again. He was angry and hurt and quick to point out how he loved Sam more than he loved me. I tried to stay calm and talk to him, but he just got worse and worse, more and more abusive. I slapped him. I was so angry. Angry for having had to take the blame in all this, angry for how my life was, and angry with him for not being able to see at least some of my pain. All he was able to see was Sam. I called Sam and swore at him. I was really mean, trying to hurt him. At that moment, I hated him. There was no excuse for what he did to us. I didn't see how this would ever work.

So, I was sitting upstairs crying. And my son, oh God, my beautiful loving son was downstairs seething with anger and hatred, and it was almost more than I could bear. I couldn't comfort him when he needed me most because he was convinced I was the cause of all this. I couldn't even see to write. Sometimes I just wanted to die.

Wednesday, February 27

I saw my priest again and our meeting was open and loving. He let me rant, be sarcastic and cry. I also found an apartment. It was nine hundred fifty dollars per month including heat and hot water. She was going to give it to me for eight hundred fifty. It was much larger than I wanted, but the plus was that if I got to a place where

I needed the kids to come with me, there would be enough room.

Caleb was better tonight. He had met with his school counselor. I apologized to Sam for my outburst. I probably would have made a Marine blush. My language was uncalled for and based purely on emotion.

My priest encouraged me to put ninety percent of my energies into rebuilding and resting myself. He said that the temptation was to focus entirely on the kids. But if I was not working to make myself healthy and whole, I would have nothing to offer the kids. He was right. I needed to be as healthy and whole as I could be. That was what they would take away from this. I thought I knew where I was going. I just needed to make certain that my decision did not come strictly out of emotion.

We also talked about my difficulty praying. He told me how, when times were good, people often took all the credit. But when times were bad, God got all the blame. It had been such a long time since things were good, I didn't remember if I had taken all the credit. He thought that it might be easier to pray, or to get back to it, by starting with the Psalms, number 78.

I needed to know that God was with me. That I was not alone. That I was worthwhile and loved.

I had been trying to pray for Sam. He spent so long doing damage that I feared would never be repaired. I prayed that somehow, he would become whole, so that not only would he survive, but he would thrive and grow. I prayed that he never became this destructive again, no matter where he ended up, and that no one else would ever be destroyed by him the way we were destroyed.

I prayed that I would heal. That I would give myself the time I needed, even though it might be years. That one day I would find somebody worth trusting. That this would not destroy any chance I had for a healthy relationship in my life and that I would give my children strength.

"Almighty God, you know that we have no power in ourselves to help ourselves: Keep us both outwardly in our bodies and inwardly in our souls, that we may be defended from all adversities which may happen to the body, and from all evil thoughts which may assault and hurt the soul; through Jesus Christ our Lord, who lives and reigns with you and the Holy Spirit, one God, for ever and ever. *Amen*"

Another fucking telephone conversation. God, he didn't remember from one day to the next what we talked about. We fought over the apartment. I just wanted some time and solitude and clarity. He was accusatory and downright mean. He actually said that I was not capable of taking care of the kids. I was so sick of this. I was sick of his games of guilt and seduction. I was really beginning to hate him. The more he pushed me to rebuild our marriage and the more he insisted that the problem was "ours," the more I was ready to say, "STOP! It's over!" At this point I didn't see any alternative but divorce. He started saying, "God-damnit! I may not be perfect, but you are no better. I am not less of a person!" I never said that. It was as if he made up his mind to get into a twelve-step program and now he got to point out how unmanageable *my* life had become. Well, the only thing that was unmanageable in my life was him. And I was not addicted enough to not let go.

I would heal in my own way, in my own time and he would not push his agenda on me.

Thursday, February 28

I promised myself that I would write each day, but I was so tired. I tried to put it all down on paper for Sam this morning. He seemed to absorb things better when they were in black and white. I called Caroline and talked to my real estate friend about the apartment. Sam wrote me a note and talked to Caleb (thank God) after a rough meeting with Josh. I don't know what happened. He seemed like a mess, although he was speaking more sensibly, more sanely, with less crap than I had heard in quite a while. I had a long talk with Caleb after Sam left. He was still looking for answers I just couldn't give him but he was respectful and loving. He seemed to have come to terms with some things after Sam spoke to him. Apparently, Caleb really heard him and then felt able to be open and accepting with me.

It was hard to believe that I had come to the end of a journal for the first time in my life. I wish with all my heart that I hadn't needed to.

BOOK TWO

Friday, February 29

A new month, a new apartment, a new journal, a new life? I was hopeful. I felt like I was able to take a step forward. I signed the lease, and I didn't drop dead or get struck by lightning.

Caroline told me she had never seen anyone work through this like me. She said I was processing and moving through things at a very rapid pace. She told me last time she was learning a lot from me. I felt really proud. If I could take this life-altering betrayal and devastation and turn it around, work through it, grow and find a positive outcome, then there really was hope. Maybe I was not lost after all.

Sam kissed me on the cheek when he hugged me. I didn't want that to happen again. Not ready. He needed to be respectful of my boundaries and I needed to make it clear, in a non-threatening, non-judgmental way, exactly what they were.

I loved my kids so much. For the first time in a very long time, I felt a glimmer of optimism.

Saturday, March 1

What a strange and full day. I started off meeting Sam at the apartment. The kids were really good about trying to make it homey. We brought photos, music, and quilts. Sam actually had to leave his uncle's house because it was sold. Talk about timing. When I think of how he fought me on this, it makes me a little irritated. So, we set up this beautiful light and open apartment that we will share as we alternate time in the house. When we were done, he told me, "You done good." "Thank you" would have been better, but at this point I'd take what I could get. Sam was emotional and weepy, which set Caleb up for an emotional, angry day.

In the evening, the kids and I took his mother to the late church service and potluck. My priest gave a homily that seemed to be speaking directly to me. The gist was that if you are overcome with fear and cannot see that God is there with you to love and support you, you may as well be blind. Of course, he was a lot more eloquent and it spoke directly to my heart.

After we got home, I ran a scan on the computer. The last one I ran was a week ago, which turned up nothing, so I was feeling confident of the same result. At first nothing came up, especially in pornography, which was always the first place I checked. But then "chats" came up with nine hits two nights ago when Sam was home with the kids. I pulled up the chats. They were all from ALT. com. No wonder he was in a much better mood than normal when I got home. Then I realized there was one hit under "personals." It was MySpace.

So now what? It was 8:15 at night with the kids in the house. Should I confront him? Did I watch for a while and see what would happen?

It looked as though this separation would just ease the way for the kids into a divorce. I would not live like this. I just wouldn't do it. And I wasn't even ranting and raving. I was tired, achy, and sad. Sad for what he was so willing to give up.

Sunday, March 2

I started the day doing another scan. I wanted to be sure the program was working correctly before I accused or confronted him. ALT.com came up as a high-risk item but not as pornography, like I would have thought. All the pages I checked last night came up in the new scan. The pages that came up last night did not show up again this morning.

I found myself printing out his registration page for ALT.com, checking and rechecking the history on the computer, only to find that he deleted entire days. He pretended to be so ignorant when it came to the computer, but it certainly had served his needs well. All this checking took hours. It was such a waste of my time and energy.

My friend Jim from The Theatre came over to help Caleb set up the wireless router for his Xbox. Caleb had gotten Sam's permission to use the old computer from the store. Before I let the kids on it, I installed NetNanny and updated the anti-virus. When I ran the scan with NetNanny, sure enough, there were lots of porn sites as well as a number of bondage photos. Jim offered to take our old computer home to fix it, but I wouldn't let him. I was terrified at what he might find.

This was no way to live. If he was not going to give this stuff up, our marriage didn't stand a chance in hell. I would wait and run another scan and see what happened. If anything showed up, that was it.

I was not going to mention it, but he knew immediately that something was wrong. Of course, he denied going on these sites on Friday. Should I have believed him or not? And then there were all the sites and bondage photos in his store computer. "Those are from a long time ago," he said. That didn't make it any better. Actually, it showed how twisted he had been for a long time. The photos were sick. Women tied down and forced open. I asked him when he got into this stuff. He sidestepped and lied to me again. He said people talk about it all the time.

"What people? I've never heard anybody talking about it."

"Guys do."

"You don't hang out with guys."

"I hear it at the coffee shops."

He was so quick with a lie. I was tempted to call him back and ask why he felt the need to keep lying. But I didn't. If he chose to keep lying, he just kept killing any hope we had.

Caroline asked me on Friday if I was afraid of people being angry with me. I was. And not just him. Anybody. I suppose that I had so little growing up, my reputation was really all I had. I was terrified that if people were angry with me then they wouldn't like me. Then I would be completely abandoned with no resources to win them back.

When I was twelve, I met a boy who made my heart race. The youngest of three brothers, he was blonde and beautiful. A golden child who seemed to be good at everything he attempted, an especially gifted musician. I was completely tongue tied whenever he was around. He was my first kiss at the end of seventh grade during a game of Spin the Bottle. For years, I admired him from afar, feeling like a self-conscious idiot whenever he was near, but still longing to bask in the glow of his nearness. My friends knew how I felt, his friends knew, our teachers knew, but I'm not sure he ever realized. There were times during the next six years when I some-times had the feeling he might be interested in me, but his mother was very clear that I was not good enough. I was from a poor fam-ily, a broken home and although I was smart, there was no guaran-tee I would go to college—a place he was headed for sure. When we were seniors in high school a mutual friend called me the day after Christmas to see if I wanted to go cross country skiing. I had never been and was very excited. We ended up at the boy's house. We skied all afternoon in the field and woods behind his house. It was a magical day. When we got back to his house, there were home-made cookies cooling on a wire rack. The sun was setting, giving the room a rosy afternoon glow. The Christmas tree was twinkling with white lights and there was a fire in the fireplace. I realized years later that I modeled much of my adult life on this snapshot I had of his mother on this one afternoon. In my quest to be "good enough" I baked cookies, kept a cozy house, trying to recreate what I felt in those few minutes of thawing our toes by the fire next to the Christmas tree, while we ate homemade cookies. I am good enough. I have to be.

I spent my life keeping the peace, making amends. I needed to stop. The people worth having were those who loved and accepted me—faults and all.

I never doubted that Sam loved me. Maybe that made it all harder. If he hadn't loved me then maybe I might have been able to come to terms with his betrayal, how thorough it was and how long it went on. But when you loved someone, how could you do this to them? Over and over and over and over and over.

My nipples were sore. Was this some kind of withdrawal from

sex? I knew, from what I'd read, that it happened to the addict. Did it happen for everyone?

Well now it was official. I sounded like a complete lunatic! I needed to stop the madness.

I was reading the Psalms as my priest suggested. It had been comforting. Not all beauty, sometimes total destruction, but always God was there.

I had this beautiful memory of the priest at our old church, MJ. She was standing on the steps of the parish hall. Sam's ex-wife had just done something particularly heinous involving Sam and the girls, for which MJ actually called her a bitch. Then she said, in her wonderfully wise and down to earth way, "Just lift it up to God."

I would try to lift it up to God.

Monday, March 3

Back to work. Thank God. There was less time to dwell. I talked a little with Sam. I tried to explain that although the stuff on the computer may be old news to him, to me it was brand new and oh, so destructive. Add that to the fact that if it actually was old, then all of this had been going on so long and that made it seem twice as devastating.

I knew he was working hard and staying focused. I was proud of him for that. I realized how painful it was to come to terms with what he did, the lives and relationships he may or may not have destroyed.

I wanted him to be completely certain that he was doing all this work for himself and not for us. As far as I was concerned, at this point there was no us. He needed to be sure that he was rebuilding the marriage because he chose to and not because he didn't want to be alone or because he was afraid of losing the kids. And I also needed to look at what I wanted. Part of me really did want our marriage back. Was this out of fear? A larger part of me was repulsed by the thought of sexual intimacy with him. I didn't know if I would ever fully trust him again. Could I live with that? Could he?

I told him that I never doubted that he loved me. That's what made this so insane. But that I would rather be friends, who were working on honesty and trust, co-parenting with love and understanding, than live in a relationship lacking all these things and based on unrealistic perceptions of each other. I hoped that gave him peace. It did me.

It was two months ago tonight that we had sex for the last time.

I wondered if any of his lovers came to his father's funeral. After his dad died at the hospital, he told me he went to the beach and stayed there all night. Did he?

This kind of thinking was so destructive. But I had no facts to put my mind to rest.

Tuesday, March 4

I went to an Al-Anon meeting tonight. I was scared and felt awkward and uncomfortable, even though everyone there was very warm and welcoming. I read aloud with them but declined to share. After all, my husband was not an alcoholic, at least not that he admitted. He was an addict. I watched and listened, taking in as much as I could. A woman around my age spoke. Her name was Leslie. She talked of the colossal mistake she had made twenty years earlier by marrying her now ex-husband. She spoke about her inner turmoil, confusion, guilt, and her need to fix everything, to make it all right. Then she shared how she had gotten to the point where she took no responsibility for his actions. She freely accepted her own choices and whatever complications and consequences arose from them, but he was on his own to live and choose as he saw fit or as his addiction commanded.

I began to feel a little connection. After the meeting was over, an older woman named Arlene came up to me and said, "You're in the right place. It *will* get easier. You will survive." I just started to cry.

Then Leslie handed me the Al-Anon book. She told me that someone had bought it for her at her first meeting and that she was doing the same for me. She hugged me.

In some ways I felt like I was suddenly not alone. In other ways I felt more isolated than ever. Alcohol isn't sex.

When I came home, I found that Caleb hadn't done any of the things I had asked him to do. He was surfing the web. A look at the history confirmed all my worst fears. He was looking for porn. Normal thirteen-year-old curiosity? Or learned from Sam? How did I tell?

"Show us your mercy, O Lord, and grant us your salvation."

Wednesday, March 5

I was so looking forward to tomorrow night. My first night in the apartment. No one to serve. A full night's sleep. No one for whom I would have to put on a happy face. A little peace. Just a little.

Faye was sleeping with me tonight. I was hoping she was not nervous about my being away for two nights. I worried about her. Caleb was over the top, demanding a great deal of focus and attention. I was afraid Faye would feel left behind. She was not quick to express herself the way her brother was, but she was easily hurt. I asked her yesterday if she was scared or upset over her daddy being away. She thought for a minute and said, "Not really. I still get to see him." She was such a love. I watched her dance. She was getting ready to leave for dance class and suddenly burst into tears. I asked what was wrong and she cried, "It's watching day!" Of course, I felt guilty that I hadn't known, but neither had she. One of the other kids just told her. I zipped off to the studio. When I arrived, she gave me the biggest, most radiant smile. I was so glad I made it. She was lovely. Tall and slim with a beautiful straight back and the most gorgeous profile. She had really grown up so much. Gone were the days of a chubby toddler in a tutu. I was very proud of her.

I spoke with Sam several times. After our first conversation, following his meeting with Josh, I thought, "something's changed." Maybe I was projecting something, but I got the distinct impression that he had changed his mind about me and saving our marriage. It wasn't anything he said, just a feeling. Of course, the "fixer" in me kicked into high gear. I had to call him several more times. Then I realized what I was doing and stopped. If that was his choice, then that was his choice. Maybe it really was a long time ago. I didn't know and probably never would. I thought I could live with that. We would see.

The dog was snoring, and I had to go help his mother pee. Yes, a couple of nights on my own would be welcome.

Thursday, March 6

It is strange where life takes us. It was my first night in the apartment. I was a little afraid and more than a little sad. But I was trying to look at it as a way to build and heal myself, my children, and possibly my marriage.

Faith came with me to take a look around. I think she wanted to make sure I wasn't staying in some disgusting little hole in the wall. She was pleasantly surprised at how light, tasteful, and big the apartment was.

I made a commitment to myself that I would use this time alone to take better care of my body, so after unpacking I went for a long walk. What a mass of emotions.

I took a forty-minute walk in a huge loop throughout the city we used to call home. Physically, it felt invigorating. Emotionally, I was all over the map. As I first began to walk, the smells of the city were very reminiscent of London, where I had taken Sam for our first Christmas as a married couple. Then as I walked along all the streets we had walked together; I had a nearly overwhelming rush of emotions. As I passed our old house I thought, *I got married here, had my son here, pushed him around town in his stroller, and LOVED every minute of my life here.* What happened?

Then I walked past the restaurant where we used to go out for nachos on a whim. We would go for long walks and window shop. We certainly didn't have any money to speak of, but we were happy. I remember one Saturday morning when I was pregnant with Caleb, jumping out of bed and walking up the street for breakfast. Sam said to me, as I was throwing some clothes on, "You know, after he's born, we won't be able to just go like this. Everything will change." I didn't believe him. I'd like to think that it was a long time before things changed. We went and did what we wanted and enjoyed life. When did we stop having fun?

I looked back over Caleb's struggles and wondered. He was such a happy, friendly kid. People commented on it all the time. Things really began to change for him in the first grade. By the second grade he was a wreck. I blamed it on his overpowering personality, his small size, his new sister, the move, the death of his grandfather. Now, as I look back, I see that it directly coincided with when Sam said he began to spiral out of control. Did Sam's emotional unavailability have something to do with Caleb's struggles? I said to Sam repeatedly over the past few years, "Can you at least pretend to like him?" How awful for Caleb. How sad for Sam. How did the healing begin? I hoped that while Sam was at the house, they could begin to reconnect and start to undo some of the damage that had been done.

God, there was just so much! It was overwhelming. No wonder Caleb was angry and sad. He was sensitive and loving. I prayed that he didn't try to hide and protect that side of himself too much.

I came home from my walk and, before dinner, thought I would have an actual, uninterrupted soak in the tub. Just as I was about to sink into the water, I realized I had left the washcloth on the rack. I stood up to reach for it and whacked my ass on a glass shelf in the tub. I almost passed out. After assuring myself that I wasn't bleeding, I had my bath. Then I made pizza. Now there I was, sitting, drinking tea, listening to some good piano music, and wondering what the kids were doing.

It was funny, but walking through town really made me realize how much I missed Sam. Not the moody, self-absorbed, pessimistic man he had become, but the passionate, fun, optimistic, kind, loving man he was. We used to talk and dream. Now we worked and survived.

One of the first things I loved about him was that I could count on him to do what he said he would do. If he said he would be there at seven o'clock, he was there at seven o'clock. It felt safe to believe him.

Friday, March 7

I survived my first night. I slept, with the assistance of sleep meds, and got up this morning to do some yoga. I actually woke up around five o'clock with a jolt of panic about His mother and the commode. It took me awhile to go back to sleep.

The kids called last night. Sam had taken them to Chuck E. Cheese for dinner. Of course, my first thought was, where did he get the money? I had one dollar in my wallet. Then I was a little resentful. His sister took his mother for him so he could do something fun with the kids. I didn't get to do fun things with the kids because his sister was not at my disposal to help with her mother.

Let it go.

I spoke with Sam a little on the phone. It was awkward. He was angry with me and bitter about this separation. There was none of that man I remembered on my walk.

I told Sam that being here alone has made me face how sad I

was. I missed my family. He was sad too. I didn't know how we were going to bridge this gap but if he would try to recover that man he lost and stay in recovery, then I would give it my all.

I was frustrated with the groups like Al-Anon for sex addiction, SA-Anon and Co-SLAA. In admitting that I was powerless over my addiction to Sam and trying to control his sex addiction, and that my life had become unmanageable, I felt like I was being sucked into a lie.

First, my *life* wasn't unmanageable, *he* was.

Second, I didn't try to control his addiction. When I found out about it, I threw him out.

Third, I was not addicted to Sam. I loved him, but I would certainly let him go if he returned to his old ways.

They said that sex addiction was a family disease. I said bullshit.

In all I have read, they talked about sex addicts losing their families or having co-addictive spouses. What about people like me? Where was the support for people who loved their spouses but called it like it was? Why was there nothing to guide them through healing? Why was there no guidance for rebuilding a trusting honest relationship unless you admitted to codependency?

My priest said the foundations of marriage was trust and honesty. Without those, there was no marriage. Everything was built from there. Where did that leave us?

Saturday, March 8

It was a better night although I woke up very sore. It was either the yoga or the massage that I got yesterday with an old gift certificate. Either way, my sore shoulders and neck have taken the focus off my bruised ass and my broken heart.

I decided that my marriage was worth fighting for. I didn't see that before. I couldn't separate who Sam was from what he had done. I didn't think I'd ever get over what he had done. But I remembered who he was, and inside all that moody, self-deprecating garbage was a good man. If he could find him, then I would do my best to forgive.

Another thing was that we needed to be on our own, in our own place. We did our best in our own house, not above my school, not his parents' house. I didn't care if we rented or bought, but we needed to be independent as a family, away from his toxic background, including his mother and sister.

When he finally felt like he could be honest with me about what he did, I would be able to stop looking back and analyzing every moment of the last ten years. I could move forward. Maybe we all could. Faith told me yesterday that if there was anyone who would be able to forgive but not forget, and work through the pain to heal the relationship, it would be me. I wanted to believe her.

Caleb and I had a wonderful evening together. We went to the apartment to put the featherbed on the bed. All the way over I was in a state of panic. I was so afraid that I would walk in on Sam and somebody. He told me he was working, but I guess when you are scared you are not terribly rational. I could feel myself acting a bit too happy and silly and hoping Caleb didn't notice. The apartment was empty. Caleb told me he didn't like it there. I didn't blame him.

Then we went to run a few errands and rent a movie. As we

were walking into the store, I told him of a time when he was probably three years old, I had taken him to a huge children's clothing
store to buy him an Easter outfit. He was at the age when he still
wore short pants and knee socks to church. We had a great time.
He picked out a suit and we got some other things for him. As we
waited in the checkout line, I looked down at him sitting in the carriage and two big tears were rolling down his little chubby cheeks.

"Oh, honey. What's wrong?"

He looked at me and barely whispered, "I thought we were
going to get an Easter outfit?"

"We did, remember? You picked it out."

As if his heart would break, he said, "But where are the ears?"

I hugged him tight and at the checkout counter picked up a
headband with two big rabbit ears. His smile made my heart ache.

Caroline told me to think of a time when I was happy and try
to figure out what happened just before, so that I could duplicate
it. I was having such a hard time with that. It seemed like everything I did was a struggle—work, home, life in general. Tonight, I
was happy. Caleb and I snuggled up on the couch and watched a
movie. There was no undercurrent, no awkwardness. Just me and
Caleb, comfortable and happy to be together. For a while I forgot
about my worries. Thank you, God.

I had a long talk with Rachel. She was angry with her father
and with Becca's indifference. She and I both think that Becca
knew or at least suspected something. Rachel was disgusted with
Sam's behavior. She was furious that he destroyed the only family
she had ever known. She wanted to tell him how she felt but didn't
want to hurt him. I tried to encourage her to tell him using "I feel"

instead of "you did." She was getting married in April. We were not invited.

Caleb was in my bed. I felt like we were connected tonight. We talked about sex. Ok, I talked, he blushed. We watched an episode of *Law and Order SVU* and it was about a fourteen-year-old boy. I was just so desperate that he not go down the same path as his father. Right now, he seemed happy and peaceful. Thank you, God.

I told Sam I needed to know that he could live on his own. I needed to know that for myself as well. I was twenty-two when we met. I lived in The City by the Sea and then New Jersey before we moved in together. How independent am I? It's time to find out.

Sunday, March 9

My priest was right. The way back is through the Psalms. I went to church and it was as if the gates of my heart opened up. I closed my eyes and began, "Oh God, you have blessed me . . ." It was as if He was sitting right next to me.

Sam and I talked in the evening. It was hard. I was trying, I really was. And God knows he has been working hard. Neither of us knew how to get through the betrayal. Maybe it was just time. Time and love.

It occurred to me that Faye had never known a time when Sam was not like this. It broke my heart to say it and his to hear it. It was time to make a change.

Caroline said I have a unique ability to "picture" my life. I saw the pink house and I could see us there. I could envision living there with the kids and all of us living there as a family. It was all good.

I went to see the first apartment that the realtor showed me.

It was tiny. I could picture Sam and I sharing it, alternating time. Even though it was not bigger than our kitchen and family room combined, I thought we could make it work. Then I saw this apartment and could see us getting through the next few difficult months here.

Maybe this was a unique gift. I didn't know. Maybe what I needed to do was picture my life with Sam. Us as a family. Maybe that would help with the process. Creative visualization. Not yet. I was still picturing him with other women. I would try.

Monday, March 10

Eliot Spitzer was on TV this morning. He was apologizing for his behavior with high-priced call girls in a scandal that rocked the governorship of New York. I watched his speech with a feeling of déjà vu. As he was speaking, his wife, the good wife, was standing by his side. She was lovely, composed, and stoic. I wondered if she was in shock. I wanted to call her and tell her, "I understand. You are not alone."

I was thinking about something that Sam said to me the other day. That he admired my spirituality. What strange twists our lives take.

When I was ten years old, I went to the Methodist church. I went alone. My sister Thea would drive me. I chose that church because, at the age of ten, they let me sing in the choir. I loved it. The next year I began to go to the Baptist church where my friends went. Again, I went alone. There was a huge weekend statewide conference called Faith at Work. The minister was asked to select two people from the parish who were spiritually ready to attend the conference with him. He chose me. I was twelve years old.

Throughout high school I went back and forth between the Baptist and Congregational churches. When I went to college, I stopped going. A friend from high school begged me to go back to church. I didn't listen. Teenage rebellion.

Then I met Sam. He was clear and open about his spirituality without being a zealot. He was living proof of what it was to be a Christian. He was good, kind, generous and compassionate. He prayed, read the Bible and the Book of Common Prayer regularly and went to church every Sunday. I wanted to be like that, sure of my faith and my place in God's plan. Slowly it began to take shape for me. As I finally became confident in my spirituality, Sam pulled away from God.

What better time for him to return than Lent? Seeing his pain, how could God not welcome him with open arms?

Tuesday, March 11

I stayed home with Faye. She was diagnosed with Fifth's Disease. Caleb was home for spring break, so I had both kids and his mother. It felt like a weekend, which I hate. His mother was toxic, and she was getting worse by the day. Twice I caught her just as she was about to sit where there was no chair. The second time she snapped at me. She could be the coldest, most self-righteous bitch. Knowing what she did to Sam destroyed what few remaining good feelings I had about her. She refused to get dressed this morning. She snapped at me about that too. Maybe it was time for a nursing home. Except that when his sister came over, she was all sweetness and light.

I invited Sam to go to church with me on Easter. I had no idea if he would be able to get through it. He was incredibly grateful. It made me uncomfortable to feel like I was holding his future in my hands. I didn't want that responsibility. After all, he certainly didn't take great care of the future of our family or of me. I didn't want to be entrusted with his.

I started my period. Easy to tell. I sounded like a horrible bitch. That's the third one during this separation. I felt sick, like I did in the beginning. Nausea, cramps, sweats. I knew that the cramps were courtesy of my period. But the rest felt just like it did in January. Like I was right on the verge of being ill all the time. Was I? I hoped that I was not picking something up on some emotional, subconscious level—more betrayal, more lies.

I needed to stop writing. I really did sound like a crazy woman.

Wednesday, March 12

I told Caroline that I journaled so that I could mark my progress. I would one day be able to look back over what I'd written and see how far I'd come. On this night, I felt as if I were regressing. Maybe it was my period, but I felt angry and bitter. One minute I was full of love for Sam and pride in his ability to look at what he had done. The next minute I was angry, hurt and still reeling from the overwhelming pain of his betrayal. A betrayal that he wouldn't even admit to out loud.

Once I was secure in his love. When things started to head south, I couldn't figure out what was wrong. Never in my wildest imaginings did I believe him capable of this.

Fear #1—If he had this secret life for eight to ten years and I was clueless, what was to stop it from happening again?

Fear #2—What would happen to us when he met someone in recovery who understood all that he was going through and all that he had been through? What would happen when they formed a bond?

Thursday, March 13

It was my night at the apartment. Sam picked Faye up from our Brownies meeting tonight. It was weird and sad. As she was getting ready to go, she came to hug me, cheeks flaming red, eyes teary, and said she was starting to not feel well. I hoped he understood how sensitive she was and responded to it.

I was lying in bed, sipping tea. Somebody downstairs just left, slamming the door. The sound scared me half to death.

Sam did something very sweet. There was a Victoria's Secret bag in my drawer. It held some new panties. There was a note telling me that he was tired of folding worn out, torn panties. That is something the old Sam would have done.

I remember when we used to spend hours looking through catalogues. He would take a pen and mark off everything I liked. We would actually buy very little, if anything, but we would mentally spend a fortune. It was dreaming and bonding.

Friday, March 14

I went to Barnes and Noble tonight. Sam had two new books about forgiveness. I thought it might be helpful if we both read the same books. I bought a book called "After the Affair"[4]. Amazingly enough, there was a profound sense of relief that I was not crazy. Of course, on the second page it was discussing different types of affairs and talked about sex addiction. The book said, "This is a specialized disorder that is beyond the scope of this book." God, would I ever find help?

Chapter one began, "When I first uncovered your secret, I stopped feeling special to you. But on a deeper level, I lost trust in the world and in myself."

There it was. My life right now.

I told Sam that I thought we needed to live independently, out of his mother's house. When we had our own house, not dependent on my school, his parents, or his sister, we were happy. We didn't have much money, but it didn't seem to matter. I was almost certain he would see this conversation as pressure to buy a new house and try to fix our problems by changing our geographical location. That wasn't it. I was trying to figure what were all the contributing factors that led us here. I needed to understand what my wants and needs actually were. That was the only way we would be able to decide if he could actually meet any of them.

Saturday, March 15

I found myself glad I bought the book, *After the Affair*. It felt as if she could see into my mind. She touched on the uncertainty, insecurity, the loss and sadness, anger and frustration, the deep despair. I no longer felt alone.

---

[4] Janis Abrahms Spring, *After the Affair*, (William Morrow: HarperCollins, 1996)

I told Sam that when he didn't call me and expected me to do all, or the majority of, the contacting, I felt as if I was the only one reaching out. He called twice later.

I went to Macy's to use the bathroom. We met my sister Hannah in Burlington so she could take Caleb for a few fun days. As I walked through the store, I saw so many cute things. I realized how long it had been since I bought anything new for myself or went on a shopping spree. I think it was when I opened my school in this location. Sam and I spent the day at the mall, and we shopped for me. That was what, four years ago?

I forgot that people regularly buy new and stylish things for themselves. I have been telling myself for such a long time that, "I don't need it." I translated that to mean, "I don't want it." I *did* want it. I wanted to look stylish and pretty. When I was in Maine, Aunt Bitsy gave me a sweater that had been hers. It was very stylish, and I got a lot of compliments on it. Was that petty? Or greedy?

Last summer, his sister told Sam that all I do is spend money. I asked Sam if he thought that was true and he said yes. I was so upset; I didn't buy new clothes. I tried really hard to find clothes on sale for the kids. I bought inexpensive groceries, packed lunches and set aside things all year for Christmas. I needed to examine this further.

It was time to open my eyes to the truth of our relationship. Had I been deceiving myself about Sam's capacity to love? Had I been excusing his behavior for too long? Was there something in my past compelling me to love and ingratiate myself with people who betrayed or bullied me? Did I have negative behavior that provoked his negative treatment?

Sunday, March 16

I felt like I had a minor personal breakthrough! Faye and I went to church on Palm Sunday. When we arrived, we gathered in the parish hall for the traditional palm-laden processional to the church. As we came in, I remembered the annual Palm Sunday bake sale. The tables were all set up and baked goods were starting to arrive. For a moment I felt a surge of panic followed closely by guilt. Then, out of nowhere, I had a moment of conscious thought. "STOP! The bake sale will be a success, with or without your cupcakes. Your ability to be Martha Stewart, even if it kills you, does not define who you are or what you are capable of." It was liberating.

I was doing a lot of reading in "After the Affair." One of the things that it says, when looking toward a decision to stay or go, was how willing Sam was to examine and discuss his infidelity. How honest was he willing to be? I needed to believe that it was not going to happen again.

Right now, I didn't. I didn't believe him. I didn't trust him. I knew he was working hard, but lying was such a large part of the fabric of who he was, I wasn't sure if he was capable of honesty or fidelity. I was afraid that it had been going on for too long and had become too much a part of his life. I felt like he was not going to be forthcoming with the truth. If I asked the right questions, he might answer them honestly, maybe. It was as if he was not willing to give up the information voluntarily. This had become a gigantic wall between us. Like his cruising for transvestites or transsexuals. I asked him, and I knew his answers were lies. All his telltale lying behaviors were there. Behaviors I wouldn't have recognized six months ago. It would be impossible for me to make a decision without knowing all the facts of his infidelity, his lying, his betrayal, his sickness. This was something he needed to put out on the table, no matter how painful. No matter the cost.

When I first found ALT.com, he brushed it off as harmless looking. I knew he was lying. I begged him to put it all out on the table so that we could deal with it. I wondered if we would be in a different place now if he had done that. I felt like I was no closer to knowing the truth about what had been going on in my marriage than I was two months ago.

Monday, March 17

I was sick yet again. I had a sinus infection and that could have developed into strep throat. I came home at noon to go to bed. Sam was there with his mother. He was kind and accommodating. He had looked at a list of things to do that I left on the dining room table, a list not necessarily meant for him, and actually began working on it. A first. He also had been doing all the laundry. Another first. It was a tremendous help. I couldn't seem to get motivated to do anything. I was so tired, I felt like I just floated around in circles, not accomplishing much at all.

We talked some. We didn't get a chance the night before. It was emotional and very painful. And oh, so necessary. When we were talking, I almost couldn't believe what our relationship had become. Would I have this feeling of disbelief forever?

I did some more reading about "facing your disfigured self" and several things stood out to me:

"Unable to connect emotionally to others"

Sam—sexually compulsive

"Unable to value yourself"

Sam—masking feelings of disgrace or inferiority

"Unable to express yourself"

Me—silencing needs to keep the peace; inside, seething frustration

"Unable to let go and have fun"

Me—unrelenting standards, running too hard and too fast, no time to stop and smell the roses.

Sam came home from his meeting. I was lying down writing. He was doing laundry. It felt extremely awkward. I was really tired, but I didn't want to just turn the light out. That would have seemed rude.

Tuesday, March 18—Rachel's birthday

I was very sick. The medicine had been making me sick to my stomach. Last night I woke up at 12:45 and was up for the night. I asked Sam if he would sleep here tonight so he could care for his mother and I could sleep through the night. So, there I was, in Caleb's bed. The last time I slept there was the last time Sam and I slept under the same roof. So much had changed and yet not. In some ways I felt closer to him than ever. He was trying so hard to reconnect. In some ways I felt as lost as I was that night two months ago, hurt, full of rage and disbelief. Where did we go from here? I felt helpless.

Wednesday, March 19

I met with Caroline. If she weren't my therapist, I would have wanted her to be my friend.

I slept the whole night last night, but when I woke up, I felt worse. It seemed to be moving into my chest. Sam was true to his word and woke me up with a cup of coffee this morning. We used to do that for each other all the time. There was much we needed to sort out. There just didn't ever seem to be enough time to talk. He had been reading my journal. It didn't really bother me. At least he knew where I was. It put me at a slight disadvantage in that I had to guess where he was.

In my meeting with Caroline, we talked about a plan to not check on him. Let him do the work he needed to do. I had to identify behavior markers that would tell if we were headed in the wrong direction and state clearly and concisely what they would be. She said to compare it to a teenager who got caught smoking pot. First you grounded him. Then, after a while, you had to let him out, but you certainly couldn't follow him around all day. You developed a list of behavior markers for him.

> If your grades drop below B-
> If you are five minutes late for curfew
> If you have dark circles under your eyes
> If you stop eating healthily, etc.

I told her how frustrated I have been with all the books that assume you were codependent or that you leave the marriage. It seemed that people like me fall between the cracks. She said that was my book. She told me after our first meeting that I would someday write a book to help others in this crazy situation. We would see.

She said again that she couldn't believe how quickly I was putting this together. She made me feel good about myself at a time when I felt unlovable and undesirable. I asked her how people get past their disgust at the thought of sex. She said that some people never do. That one of the realities about the relationship that Sam and I put together is that it may not include sex. As long as the "betrayal movie" kept playing in my mind, I would have to accept that. She also said that in time the movie will be covered over by new, better memories. Maybe.

She also thought my feelings about the house and our dependent living situation were insightful. Whether we ended up in one house or two, we needed to have our own space, where we were free to make our own lives.

Sam was a master manipulator and deceiver. That was simply a fact. Neither good nor bad, but a fact that needed to remain out on the table forever.

Friday, March 21

Pneumonia. A very scary word and I had it. I spent much of last night thinking of a young mother I knew at school and how pneumonia killed her in only a week. I was terrified.

Sam was at the house taking care of me. I slept most of the day.

It was funny, Caroline and I were talking on Wednesday about his mother and how some people with no reason to live seemed to hang on forever. It was often the people who had so much to offer that got taken too soon. I prayed I was not one of them.

Monday, March 24

Easter came and went. I was in bed, exhausted.

I was at a total loss.

Sam had been here since Thursday night taking care of me. He had been wonderful, kind, considerate, loving, attentive. We had some good talks. I was beginning to think there was something wrong with me, not letting our love take us past all the mistrust.

He had a trial day for a new job. I was anxiously waiting for him to come home to hear all about it. We were talking of the future and looking there together.

Caleb had a dentist appointment that I had rescheduled from last November. Still feeling sick, I decided to drive him over and wait in the car for him. Sam had my car, so we took his. Waiting there, I looked through the books that he was reading. It was one way to help stay on the same page. He left his red duffle bag in the car. I looked in it and found two porn films and a new corkscrew. I couldn't have cared less about the corkscrew, except that I asked him not to drink and he agreed. The videos were another matter. This was how it all began—collecting porn. I just couldn't understand how someone couldn't get through the day without sex. I didn't understand why someone would consciously put their marriage and family on the line to buy pornography. This was not his uncontrollable addiction. He was going to therapy, to twelve-step meetings. This was a decision.

If this was the lifestyle he chose, that was fine. It was not my choice and I would not be dragged into it. He said he had been sober since January 14. Lies. Lies. Lies. Lies. Lies. Lies. Lies. Lies.

I had a good mind to go to Gabriel's house and say, "Gee, we felt so guilty about kissing. If my marriage doesn't matter to him, maybe it shouldn't matter to me either. Let's just have sex and get it over with."

That would solve nothing, and I would hate myself. Besides, it had never been Gabriel I wanted.

I couldn't believe I was back in this position, having to confront, ask and sort through lies. I wouldn't do it. I was worth more. I deserved somebody who loved me honestly, wholly.

He was a master manipulator and deceiver. I wouldn't forget it again.

Tuesday, March 25

He said the videos were Frank's, a client at the group home where he worked. He said that Frank regularly bought porn and dirty magazines and the staff were required to take them home to screen them for violence. I was not sure I believed that. What agency would ask that of its staff? I could not be the only one who took issue with my husband frequenting adult video stores with his clients. Especially since his sex addiction had been brought out into the open.

Was he being truthful? Or was he lying again? How did I tell?

That brought up a good point. What was Sam's definition of sobriety? What was mine? Could they work together? He made it sound as if he was not going to avoid porn. I think he saw his addiction as only his physical infidelity. But to me it was so much

more. It was also his need for porn that didn't involve me. He said
he only watched it alone because after a while I wouldn't watch it
with him. That was a lie, and he was still in denial about what was
controlling him. I took issue with his massive collection of porn
when we lived above my school. I made him throw it out when we
moved, two big boxes, at least fifty videos. I found a garbage bag
full of it under the bed, some under the couch, in his trunk, in a
bag beside the bed. NO MORE PORN. It was the foundation for
secrecy—the secret life.

I had already put a block on the computer, which I would keep
on. It blocked out adult, nudity, violence, hate, personal and chat
sites.

When I told him that I was not sure that I would be able to
have sex with him anytime soon, he got angry and said, "I won't
live in a sexless marriage!" I really resented the pressure put on
me to come to terms with what he did and to do it quickly. He
spent nearly ten years shitting on me and our marriage and I was
supposed to get over it in ten weeks? I really wanted to find a way
to make this work, but I wasn't sure I could. I told him I needed to
know exactly what he did and with whom. It was not the first time
I had said it. Without that, how would we move forward?

I had always thought that he was the most loving, generous,
articulate, intelligent man I knew. I told everybody, and in front of
him too. Maybe I didn't tell him enough. All I knew is that I didn't
know anything. I couldn't trust him, and I felt lost again and alone.
I resented his referrals to "our" problems. I didn't sleep with anyone. I didn't solicit sex. I didn't answer personal ads or close my
store to have sex in the back. I did get too close to Gabriel. I would

shamefully admit that. Yes, we made out. That was the end of it. How was that different from his relationship with Bonnie that he kept up our entire married life? He was sleeping with Bonnie. I was not sleeping with Gabriel. I had to stop writing. I was getting too angry and resentful. I would admit to my part in the breakdown of our relationship, but this is not "our" problem.

Wednesday, March 26

I looked in the mirror and didn't like what I saw. I looked like shit. I felt like I had been sick forever and I looked like it. Anyone who suffered excessive pride needed only to get pneumonia. I used to think I was a little bit pretty. There was nothing pretty there now. I felt very sick this morning and so tired. I got into bed and my legs began to sweat. I feared a relapse. God, I hoped not.

In some ways I would really have loved to have Sam in bed with me. The warmth of his body, the rhythm of his breathing. I felt like I would heal so much faster. But I didn't trust him. Not yet. I was afraid.

Thursday, March 27

I went back to the doctor. By the time my appointment rolled around at 1:00, I had already had two naps. The weeks of sleep deprivation had finally caught up with me. My body was screaming, "STOP!" The doctor said I was healing. I still had pneumonia, but it was, ever so slowly, getting better.

Sam took me to the doctor and then made dinner after my third nap. I was telling him about the plans Hannah and I were making for Thea's fiftieth birthday party, when out of nowhere, I got a flash of his MySpace page: forty-nine and single. All the hurt and loss came welling up inside me. I knew that I carried a lot of baggage from my father's abandonment and this only added to it. I couldn't help my father leaving. I was only a little girl. Sam's rejection was of Josie, the grown woman. It was more painful than anything I had ever experienced. I was the mother of his children, the keeper of his home, the caregiver of his mother, and for a long time, the breadwinner. I thought I was also his best friend, his confidant, his love.

For years we had been living a lie, an illusion of a relationship. His lies kept his secrets safe for at least nine years. Where did we honestly go from there? How did we heal? Was it possible? I had no truths, no confessions. I didn't even think we were on the same page as far as definitions of relationships. I saw the kids happy to have him around and felt guilty and selfish.

So, he left to get Faye, gave me a hug, and whispered, "Sorry." Again, where did that leave me? How sorry was he? And sorry for what? Sorry for what he did or sorry he got caught? If I hadn't stumbled upon his infidelity and betrayal, it would still be going on now and I would still be ignorant and frustrated.

I think that the nine years of lying did much more damage than the nine years of infidelity. Had he been unfaithful and then been honest, we could have taken a look at the situation, painfully, and figured out the next step. But because he lied to cover it all up, he could have lied about anything and everything that went on. Now as we were looking at our marriage and trying to untangle the mess, how could I believe anything that came out of his mouth?

There was no way of judging his honesty. He had lied to me,

to his family, to his boss, and his priest. Did he lie to his friends? He lied to Dan. Did he lie to Josh?

Maybe we were too close too soon. I needed to get well so that we could put some space between us again.

Just when I thought we might have a chance, the despair, abandonment, and hurt threatened to overwhelm me again.

Friday, March 28

I was sad. I felt overwhelmed, bogged down and depressed. Sam's inability or unwillingness to talk about anything other than to say "sorry" just added to the feeling of isolation.

I dreamed last night that we were making love. I wanted him to know that I found him sexy and desirable. In the middle of it all he got up and walked out. Abandoned even in my dreams.

Without being able to talk this out with him, I felt like I had not been able to work through it and deal with it.

I talked with Sam when he was driving to pick up Caleb and his schoolmates for the carpool. I told him how isolated I felt when these negative feelings and memories come bubbling to the surface. I told him that every book I've read states that there can be no healing until the infidelity and betrayals are all put on the table and examined. I half expected him to get exasperated and say, "God, would you get off it already?"

Why did I do that? I was always selling him short. He was capable of so much and I didn't give him nearly enough credit. Why did I think that he wouldn't jump at the chance to show his love and support? I guess I knew how fragile he was. There was a part of me that was not willing to add to his grief and shame at the expense of my own sense of self. That was not healthy. I needed to trust him with the abandonment and betrayal I felt, without grinding him down. He needed to trust that I would not explode in self-righteous, guilt-inducing anger. He said he was so afraid of my reaction. It didn't make sense. In his fear, he drove me toward the very reaction he was most afraid of, ensuring failure for us both.

Saturday, March 29

I felt like I turned a corner. I got dressed and went outside to sit in the sun for a while and it felt so good. Then I had a nap and a long hot bath.

I had a great talk with Shawn. I miss him. He has been such a good friend. I did a lot of thinking about The Theatre lately. It nearly killed my marriage and my spirit. I loved performing but it just wasn't worth it. Then I thought back to the Shakespeare Theatre. Was it really so different? The director used to hit on me all the time. When we were having sex, Sam liked to hear stories about my leading man and me. Did he know that they were completely made up? Was this sickness within the theater or within our relationship and ourselves? Even though there was a part of me that thought, "I'm just not enough for him," the sex was hot and often. But even then, it was never just us in our bed. Maybe fantasies were something that should never have been shared. Then the line between fantasy and reality would never have been crossed.

Shawn said something to me. Maybe in the end this would be the best thing that ever happened to us—a wake-up call that would actually save and improve our marriage. Time would tell.

Sunday, March 30

Broke some more ground. Had fun. Just Sam and me.

He came home from church and asked if I would like to take a drive to see the pink house. We ended up driving around, going to an open house and then over to see the pink house I'd looked at. My little pink house was sold. But the open house we went to was fabulous! It was a big old Victorian with lots of large rooms, windows everywhere, open and bright, beautiful floors, just enough yard and ready to move in. We both completely fell in love. The one minor glitch was the price tag of half a million dollars. Oh, well. It was a great day and I really enjoyed being together. He held my hand on the way home. I was a little uncomfortable with that, but I didn't say anything. I didn't want to ruin the moment.

Tonight, I was thinking about our frustrating conversation the other day when I found the porn in his car. He said that if I expected perfection in his recovery, then I was going to be disappointed. I had been processing this for about a week. Yes, I supposed I did expect perfection in this. Fidelity. It was a black and white issue. You were faithful or you were not. I didn't expect him to be perfect in any other way, but I did expect fidelity. And I believed, were the tables turned, the situation reversed, he would expect and demand no less from me.

Monday, March 31

I went back to work. I was exhausted and everything ached. Sam was sweet, bringing me coffee to work. I was able to tell him that I have been uncomfortable getting too close, too soon. I have been afraid that the work that needs to get done will not. I was just not ready. He was great. I felt like such a schmuck after he had taken such good care of me. I didn't want it to feel like a slap in the face.

Tonight, before he left for his meeting, we were making dinner and talking. I told him that Gabriel had called me, but I hadn't returned his call. Sam said that he could not control my choices. "I know that," I told him, "but if we are going to follow the guidelines in *Emotional Infidelity*[5], then there are things we need to give up. My friendship with Gabriel is one of those things." If Sam had that kind of a close female friend, I would probably be less than understanding, especially now, knowing where his friendships ended up.

He told me that reading *Forgive for Love*[6] made him realize that he could only be responsible for his own choices and decisions. That he had to trust that I would make the decision each day to love him and put him first. I said that was part of the problem. For a very long time, he made the decision each day not to love me and put me first. He said he understood. I don't think he could possibly understand how it felt. Try to understand, maybe. But never fully understand what it felt like for the one you loved to choose anyone but you for years, keeping you in the dark. It was much more than devastating. And this is written without anger or hurt. A fact of my life. Something that I have been trying hard to come to terms with.

---

[5] M. Gary Neuman, *Emotional Infidelity: How to Affair-Proof Your Marriage*, (Random House: Three Rivers Press 2001)

[6] Frederic Luskin, *Forgive for Love: The Missing Ingredient for a Healthy and Lasting Relationship*, (HarperCollins 2007)

Wednesday, April 2

I began this day with so little energy that I felt like I was battling pneumonia all over again.

I met with Caroline. When I was on my way there I thought, *what would we find to talk about?* And then the hour flew by as I gave voice to my thoughts and realizations, my hopes, and plans, of all that I was unsure of and the very little bit I felt that I knew.

One thing I knew was that Sam and I had to be separated. When we were together it was wonderful, just where I wanted to be. It was also confusing, being intertwined and without boundaries, buying lingerie, touches that felt too intimate, hand holding. If we were to go on like that, we would risk falling into the same old dysfunctional pattern. Nothing worked on or worked through. Then, when unresolved rage and hurt erupted, he would be confused, thinking that was all behind us, and I would build resentment.

I told Caroline about my trip to Macy's and how I seemed only to recognize my needs and wants either when I ran headlong into one or else by coming to realize what they weren't.

The important thing to remember was that we had both been working on the same thing—reconciliation. It could not be rushed; particularly by Sam's need to put it all back together quickly, as if nothing ever happened. He didn't want to feel too uncomfortable for too long. Baby steps. If I was uncomfortable holding his hand, then the first goal was to become comfortable with that again. I would not be okay with that until I knew where his hands had been. When I could hold hands again, then we would be able to move on to the next thing. Baby steps. Rebuilding trust and intimacy.

We talked about the porn I found. When figuring out where

we were, what was I entitled to? Did I have the right to check his phone? His credit card statements? Call his supervisor about the porn? None of these were things I ever wanted to do!

As we separate, Caroline said to start over. Date as if we were just getting to know one another. How would we treat someone we were interested in? Someone we liked and respected and wanted to find out more about? Not by buying them lingerie and asking to see them in it. Baby steps.

We would work with Dan. We would try to put this together. Maybe it would work. Maybe not.

When we talked about the hand holding in the car, I told her that it made me very uncomfortable, but I didn't say anything to him for several reasons.

- I didn't want to hurt his feelings.
- I wasn't sure why I was uncomfortable. Was it me? Him? Us?
- I didn't want to spoil the great day.

She said I gave him a gift. I didn't leave my hand there because I was afraid to take it out. I made a conscious decision and then talked to him about it later.

More conscious thought is good.

Thursday, April 3

I felt like a wrung-out sponge.

I was back at the apartment, a place I did not plan to be until after vacation. It was 8:00 and it was all I could do to stay awake to write this down, but it was far too important to forget.

Sam was returning my car to school this afternoon as I was pulling out in his. He already seemed tense about a phone conversation we had earlier. Now I don't even remember what was said—how unlike me. As he stood at the car door talking to me, I saw that he had at least one, if not two, cell phone bills tucked into his book. I asked him if he was collecting phone bills. He said he was checking the phone calls—evasive. "Checking for what?" I asked. He said, "Looking for certain numbers." Still evasive, but I knew what he was doing, and his avoidance was starting to piss me off. I asked what numbers he was looking for. He said he was adding up minutes between mine and Gabriel's phones. I replied, "You didn't find many did you?" He was terse, "There were quite a few."

He was checking up on me. I lost it! That little fuck could shit all over our relationship and all over me and then try to relieve his guilt by turning it around on me. I already told him that Gabriel and I made out. I told him that I had chosen to end that friendship. He said that he didn't remember my telling him about the kissing. More lies! It was in his journal!

I drove away. I was too angry to have a conversation. When I got home, I told him I was going to the apartment. I tried to make it clear that I was not going to take the blame for this, no matter how he tried to turn it around and pin it on me. I was a raving lunatic. All my anger and frustration about still not being any closer to having answers came pouring out.

As my tirade subsided, we actually began to talk. He tried to explain his terrible insecurities about Gabriel. I told him that I was not interested in a relationship with Gabriel. Gabriel was filling a need in me that Sam had, for a long, long time, refused to fill.

Gabriel listened and talked with me. He made me feel like I was worth listening to and that my opinions mattered, even though he rarely agreed with me.

We talked about the hand holding issue, Sam actually brought it up, and his need for physical contact. That is a need I thought I could fulfill, if we could take the time to work through this. It was a need that I had also, close physical contact, not necessarily sexual. A need to be held and touched. He said that we made a big mistake when we stopped focusing on our marriage. I tried to explain that when Faye was born and he lost his job, we went into survival mode. We have been there ever since.

I went back to work full time when Faye was six weeks old. By the time she was four months, I was working from 7:30 till 4:30 at my school and then from 7:00 till 11:30 at The Theatre. I was nursing full time, cooking, and cleaning, doing laundry, and we had a busy five-year-old as well. I had not stopped since.

I knew there were things that were taking away from our marriage. That's why I bought the book, *101 Nights of Grrreat Romance*[7]. I did one activity, then we each took another activity to do. We decided to take turns each week. His turn was the next week. He never did it.

I told him that I was glad he was coming to all these realizations about our relationship. I was also frustrated that these are all things that I tried to tell him over the years. After a long time of him not listening, I just stopped talking.

I had to stop writing. I would start crying again. I just wanted to go to sleep.

---

[7] Laura Corn, *101 Nights of Grrreat Romance*, (Doubleday, 1997)

Friday, April 4

Suicide. That's what Sam said he was trying to commit. For nine years.

I felt like I tried to show him through words and actions how much I loved him, how worthy he was. I didn't know what else to do. He said that he had to look within himself, but I knew that he had also been looking to me. I told him that when Caroline said something about my life, I started to cry and choked out, "This is not my life. That, back there, and that, way up there is my life. *This* is not my life!" She said it was like traveling through a pitch-black tunnel and all you can see is the small area lit by your head-lights. Eventually you will come out on the other side. Hopefully together. She said that I had not let him drag me down into his shit. I had my work to do and he had his. It was separate from the work we had to do together. It had been a long time since I woke up with my eyes so swollen.

A healing evening, after a sad miserable start to the day. I called Sam to tell him he needed to let me know what Faye was doing after school. After talking for a few minutes, he asked if he could bring me anything. "Coffee," I said. He laughed. When I returned to work last week, Sam brought me coffee in the middle of the morning. My assistant, in surprise said, "But she already brushed her teeth!" Another teacher said the same thing to him. I explained to him that after I brush my teeth, I don't drink coffee or soda. My teeth were too sensitive to bleach and, because I per-formed all the time, I didn't want the stains.

How was it that the girls who worked for me knew this about me, but my husband of fourteen years didn't? This was exactly the picture that "Emotional Infidelity" was trying to paint. It was not lost on either of us.

So, when I asked him to bring me coffee this morning, I hoped he knew that it was because I wanted to see him. We talked for a little bit. Healing talk, full of sadness. My eyes were still very swollen and sore. Afterwards, I was able to focus on work and nothing else. For the first time in a long time, I felt productive and capable.

After work I went home to get a change of clothes for the next day. We talked a bit more. Our checking account was about to be overdrawn so I told him I would make a deposit.

"From your school?"

"No, my sister Kate gave me some money when I was in Maine and I opened my own bank account. I was tired of feeling so vulnerable. I needed to know I had choices."

Silence. I thought he was going to rant and rave. He didn't. He told me he was completely surprised, but he wasn't angry. I tried not to rush to explain myself to avoid his wrath. I guess I didn't do very well, because he looked at me and said again, "I'm not angry."

"I didn't know what you were going to do," I replied," I had to make sure I could take care of me and the kids. There were a few weeks when there were fourteen dollars in the checking account, and I had no cash. I had no way to pay bills or buy groceries. I was feeding the kids on the forty dollars your mother gave me each week."

Then I told him that, hopefully, it was getting better. He said I should have told him. I said I thought he knew. And why was it up to me to tell him? It was *our* checking account. And at that time, we weren't exactly speaking. It was hard to talk and not get defensive, but we did, and it was healing. I told him that my school was finally running in the black, and hopefully, financial rewards would not be far behind. His eyes welled up and he thanked me for sharing with him. He said I hadn't shared any information about my business with him in a long time. I told him I didn't think he was interested. We really were in survival mode.

I had planned to go to a movie alone that evening, but I asked if he would like to go together as a family. And we did. It was fun and relaxed, even as we chatted afterward. When it came time to say goodnight, I had a bout of inner panic. I didn't want to leave the kids or him. I didn't want them to drive home and talk and giggle in the car, then tuck each other in or snuggle up. Not while I drove to the apartment by myself. I hoped one of the kids would say, "Can't I come and sleep with you Mom?" But they didn't. And I went to the apartment alone.

Now there I was, in bed, alone, in this apartment. I wanted to be at home with my family—with all the people I loved and missed so much my heart ached. But I had important work to do. I needed to discover who I was and what my wants and needs were.

Saturday, April 5

I got up in the morning and went for an extended walk. I walked the long way to the bank and then back along familiar streets. I didn't walk past our old house. It was as if I had already acknowledged the pain in that loss and was ready to move on. It was my first walk since being sick and it felt good. As I was walking, I noticed how many stores were empty with "For Rent" and "For Sale" signs in the windows. They were all over the place. It seemed sort of symbolic somehow. Maybe it really was time for us to move on.

After I got back to the apartment, I decided to go to Barnes and Noble. Sam had been talking about wanting to build a post and beam house. I wanted to see if I could find a book on the subject. I also wanted to get him a new journal. I searched for a couple of hours but couldn't find exactly the book I was looking for, so I got a book about designing family spaces instead, as well as a magazine of home plans. I looked all the journals over carefully. He has been writing in a spiral notebook. He needed something better, something more special. After much deliberation, I finally chose one with a leather cover, printed all over with antique typewriters and type. Then it took even longer to pick out just the right card. I wanted it to be special. I took it back to the apartment and left it on the bed for him. I wrote in the card,

"It is as important where you write as what you write. Your thoughts, dreams, hopes, fears, prayers, and plans deserve more than just a notebook."

I hoped he liked it. I was a little worried. It was now 10:30 at night. I thought he would get back to the apartment a little after he got out of work at 9:00, find it and give me a call. I hadn't heard from him. Now, of course, my brain was in overdrive. Did he go back to the apartment? Did he make a stop? Hook up? God, I hoped not.

Sunday, April 6

What a wonderful day! I was lying there next to a warm sleeping Faye. The dog was snoring. I had just taken his mother to the bathroom and was counting my blessings. I asked Sam if he would like to go to church with us and if he would plan a family activity. He arrived at 9:00 and immediately took me into his arms with a thankful hug for the journal. He got it the night before but was afraid to call because he didn't want to wake me. He was very teary, and it was a moment I wouldn't have swapped for anything. Church was comfortable. He seemed at ease there for the first time ever. I got very emotional toward the end of the service, but it was not overwhelming. We seemed just fine.

We came home and tried to decide what to do. He was planning to go out to the point to fly kites, but it was cloudy and raw. We got in the car and drove over the bridge to a huge state park. Caleb wanted to try to fly kites, despite the weather. He did great. We walked a little on the rocks and then Faye wanted to try her kite. They had so much fun. There was a guy who was trying to fly a really big trick kite. It was so windy that the kite took off, pulling him across the field and through the mud on his bottom. We all laughed. Then we drove to the next town and showed the kids the big Victorian house we had fallen in love with and then headed home. After a stop at the market, we arrived at home. I was exhausted, like I might have been a week ago. I lay down for a bit.

After dinner, Sam and I watched a movie. I asked him if he wanted to stay because it was so late, but he decided to go back to the apartment. I hoped I hadn't said anything wrong. I felt like it was a wonderful, hopeful day without pressure or underlying expectation.

Now I lay in bed, listening to the dog snore and Faye breathe. She was lying on her stomach with her head turned toward me.

Her lashes dark and thick on her flushed cheeks and her hair fanned out behind her. She was truly lovely. She stayed at a friend's house the night before. The mother called me late to tell me that she had scolded her husband for something, and Faye had said to her friend that she needed to watch that fighting or her mom and dad might end up like Sam and me. I decided to make a conscious effort to talk with her each day and *really* hear what she was saying. I didn't want her to be afraid.

Tuesday, April 8

I was finally packed and ready to go to Arizona to ride home with my mother. I couldn't wait.

What a bizarre day. It started with a call from Gabriel. I was sure that bumping into him last night, and Sam's seeing him this morning at the coffee shop, triggered the call. We talked for a little bit, mostly about him and his wife, and I got off the phone as quickly as I could without being rude. After we hung up, I called Sam to tell him Gabriel had called. I didn't want him to stress or see it on the phone bill and think I was keeping things from him. He got all tense and weird. I knew he hadn't believed me about my level of involvement with Gabriel, but there was nothing I could do about it. I would not admit to something I hadn't done so he could feel better about himself and his own behavior.

Then, when I was coming home, I called Sam to tell him I had to pick up a few things from the apartment. He again got all weird and told me that there was a porn video on the table. He said it was left over from the ones from work and that he had left it at the apartment. He said it had been there for a while. Lies! Lies! Lies!

There was not porn there before. I felt deflated. I thought we were making such progress. He couldn't have both worlds. He needed to decide what it was he wanted.

I tried to explain that I was not judging or trying to control anything but my own life. But if this is what he has chosen, then that was ok. It was not what I have chosen. My life would not contain secrets, shame, or guilt.

He was cycling, just as Caroline predicted. Could I handle this? He was feeling frustrated and lost. He could relapse, backtrack, or act out. Then what?

Wednesday, April 9

We were on the plane from Chicago to Tucson and it was a long and painful flight. My body ached, my legs hurt, and my heart was sad. Sam was a disaster when he came over in the morning. He hadn't slept and looked emotionally spent. I just didn't understand the need for porn or sex to get through the day. I told him I can't fathom how he could be so willing to give up his family to fulfill a need like that. We used to watch it together occasionally and it was fun at the time. Now it was so dirty and shameful to me that I wondered if I would ever be able to look at it again. I was glad to be going away for a week and a half. I told him I absolutely did not want to have to check up on him each day. I said I was trying to let him come clean in his own words, in his own time. That he could use it as a starting point for honesty.

He began to cry this morning and said, "I love you so much." I told him I loved him too, deeply, and completely. He said, "You are so good. I don't deserve you." I explained that as long as he

believed that, he would never stop pushing me away. So complicated.

Gabriel called my school this morning. He said he had forgotten to tell me yesterday that he ran into Sam at the coffee shop.
He said he had given Sam a hundred dollars toward what he owed
from his store. I told him I was glad he had a chance to talk because
Sam feels so alienated. He said, "You know me. I would never
alienate him."

Sam put a hundred dollars in my wallet this morning. I was
very touched. When I asked him where he got the money, he said
he had been saving up for my trip. I was sure he had been, but why
not just say Gabriel gave it to him? I remember him saying something about needing to get a bill to Gabriel, but I honestly didn't
remember him saying anything about a hundred dollars. Should
ask or just let this one go? I would let it go. He told me last night
that Gabriel was a big insecurity for him. I told him there were
several big insecurities for me—porn, masturbation, the computer,
the cell phone, every minute he was away from me.

Why couldn't things just be easy? Why couldn't it just be us?
Loving, giving, sharing.

I couldn't wait for the flight to be over. Everything hurt and I
was exhausted. Period number four.

Thursday, April 10

Faye let us sleep until seven a.m. What a peach! We got up
and puttered around for a bit and then went off for a walk with
my mother and her neighbor. I found myself wishing that Sam and
Caleb were there with us. I talked to them before we left. Sam said

he missed me. I knew he loved me. God, I hoped that was enough.

We went to The Gaslight Theater in Tucson later. What an incredible evening. I kept thinking how much fun it would be to put together a company like this. I could picture myself as part of this company or one of our own making.

Sam would probably never be interested. Not serious enough for him. Oh well. He sounded good on the phone. I hoped and prayed that all the positive changes he had made to reconnect to the family were not temporary. Please God, do not let him drop this ball. Make the love of his family motivation enough to work hard.

Friday, April 11

Yesterday, when we were taking a walk, my mother told Faye the story of forgetting me at Brownies. I was in second grade and my mother was out of the hospital, so I had already turned eight. My mother had two brain tumors when I was growing up. One when I was in the second grade and one when I was a freshman in high school. I went to Brownies one afternoon a week in a church down the street from my school. My little sister Hannah and I were living with our aunt and uncle in the city when my mother was in the hospital. Our older brother and sisters were at my grandparent's. It was an uncomfortable time for me. I felt scared and out of place almost all the time. One day when Brownies was over, everybody, including the adults, left. I went around to the front steps of the church to wait for my mother. I remember that I had a doll with me, which I was clinging to. I waited for what seemed hours. It started to get dark. As an adult, I assumed that it had only been a few minutes and my child's brain had magnified the time. But my mother, when telling the story, said to me, "How long were you there?"

I asked, "What time did you pick me up?"

"Oh, five thirty or six."

I got out of school somewhere around three and went straight to Brownies. I was sure the meeting lasted no more than an hour or an hour and a half. So, I stood on the church steps, terrified, for probably an hour while it got dark. God, no wonder I suffered from fear of abandonment. I remember thinking, "*I'll be a good girl. Please don't leave me. I'll do better.*"

Saturday, April 12

It was beautiful in Arizona but the friction was already starting to build between my mother and my sister. My sister lived in my mother's house in Maine. As much as they loved each other, it rarely works when an adult woman shares her mother's home. The tension was crazy! I found myself acting fearful like a little kid again, trying not to set anyone off. It was strange that my mother and sister had become so much alike. They both had the most wonderful, loving, creative souls that were hidden behind masks of negativity. What a waste of absolutely beautiful people.

Was I like that? Did I criticize too much? Did I make my kids feel uncomfortable or like they had to keep trying to maintain peace? I genuinely hoped not, but it would be something I needed to think about and look at. The only person I could change was myself and it was my goal to be the healthiest, most loving person I could be.

I talked to Sam tonight and shared what I could about the Brownies story. Maybe if he understood why and where my fear of abandonment started, he might be able to stay focused. God willing.

Sunday, April 13

What a strange and upsetting day. We went back to Tubac. While we were there, Sam called. He was upset because Caleb had been online cruising for porn and Sam was sure I would think it was him. Of course, my first reaction was to panic that my son was inheriting his father's addiction and was never going to be able to have a healthy, truthful, and loving relationship. My next knee-jerk reaction was to try and fix it—have Sam put Caleb on the phone or tell him how it should be handled, what to say, etc. I didn't do either of those things. I stayed calm and tried to remain unemotional, telling him that he should talk with Caleb and that he might want to let him know what the consequences of that kind of secretive behavior could be. When we hung up, I was amazed at how calm I felt. I had absolute faith in Sam's ability to handle it.

We went to dinner at my mother's neighbor's house. I had told Sam that we were going out, but he could call me later. My phone rang. It was Caleb. I excused myself to the other room to say goodnight to him. Afterward, he put Sam on the phone. Sam told me that he had talked to Caleb, who at first denied everything, but then admitted to cruising. Sam tried to explain the difference between healthy curiosity and unhealthy interests. He finally ended up telling Caleb, "You can't go on those sites because Mom will think it's me. You want us to get back together, don't you?" He said Caleb seemed to understand. I felt depressed. I had been unwillingly put into the role of law enforcement, judge, and jury.

I tried to explain my frustration to Sam without getting emotional. After all, I was in the middle of a dinner party. All he could hear was my unemotional tone which he read as I'm pissed, and it was all his fault. Now, I was stuck in a conversation that was going nowhere, because he was not actually hearing me; he was projecting his fears onto me. I was at a dinner party where my mother was starting to think that something was wrong, and the old panic of "I have to fix this" was starting to set in. It was all I could do not to hang up on him and just walk out of the party. I didn't. After twenty minutes of going 'round and 'round we hung up. The evening was in shambles and now I had to convince everyone that I was okay. FUCK! I was tired of this shit!

We got back to my mother's and I had Faye call Sam to say goodnight. I just wanted to talk to him and see if he was still a wreck. He seemed better. I told him that I tried, against my usual reactions, to step back and let him handle things on his own. He misread my calmness as being angry, and there was nothing I could say to convince him otherwise. I told him to try and remember that we were working toward the same goal. I told him I loved him. I really did. I was just sometimes at a loss as to what to say or do. Like I said to Caroline, "This is *not* my life." But Caroline was right. This *was* my life, like it or not. I needed to pull it together and deal with it.

Monday, April 14

We just got back from dinner with my aunt and uncle. They had a wonderful knack for making us feel special.

I spoke with Sam. He was much better—loving, more secure, more confident. I told him I loved him. Are we at the end of the cycle? Will it be done when I get home? Will the real Sam please stand up? I hoped, in the end, it was the Sam I knew and loved so dearly. He told me that he really appreciated how well I communicated with Caleb. I wanted to tell him that I love how far he has come in rebuilding his relationship with Caleb, but it would have sounded insincere, after his compliment, so I just said nothing. A missed opportunity to appreciate him and let him know. I would try not to let that happen again. Everyone needed to feel loved, valued and appreciated.

Tuesday, April 15

It was our last full day here and Faye was asked by my mother to pick what we were going to do for the day. She chose Old Tucson and then swimming, so off we went. I couldn't wait to get home. I couldn't wait to read what I needed to read, do the work I needed to do, hug my husband, and hug and kiss my son. I couldn't wait to be in a place where I had a voice again.

Wednesday, April 16—Roswell, NM

Last night I dreamed of Gabriel. It was a strange dream, the kind of vivid dream you have when you wake up too early and then doze off again. He came in to wherever I was, just out of the shower, wearing only a towel. He walked over to me and kissed

me. It was a long passionate kiss. Dropping the towel, he said,"
Look what you do to me. You know how much I want you," and
turned, walking into another room where he said he would wait
for me. I stood there not knowing what to do. He was very sexy,
but he was not who I wanted. I knew I turned him on, just me,
no fantasies. He wanted me and that was nearly overwhelming. I
stood there trying to decide—did I go in or not? My husband was
not honest. We had no trust, no fidelity. What was stopping me?
Then I woke up.

I knew that I did not want a relationship with Gabriel. I never
have. He gave me what I was craving in my marriage—conversation, connection, affection. As we started our drive home, I realized
how anxious I was to get there. Where was Sam? Had he addressed
any of this stuff? Was he ready to work with me and make changes,
not only in our home, but in our relationship? I hoped and prayed
that we could repair this torn and nearly decimated marriage. So
much hinged on him.

Thursday, April 17—Oklahoma City

I couldn't wait to get home. I didn't sleep at all last night
because my mind was racing. I was so anxious to be home where
there was some semblance of peace and love. A teacher at my
school called me and asked if I had a good time. I said yes. although
I'm not so sure that "good time" is how I would have described it.
I loved getting out of town, even though the flight was grueling. I
really enjoyed the theater and some of the things we did. She said,
"Some time and motherly love are just what you needed."

I talked with Sam. He said he met with Josh and they began to work on Sam's need to lie. I was glad to hear it. That was a major concern for me. He lied about so much. If I could not trust him, what basis did we have for our life together? I asked him to make an appointment with Dan. He said he would. So much was riding on Sam and his ability to change his behavior. I knew he wanted to. I hoped that was enough.

Friday, April 18—Davison, TN

I felt so sad. My marriage was a mess, and my son was a wreck. Caleb's best friend picked on him and he responded by punching him in the face. I just felt sick at the state of my life.

Mom and I talked a little, finally. I actually let myself be vulnerable and she rose to the occasion. She said she doesn't understand what happened, but she knows something did. I don't know. Maybe, like Hannah, she thought I had an affair with Gabriel. Funny how quick Hannah was to think poorly of me. I hoped my mother didn't think the same. There was nothing I could do about it. I just had to live the best way I knew how, cleanly and honestly.

Caroline said I have a unique ability to see a scenario and picture myself there. Escapism? Okay. Enough feeling sorry for myself. Time for action!

Saturday, April 19—Chambersburg PA

Exhausted—both physically and mentally.

Thank God for Faye. She was an absolute joy this whole trip. Bright, sunny, and full of love and laughter.

I talked with Sam several times. I was looking forward to getting home. I would really like to just have him hold me and let me cry, but we didn't leave on an honest note. I knew he would like nothing better than to hold me, but I couldn't trust him. I couldn't trust that he would put me first, me and the kids. Maybe we could talk tomorrow. I would try to just listen. I had a week and a half of unshed tears. Everything made me emotional. Just the thought of Caleb, home making dinner tonight, made my eyes prickle with tears.

I rode through Tennessee and Kentucky. Both are beautiful. A fresh start. That was where my mind was—starting again. One house? Or two? Would this be a geographic fix? Or a true new start?

We must have passed a dozen huge signs on the roadside advertising "adult bookstores with truck parking." There was one in particular in Kentucky, and opposite it, on the other side of the highway, was another billboard that read "Hell is Real." Interesting.

Sunday, April 20

We arrived home and I was so relieved I could cry. After sitting in the car for four days, I desperately needed a walk. I invited Sam to walk with me. It was soothing. We walked and talked for an hour. He was kind and attentive. I was grateful.

When I arrived at home, he was putting groceries away. He looked and smelled good. The house was fine. There were fresh flowers in the kitchen and beside the bed. He was warm, hugging me and rubbing my back.

As far as our family, I felt like I could trust him to feed and care for the kids as well as his mother and keep up the house. I told him this. I still had no way of trusting him when it came to our relationship. In some ways he was open and honest with me. In other ways he was still the master manipulator and deceiver. I found that I was really looking forward to both of us working with Dan. I was hopeful. I really wanted to stay married, but I couldn't do that without honesty and trust.

Monday, April 21

The ten days I spent with my mother were a gift. For the first time, I heard her tell the story of leaving me at Brownies. I was able to see how dysfunctional my family was and how I was both different and yet the same—peacemaker/survivor.

My father left when I was five. They were divorced when I was six. My mother had her first brain tumor when I was seven, and I was separated from my siblings and moved to the city. My mother went into the hospital and after she came out, she left me on the steps at Brownies. I didn't see my father again until I was ten. At twelve, my stepmother told me I was too big to sit in his lap. When I was fourteen, my mother had another brain tumor and I went to live with a local family, friends of my mothers. At twenty, my father severed ties with me. When I was twenty-two, I met Sam. I told him that I just wanted someone who would let me love him. He knew most of this story before we got married. Knowing all this, how could he have abandoned me so completely—physically, emotionally, and financially? He said he loves me. *Now* he loves me. Why? What is different?

The first thing we needed to decide with Dan was what goal we were working toward. Married or divorced? That should be the first step. If we do decide to stay together, how would we define "committed relationship?"

Some things to address were my discomfort over why, when we were there for counseling twice before, none of this raised a red flag for Dan.

In the end, it all rested on Sam's ability to own and discuss his infidelities. There was no hope of reconciliation without full disclosure. Even then, how would I ever be able to trust him? He had earned my trust in his ability to take care of the kids and the house. I would not spend the rest of my life checking up. That was mothering him. I didn't want another child. I wanted a partner. I was worth at least that.

Tuesday, April 22

I took Faye to dance class. I really had to go to the bathroom, so I drove over to the apartment. I hesitated, afraid to go in, afraid of what I might find. I finally went in and went to the bathroom. I didn't want to look around, but I did. I was relieved to find nothing. It really was a relief but for some reason, I didn't trust not finding something. Sounds crazy. Maybe I was crazy. More often than not, I felt like it.

I was thinking about my trip out west. I was feeling very badly about the porn and the lies when I left. It was just so easy when I returned to slip back into a warm, loving "play at relationship" with Sam. It felt familiar and happy. When he got word yesterday that he didn't get the job he had applied and interviewed for, I fell right back into cheering him up and trying to get him to look at other possibilities. We talked of getting his degree, living in England. Dreams. I had never been able to motivate him before and now it wasn't my job. If he wanted a better job, he needed to find one. Sophie said that the test he needed to complete for his certification could mean a difference of thirty to forty thousand dollars per year. He needed to get up, be a man, and support his family. We were no closer to being in a debt reduction program than we were before. He closed his store December 31st. Next week would be May 1st. How much had *really* changed?

I felt like I was all over the map!

His mother went to the ER tonight. She was coughing and sounded terrible. His sister called and said she had a fever of 101.8. When I got home from Arizona, I commented to Sam how bad she looked. I was not sure, at ninety-two years old, she would survive a case of pneumonia or bronchitis. It was very scary. We were not ready to deal with the consequences of losing Sam's mother or our living situation.

Caleb's report card came. Honor roll. I was so proud of him. There was also a report listing the results of his Stanford Achievement Tests. He tested "post high school" in all but three categories. In those three areas, he scored in grades ranging from 10.5—12.2. No wonder he had a hard time connecting with other thirteen-year-olds. He was amazing.

Wednesday, April 23

It was a relatively good day. Sam brought his mother home at 1:30 in the morning. She had pneumonia. Why they didn't insist on admitting her was beyond me. She was disoriented. Now we were back to twenty-four-hour care. Stress and strain.

Becca was planning to come home tomorrow, and Sam told me she was leaving on Sunday. I was relieved. It was not that I didn't love her and want her to stay. I loved her to pieces and really missed her. I was just not up for one more person, one more opinion, one more stress in this house. She could actually share the apartment if she wanted to stay. Besides, Faye got jostled about every summer when Becca arrived. I would have loved to see Faye keep her own space. But it would be good to see Becca. I wondered if Sam was nervous to see her and if he would tell her the whole story.

His mother called me into her room. I had to put her teeth in the cup. I added water and Efferdent but she was confused. She told me her teeth weren't soaking. She insisted there was no water in the cup as she was pointing to her mouth. Over and over. I tried to reassure her. Sick *and* crazy.

I was looking forward to a couple of nights on my own. I felt like I was stalled. I was anxious to see Caroline tomorrow and to meet with Dan on Friday. Sam and I were planning a date, I think, for Friday night. What if our session didn't go well?

I was very tired and just need to sleep. I bought my next journal. Hard to believe. Almost four months and two full journals and I still knew as little about what happened with my husband as I did at the beginning. It all centered on that. Didn't he understand?

Thursday, April 24

I met with Caroline—a little clarity. Dan invited her to our session tomorrow. I was actually relieved. Hopefully, we would be able to stay on track and make a plan. We needed to be absolutely specific, like a business plan. Very romantic. She asked me to come up with several possible scenarios:

> We stay together. Full disclosure. We work with Dan, Josh, and Caroline. We set up a system of checks and balances to measure progress, both internal and external, as well as honesty. He stays connected.
>
> We divorce and go our separate ways, each one doing what individual work he or she thinks needs to be done. Friends and co-parents.
>
> We divorce. We each work individually. Later, if and when he had acted out as much as he needed, or decided he is ready for full disclosure, we start over from the beginning.
>
> We stay married but live as friends.

I knew my wish would be to put our marriage back together. I hoped we would be able to figure out what I was able to live with and what he was able to live without.

I told Caroline about the "being left at Brownies" story and about my fear of abandonment. She thought it would be interesting to contact women I liked and respected and ask each one to write a brief story that characterized their relationship with their mother. It would be fascinating.

I told Caroline that I felt as if I was on the outside looking in. I couldn't seem to get motivated about anything. She said this was just a new phase, just another step I needed to take in the process. It made me wonder: would I ever arrive at a destination? Maybe it was just all one continuous journey, a process that never ended. God, that was depressing. She said I had been operating in a super heightened state and that it was time to feel the letdown that was bound to happen. She said Sam would be feeling it, too, if he was truly progressing.

We talked about the cycling that began before I left and how it was probably a good thing. She described what Sam and I were going through as a type of dance. We move backward and forward at opposite times. It was all so complicated, and I was tired.

Internal work, as opposed to, or in conjunction with, external work.

Caroline said that to meet someone with the same kind of personal intensity was rare. That is what Sam and I had. The rest were just details.

Friday, April 25

We began a new phase of our journey. We met with Dan. I was scared.

What if, after all this work, Sam just couldn't bring himself to make a full disclosure? Did I really dare to walk away? I knew I was worth so much more. I knew I would feel sad and broken. I couldn't even write this without my eyes prickling with tears. I also knew that I was a survivor. I had lived through abandonment and survived. That is why he chose me, because I was strong.

As much as I wanted this marriage to work, I also needed to be realistic. Sam and I were both human, with human frailties. Our relationship, for so long, had been Sam doing what he wanted or needed to fulfill whatever was going on with him, and me picking up the pieces and holding us all together.

I couldn't live like that again.

I loved him so much.

I wouldn't live like that again.

I wondered if we were headed off to Dan with common goals. Would he be honest in the sessions? How would I know? How would I trust?

This day already felt different. I hoped that I could approach it with the same kind of openness and integrity, honesty, and compassion that I was expecting of him.

I started this journal almost two months ago, when we got this apartment. Now it was done, and we begin a new book.

BOOK THREE

How to begin this new chapter? It was a long day—emotional, exhausting. I rushed out of school to get to my meeting with Sam, Dan, and Caroline. When I pulled into the parking lot, I realized I didn't see Sam's car, so I called him. Dan's office had moved and they were all over at the new location waiting for me. I could feel my frustration level rising. I was already late for an important meeting, possibly the most important meeting of my life, and nobody had bothered to tell me where the meeting was. I felt like I wasn't important enough to tell, and now I was late. So, our already short meeting was shorter by fifteen minutes.

When we began, Sam immediately began to voice his distrust and frustration at being blindsided by Caroline's inclusion. I wanted to say, "Wait a minute! You found out when I did that she was invited, and I gave you the opportunity to say no." But I kept my mouth shut. He was anxious and uncomfortable, a situation that could easily trigger lying or acting out. I tried to be honest and supportive at the same time. I don't think I succeeded very well. He pompously leaned back in his chair, one ankle resting on the other knee, fingers locked behind his head, elbows out to the sides. When he started saying that there were things throughout our marriage that needed addressing, I almost lost it. He was so defensive and accusatory. If he was still looking for ways to pin his addiction on others, then he was certainly not making the progress it was necessary to make. The whole thing was stressful and incredibly painful. I was so stressed out that I was trembling uncontrollably the entire time.

After the meeting, Sam and I hugged and sat in the car talking for a bit. As bad as the meeting felt, I wanted to make sure that we weren't leaving with unresolved hostility. Later, we went on our first date. He took me to a lovely little Italian restaurant. We talked a lot. About his mother, among other things. We had a really nice evening. Now I was back at the apartment, exhausted and feeling a little sick. Wouldn't that just take the cake? A touch of food poisoning on our first date?

Saturday, April 26

I was up all night with a miserable stomachache. I didn't know if it was a result of the dinner or the tension of the day. Either way, I was exhausted.

What a strange day. When I arrived at home, Sam was distant and moody. After prompting him to talk, he admitted to fears about our relationship. I had tremendous fears also, as well as new resentments building. I feared he would act out again. I feared I would never get over this betrayal and be able to forgive him. I feared I would not be able to meet his needs, particularly his sexual needs. I feared that he would want to do all that bizarre sexual stuff on the website. I feared that I would begin to trust him again and he would betray me all over again. I feared that he would come to realize that he was trying to rebuild our marriage out of guilt and fear of being alone, and he would wake up one day and change his mind. I feared that he would make me feel that his infidelity was all my fault.

I was beginning to resent his insistence that there have been things going on in our marriage for a long time that have been unhealthy. No shit. I knew that we need to look at and address those things. However, I was feeling like he was using those issues to somehow lessen the effect, or justify, what he had done and I didn't know what to do about it. I was certain that the next accusation would be that I was in denial.

He left his old journal open on the dining room table, odd, and I looked through it again. At one point he said that I have so many needs, probably left over from my childhood abandonment, and that I expected that he should be able to meet them all. He said that no one could ever do that. Honestly, how could he say that he loved me and yet know so little about me? I don't live in some la-la land. I was perfectly aware that it would be impossible to meet all of someone's needs, nor did I expect him to. How could I communicate so he could hear me? I wanted a partner. For the last ten years he met very few of my needs—emotional, spiritual, financial. My complaint was not that he was not meeting my needs. My complaint was that he wasn't doing anything. He wasn't earning a living, wasn't going to church with us, spent as little time as possible with us, and even that was spent reading (napping) or in other solitary pursuits. His whole attitude reminded me of when I dragged him off to Dan the first time. I almost fell on the floor when he said to Dan, "I know I need to go out and earn more to support my family, but part of me thinks, why should I?"

My thoughts were in a jumble. I thought we had a good night

last night, after a very upsetting meeting. And once again, I felt like I was all over the map. And to top it all off, tonight Becca was singing his praises. She was acting like I was some kind of ungrateful shit who refused to acknowledge her father's hard work and changes. I felt like I was praising him all the time. Did his mood have anything to do with the fact that they spent the morning together? And why did he rush to put his bag in the car when I came home? Was there something he didn't want me to see?

In the back of his journal, written very softly in pencil, are the numbers of my landlord at school, my financial planner, Shawn, and Gabriel's house. He either was doing more checking up on me than I thought, or he thinks that, like him, I have slept with every man I have come into contact with. Fine. I didn't care. He could keep checking. I had nothing to hide. I even took the new phone bill and highlighted the five or six calls I had with Gabriel.

I WON'T LIVE LIKE THIS!

This is not how I thought I would open this new book. Yesterday morning I was full of hope and love. Now I was just tired and angry.

Sunday, April 27—A better day

I did not sleep well at all last night. My stomach was still bothering me, my mind was racing, and I was feeling angry and hurt.

This morning we all went to church together. I felt sad and disconnected. Becca and Caleb sat between Sam and me. I could feel Becca's irritation. I just wanted to say to her, "Why didn't you just stay home?" Maybe I was being overly sensitive, but I felt like she was looking upon me with total disdain.

After church Sam and I talked and cried for a long time. I tried to explain how I was feeling and tried really hard to hear him. Part of the problem was that we had been so wrapped up in our own pain that we couldn't hear, much less help, the other. I hoped he understood that I was not ignoring the issues we have had as a couple and that I was willing to work on them when the time came.

After our talk/cry, it seemed easier and more peaceful.

He and I went off to Home Depot and had a very good time. We had been trying to reserve Sunday for family time, so we went to buy paint for his mother's room, the living room and dining room. Afterwards, we went home to pick up the kids to go bowling. Caleb was moody, Faye was silly, and Becca was disconnected. While we were bowling, Becca was taking pictures, mostly of Sam and some of the kids. Every time I got up to bowl, she put the camera away. It felt like a slap. I guess that it upset me so much because she was the one who helped him set up the email account. She may or may not have had any idea what was going on. I don't know. Then, for the last four months, while we have struggled so much, she seemed disinterested. Now, it was like I was dealing with Caleb in the beginning all over again, minus the raging anger. She knew so little about me but maybe she didn't care. That made me sad. Anyway, I couldn't dwell on Becca. I had to focus on Sam, me, and my children. Funny, until now I never differentiated between his children and mine. I had to take care of my kids, and I had to focus on the positive talk we had. I prayed that it would bring about more growth and healing. Please God.

Monday, April 28

What a positive day! Work was good. I spoke to Sam a couple of times. I took Caleb to the carpool this morning and no one was there. I was afraid we had missed it, so I tried calling one of the boys in the carpool but got no answer. I didn't have Jasper's phone number, but I called Gabriel, who assured me that they were not there yet. Then I called Sam to tell him I had called Gabriel. He said I didn't have to do that. I told him I was willing to do that because he felt so insecure. I told him there is nothing else I can do but tell the truth. If he doesn't believe me, there is nothing more I can do. I told him that if Gabriel was who I wanted, I would already be gone. That finally seemed to reach him. I hoped so.

When we were on the phone he said, "I love you." I didn't say it back and he mentioned it. I felt pressured and tried not to give in to it. It was like yesterday when he said something about painting my nails. I wanted to say, "I will paint my nails if, and only if, I choose. And I will paint them any color I choose." STOP. His manipulation or my overreaction?

I was thinking that one of the reasons I was so angry the other night is because of what I read in Sam's journal. I wished he would have talked to me and asked me about the things that were weighing heavily on his heart, instead of writing about it and leaving his journal open on the table.

I just didn't understand why this was so hard. Why was he still hiding? Would I be able to drop my guard a little when he made his disclosure? I hoped so. I knew my distance hurt him. After all he had hurt me, torn me to ribbons really, I didn't want to hurt him. I loved him.

Tuesday, April 29

I was such a shit. I had finally gotten a good night's sleep and had had a fairly good start to the day. Just before Sam arrived to pick up Caleb and Becca, Caleb was rude, and I snapped at him. I was flustered when Sam came in, and when he leaned in to hug me, I gave him a little kiss on the lips. It was nice and very natural, and it was absolutely, positively the wrong thing to do. I felt like I completely set him up for a downfall by doing something I am in no way ready to do. When I told him that (I was trying to be honest) I could see the hurt and disappointment on his face. I felt terrible. I called him later to apologize and he said not to worry about it, but I still felt like crap.

I spent a lot of my day thinking about Sunday and how much fun we had out shopping for paint. We were relaxed, just enjoying the day. It really was fun. He must have been reading my mind, because when I spoke to him later in the day, he said the exact same thing. It was nice.

Becca called me later in the evening. She had gone back to New York and said she wanted to tell me how impressed she was that her father and I were working so hard to rebuild our marriage. She said she appreciated my strength—that they both do, she and Rachel. She added that Caleb and Faye would in time. She must have been talking with Rachel because this is certainly not what she projected while she was here. Maybe she just felt awkward. After all, I was the wicked stepmother and she needed to remain loyal to her father. She got all weepy talking to me which, in turn, made me cry.

Tonight, my sister Hannah called. She asked me how things

were going. I should have known better than to tell her anything. I was so glad I never told her the details. I told her that Sam and I were working hard, that we had been to our first therapist meeting together, and that we had been on our first date. She said, "Well, you don't sound very upbeat." I replied, "Oh, I really am, but it all hinges on Sam right at this moment." Then she hit me with," Don't even think that it's all his fault. Don't put all the blame on him." It felt like she punched me in the chest. I said," I am fully aware that it takes two people to make a relationship," to which she replied," And two people to make a divorce."

I was really struggling. I have tried hard to be a good person, to be kind and giving. I always try to lift other people up and to be as loving as I can. What was I doing wrong that everyone was so quick to think the worst of me? Was I fooling myself? Sam told me how good he thinks I am and, almost in the next breath, how I have made problems in this marriage from way back.

"I am not going to let who I am be determined by what other people think." Sam just said this.

This is the hardest thing I have ever done.

Wednesday, April 30

If I were a child, I would just say, "Ok. I'm tired of this game. I don't want to play anymore." I constantly felt physically and emotionally exhausted.

Hannah called me this morning to apologize. I wanted to tell her how insensitive and hurtful she was, but I didn't. I would just avoid all future personal conversations. What good would come from making another relationship mess in my life? I was already feeling isolated enough. I didn't need more.

I talked with Sam this morning about laying his cards on the table and using that moment as a place to start new and fresh—no more infidelity, no more lies. What if he couldn't stop lying?

Caroline asked me to figure out what I could live with.

Porn? Possibly. What would it mean to be sober in SA? Abstinence? I knew from my reading that there is a period of time when that is recommended.

Infidelity (acting out, sleeping around, getting a little, having an affair, a fling)? No. Not even once.

Dishonesty? No. If there was no honesty, there was no trust. No trust equals no marriage.

It was all so complicated. I was feeling more and more exhausted each day. I was terrified of our appointment together on Friday and yet looking forward to it at the same time. What if it were to happen again? What if he felt nervous and anxious and appeared closed down and almost hostile again? I just wanted us to begin the work we need to do. What if he wouldn't make a disclosure? Should I ask for some kind of deadline? He would feel pressured and ganged up on. I just hoped he wouldn't force a position like that. It did nothing to help his cause.

It was interesting to think back over the conversations we had over the previous four months; we have each shed so many tears. He cried over hurting me and hurting the kids, but I don't have any recollection of him crying over what he did. I remember saying to him, "If I were you, I would be on my hands and knees right now sobbing for forgiveness." He just looked at me.

I have kept coming back to what it said about infidelity and breach of trust in "Emotional Infidelity." I needed to feel and know that it was over and not going to happen again. "Fool me once, shame on you. Fool me twice, shame on me."

Thursday, May 1

This was such a raw emotional week. I called Sam to see if he would bring a game over for me. He was having coffee at The Creamery. My mind immediately thought, "With whom?" but I didn't ask. When he arrived at my school, he was empty-handed. He had driven home only to find the door locked. Although in the past we never locked our doors, I now locked it at night when I was alone and forgot to open it this morning. I felt bad, knowing he had driven there only to turn around and drive all the way back, turn around again and bring me the game. I said I was sorry right away, but he said it had been a good thing. He had been driving back to me feeling anger and resentment build up. All of a sudden, he just said, "Stop!" He said he realized it was just a mistake and that there was no need for those extreme feelings. How liberating. I remembered feeling that exact same way about the church bake sale. I was thrilled for him and proud of him, although I still felt bad about the locked door.

I called him after his meeting with Josh to see how he was doing. He had said if I wanted to know what they were doing to just ask, so I did. Josh tried, I think, to prepare him for our meeting the next day. He was planning on making his disclosure then. They talked about telling all vs. not telling.

Not telling = end of marriage

Telling = possible end of marriage, possible reconciliation

I hoped I was strong enough to hear what he had to say—really hear it, process it, believe it.

He said he was worried about hurting me more. Josh said it wasn't about me. This was about Sam. I was grateful to Josh for saying it and to Sam for hearing it.

I was scared to death about tomorrow. As MJ says, I will just have to lift it up to God.

I went for a walk with one of my teachers. As we walked around the wildlife refuge, we saw five deer. Strange—I had lived there for eighteen years and never knew it was there. For the last seven years I had lived fewer than five miles away. It was beautiful and peaceful. It reminded me why I lived there.

I went to see my hairdresser Jill. Her mother-in-law, who was difficult and pessimistic, had been living with her for the last three weeks. She sounded like a carbon copy of Sam's mother. But although they had never been close, Jill tried to see God's reason in everything. Maybe it was a time for healing.

I would like to be more like that. I would like to be able to trust that there is a reason for everything. Maybe his mother was meant to be living with us as Sam underwent this horrific work. Perhaps he would come to terms with her emotional abandonment and neglect. Maybe Sam and I were meant to go through this. I wondered if it would strengthen our relationship, whatever that relationship ended up being.

When he was so upset and scared, I told him to try to envision us living in that big Victorian house. Picture it at holidays, filled with family and noise, laughter, and color. I also have pictured it tranquil and serene—HOME. I wished so much that there was a way to make it happen.

We must not stop working. We began and now we need to do something totally out of character—complete the work.

> debt consolidation
> work on house, paint, garden, etc.
> work on self
> work to open new school
> work on rebuilding our kids
> We'll see what happens.

Friday, May 2

Well, I asked for it and he gave it to me. The truth.

After the top blew off my life last January, I thought it would be impossible to feel more betrayed but I did. It wasn't what he said—most of it I knew—it was the timeline. He had his first infidelity in our marriage before I was pregnant with Faye. We married in August of 1993 and I got pregnant with Faye in September of 1998. That was exactly five years. Not much of a monogamous relationship. Ginny—not part of the cycle. Before we moved, before he lost his job, before Faye was born, before his dad died. His choice. Devastating.

I went for a long walk. It was the same route I walked on my first night in the apartment. I remember walking by our old house and thinking, "We were happy there." It's different now. I realized that in the four different places we had lived together, he had been unfaithful in each one.

I wanted to be done. I wanted this nightmare of betrayal to be over. I wanted to walk away and never look back. I was exhausted. They say your body does its best healing while you sleep. I hope so.

Saturday, May 3

I think if it weren't for Sophie, I would have jumped off the bridge by now. She called me last night. She had Faye with her and Sam asked her to call, so I went to her house. Just like that first walk around the city when she and I talked about how sad I was and how much I missed my family, we talked about how sad I was and how fresh the betrayal seemed. At her house we ate, enjoyed the silliness of the girls, and talked a lot about home improvement. Sometimes it seemed like nothing ever happened. The world went on and nobody noticed your pain. How sad.

She said she believed Sam had genuinely loved me for the last ten years. I agreed. But that love, and the love I had for him, apparently was never enough. How on earth would it possibly be enough now? And how much should one person be asked to take? Dan said trust equals time. Would my anxiety level ever come down to a place where, if he was late or I couldn't reach him, I would stop wondering if he was with someone else?

Yesterday at this time I had such hopes for our future. To find out that he was already being unfaithful at a time when our marriage was in a good place brings all those hopes and dreams to a screeching halt.

How did I not know and how did Dan not know? Was Sam really that good a liar? If that were the case, how would I know if it happened again? During the meeting, I choked out that if he ever does this again, I will leave him. He said if he ever does this again, he will kill himself. I said if he ever lied to me again, I would leave him and I meant it. One small lie opens the door to more and more and I won't do this again. I won't go through this again. It would kill me.

The end of a long surreal day. Sam and I talked on the phone for over an hour this morning. In some ways, I couldn't believe he had the balls to call me but I'm glad he did. He answered some questions and seemed to be honest. I just didn't know for sure.

I was glad it was all out on the table. It seemed to have lifted the burden from him a bit. I told him that I was worried about my anxiety level if he was late or unreachable. He said he wanted me to ask immediately if I had doubts. That seemed fine for the time being, but what about in a year? Or five? Or ten? How understanding would he be then?

I wanted to know where these women came from. Who the hell goes into a store and ends up fucking the owner? Or giving him a blowjob in the bathroom? Did he ever stop to think about where a person like that had been? It was shocking to me that there really were women like that in the world. I supposed as long as there are men like Sam who respond to them, they will be there. It turned my stomach.

I really didn't know what to do about this "Ginny" thing. Sophie and I ended up watching baby movies. There was Caleb at two and a half and I thought, "*That is what you were so willing to give up. That innocent trusting baby and a wife who adored you.*" Then there were videos of Faye as a baby. He was already sleeping around. My past and the stories of my children's babyhood all seem different to me now.

It was four months ago that we made love for the last time.

Sunday, May 4

I was lying there with my pencil poised above the paper, hesitating. How to begin? What to write?

This day was so long, it seemed like it started yesterday. I felt like I was in a permanent state of confusion. I married a man I adored, a man I was certain adored me. We were so full of love; we tried to give each other everything. We gave each other support, strength, and a beautiful son. The world was a kind and happy place. I was so full of love that sometimes it would overflow and leak out of my eyes.

The man I married decided it would be more fun to make love to someone else. Of course, I didn't know. I just kept on loving and giving and thinking my world was perfect. Then, slowly, things began to not be so perfect. My business needed a new home, so we moved. We unexpectedly had a beautiful daughter. The man I loved lost his job and with it, his identity. I tried to give him support, strength and love like before, but I was tired and it wasn't enough. He told me I was nagging and cold. He began to withdraw and even my love and our beautiful children couldn't bring him back. Our beautiful son began to struggle and I thought it was insecurity. The man I married said it was ego. I still adored the man but he was distant. He couldn't hear me sometimes, so I began to shout. Then, I just stopped talking. I was sad and he didn't seem to care. I found someone else I could talk to but I felt bad. I only wanted the man I married. We were all so sad all the time, but nobody knew. Then my world completely shattered. I discovered that the man I married, the man I adored, had shared his body with many women. I was shattered—I *am* shattered, broken. Then, the man I married decided that I really am the one he adores. I didn't know what to do, what to think. Now, instead of love overflowing and leaking out of my eyes, pain was running down my cheeks.

Monday, May 5

Four months ago yesterday, I checked into ambulatory surgery. I had my urethra lifted due to a complication of pregnancy. I was too young to be peeing myself and too self-conscious for oral sex. How ironic—I haven't had sex since.

Also ironic—we checked Faye in there to say goodbye to the bump on her finger that had been there her whole life. It seemed right and normal that Sam and I would take her together. There didn't appear to be any awkwardness. We were just there together. Watching them wheel her away was scary. She looked so small. I don't think I was ever as proud of her as I was. She was brave and sweet and perfectly beautiful. The surgeon kept calling her "My Princess," and several nurses, the recovery nurse in particular, kept saying, "Oh, you are *so* beautiful!" And she was, inside and out.

Sam had to leave early to meet the plumber at the house. When we were discharged the nurse said, "Is that man coming back?"

"My husband? Yes, he's coming to get us."

I was puzzled. It seemed obvious to me that he was my husband and Faye's father. Then I realized that neither of us was wearing a wedding ring. How could she know we were together? Caleb also asked me tonight where my rings are. He told me he wants me to put them back on. Then he had a rough, emotional night.

I missed wearing my rings. They were the only "real" jewelry

I owned. I was proud to get them. I felt so loved. I tried to return that feeling to Sam by getting him a ring. I was afraid he wouldn't like it, but it was the only one I could afford. When he lost it, I was sad and felt a little rejected. Maybe more than a little. After his father died, Sam wore his dad's wedding ring. I wondered if he missed wearing it. Did he wear it when he was having sex with other women? Did they care? I guessed not.

Tuesday, May 6

I got a chance to meet with Caroline. It was much needed and I felt like we covered a lot. She read the letter. We talked about writing a marriage contract. I told her after Sam's disclosure I got up in his face and told him if he ever did this again or lied to me again, I would leave him. She thought it was good to voice what I will and will not tolerate. She thought that maybe we needed to have some kind of a touch point at the end of each day, where he could have a chance to confess if he slipped up and lied or struggled that day. I thought that would work for us. We talked about how hard he was truly working and how his disclosure seemed to lighten his burden. She gave me credit for always being sensitive to his feelings and also for never abandoning him or our marriage and running away. I loved him. I wanted to make our marriage work. Now we just needed a plan and a rule book.

Wednesday, May 7

I re-read Sam's letter and truly, it sickened me. There was just so much I didn't understand. How to get past it? How to keep moving forward?

He said he was excited to go to Maine as a family. I was certainly not used to this "new Sam." It was hard not to be suspect. He told me he wanted to make me happy and it made me stop and think. I had been unhappy for so long while trying to pretend to be happy—could I recognize and embrace happiness when and if it came? God, I hoped so.

I had a full, crazy day scheduled for the next day and I needed some sleep. I felt a great sense of pride and accomplishment about how far we had all come together.

Thursday, May 8

Now what? I was up half the night with Faye. I was scared to death she was having some weird kind of reaction because she was so wobbly and in so much pain. To make matters worse, she got up in the dark to go to the bathroom. While she was in there, his mother began having a nightmare and started to yell. Faye was terrified.

I worked all day, held a rehearsal, and then ran Brownies. Twelve hours without so much as a break. I was nervous because my mother was coming, and I didn't know if it would be stressful for Sam. I didn't want it to be. When I got home, things seemed fine; everyone was in a great mood. I was tired and had miserable cramps, but I was glad things were going well.

Then, when Sam was getting ready to leave, I told him Caleb had been upset he was not sleeping here tonight. I explained that I had told Caleb I would make it up to him. All of a sudden, it was like flipping a switch with Sam. He started getting moody and cool. I asked what was wrong and he said he was getting mixed signals from me and he was frustrated and confused. You could've knocked me over with a feather. And then I did my usual scrambling to make amends while Moody Judy played the hurt card.

I didn't understand. I asked him to bring me coffee in the morning just so I could see him. I told him how proud I was of him and how much I loved him. I always told him whenever anyone had said anything nice about him. I didn't know what else I was supposed to do.

He said he felt frustrated that things are not moving faster. For God's sake, he made his disclosure six days ago, telling me about all the sexual partners he had had during our marriage. What was I supposed to do? Jump back into bed with him? That was exactly what I was afraid of, that he would be impatient and irritated with my recovery process.

Then he said to me that anytime he had a negative thought I perceived it as if he was pissed at me. It was true– I did. It was difficult to interpret it any other way when he pursed his lips and stared off to one side of me like he couldn't even bear to look at me. He read my journal. He knew where I was. Was he playing me? I was too tired to think about this. I was always so fucking tired and I hated it.

Then, I walked him to the car and he was back to his fun self. I guess Caleb heard our whole conversation in the kitchen and told him he was being dumb. Whether he meant just Sam or both of us, I don't know, but it seemed to snap him out of it. Talk about conflicting messages. Once again, I felt like a crazy person.

Friday, May 9

At five o'clock in morning, I lay awake wondering why I always felt he was angry at me. It seemed that over the last ten years, Sam would get angry in order to protect himself and push me away. He would portray me as nagging and bitchy and he would put up his wall or say really mean things. It was hurtful for so long that I began to try to avoid it as much as I could. I shared this revelation with him this morning and he listened. It was a stressful day. It had actually been a very stressful week.

We met with Dan and Caroline and talked about what happened last night. They both seemed to think it was a good learning opportunity. If Sam had been able to say something the minute he sensed a change in me, I could have tried to target whatever it was that I did. We could have avoided the "what did I do now" scenario that went on in me all night. I felt good after the session. Perhaps we were moving in the right direction.

Saturday, May 10

It was important that we were each finding ways to verbalize our fears and anxieties, so that we could give the other person a way to respond and reassure. It was doubly important for Sam, so that I didn't unwittingly set off a relapse. Caroline said that we get to write our own rulebook. The number one rule I wanted was honesty—in all things—not just of the big ones. That meant if Sam and/or I were suffering from anxiety or fear, it would get expressed—immediately.

My mother was really searching for information about what was going on between us but I didn't give her any. She probably guessed a little, but she was not getting it from me. I tried hard to remain guarded without appearing guarded. It was tiring and I found myself relieved when she left.

I sewed the memory pillows. *After my father-in-law died, I quilted his clothes into pillows for his grandchildren. Then I began to make these "memory pillows" for anyone who wanted or needed them after losing someone they loved.* It felt good and healing to be doing something for someone else. I also made a beautiful tart to take to Maine the next day. Maybe some part of me was coming back to life. Sam was staying here so that we could get an early start. I was so glad to have him here. I wished I was brave enough to let him, or ask him, to hold me. I really missed the physical contact—not sexual—just touching and feeling close and connected.

Sunday, May 11—Mother's Day

We got up early and drove to Maine. The kids had fun and so did Sam and I. Sam was present emotionally and interacted with everybody. I hadn't seen that side of him in so long. It was great.

I had an indication of just how disconnected he had been when we were in the backyard. He looked at my mother's little fountain and asked if it was new. I said no and told him it had been there about five years or so. Then Thea said Mom got it for her retirement and I remembered I went to my mother's retirement party when Faye was two weeks old. She would be nine in less than a month

I asked him on the way home how old Emily is. He said twenty or twenty-one. I wasn't quite expecting her to be so young. Younger than Becca. No wonder he could barely stand to look at himself in the mirror. She was a baby.

In the evening, we talked a little bit about my being tired. I started to feel he was being a little accusatory, like "you can muster up the energy at The Theatre but not at home." I wasn't going there and I told him that. I said I felt like he was being accusatory and that we were slipping into an old argument. It has been four months of emotional strain and sleep deprivation on top of ten years of ridiculous energy levels and overwhelming hours of responsibility. During our meeting on Friday, when I was talking about doing, feeling, managing, or handling things, twice Dan looked at me and said, "That's exhausting." I hoped as time went on and we could share more and more it would become less exhausting.

Anyway, it was a beautiful day, and I was proud to be mother to my kids and "wicked stepmother" to Rachel and Becca, both of whom called me.

Monday, May 12

I was trying to be conscious of what my exhausted body was telling me. I knew I needed to eat right. No more sugar or caffeine to boost me up because they also made me crash. I also needed to exercise—walk, bike, whatever—thirty minutes every day. Finally, but even more importantly, I needed to get some proper sleep. After all, I was dealing with six years of sleep deprivation. It was like having an infant in the house. I had to get up at six a.m. so I needed to be ready to go to sleep by ten p.m. This would be the hardest one!

Faye had her bridging ceremony for Brownies in the evening.

My baby was no longer a Brownie. She was now a Junior Girl Scout. So proud.

I rehearsed the kids for the variety show on Friday. Faye was cute. She told me she feels frustrated when her friends act silly. She said that she knew how hard I worked on the choreography and she didn't want me to have to change everything again. I made sure she knew how great that made me feel. Then on the way home, she said that when I was talking the night before about how swollen her finger was, it scared her. I was pleased, not about scaring her, but because maybe she was finally able to express herself. I certainly hoped so.

Sam told me he said several times that he was waiting for me to plan the next date. How did I miss that? I needed to get out of my own little world and listen better. We were going to have a date on Sunday night. I needed to get a sitter and start making some plans. I wanted it to be really special. What could I do with no money? I'd have to be creative.

Tuesday, May 13

I went walking in The City by the Sea while Faye was in dance class. I knew exercise would help boost my energy so, while Faye was dancing, I took advantage of the hour I had. Instead of going to the grocery store or running home to make dinner, I decided to do something for myself and go for a long walk. I thought it would help me feel refreshed and energized. All it did was leave me feeling sad and angry.

I had not walked, or even been, in The City by the Sea since the night of Sam's disclosure, about Ginny, eleven days ago. Everywhere I went there were memories: strolling around downtown, our church, and the big square, pushing the kids on the swings at the library park. All those early years thinking I had such a charmed life, an amazing husband I adored who adored me, and the most beautiful little boy and then little girl.

So, while I was pushing my children around The City by the Sea in a carriage, thinking no one was as lucky as I was—so fucking naïve—my husband was screwing anybody who would flirt with him.

It made me sick all over again. I felt like I had just taken five steps backward. I wanted to tell him that it was over. Anyone who had that little regard for me and my children had no right to be a part of my life.

I walked a different route, down to the water and along the harbor, up behind the library, weaving in and out of side streets, until I got to the park where I just sat and cried. I was so unbearably sad that all I had, and all I thought I had, was just gone, with the snap of the fingers, like it never existed. Even as I was writing this, my chest was tight and my throat ached with unshed tears. Was this my relapse? All of a sudden, I just felt like giving up.

Sam had been talking about my fatigue level and getting things checked with the doctor. I was reading it as "when we finally do get back together, you need to have enough left at the end of the day for sex." Is that what he was really saying or was it my knee-jerk reaction because it had been a long-standing complaint with him?

I knew what was wrong. I had been killing myself for the last ten years and my body had given out. Everybody had told me that, including my doctors. Sam didn't believe it. Why? Would that be just one more thing he was responsible for? After he lost his job in July 1999, I went back to work full time. In October 1999, I took a second job and I was still nursing my baby. Two jobs, two kids, running a business and the house—I just couldn't do it anymore. After I had pneumonia, he said he had a better concept of what I did. That was nothing! Add to that the theater, running my school, teaching, and keeping up with the kids' schools and lessons. Too much, too long.

I sounded like some bitter bitch. Maybe that was my reward for the life I'd lived. One thing I knew was that I would never be able to live here. I looked at every place I went and thought, *Was it here? Did they flirt here?* Was he happy here or was it all a lie? A cover? I understood now why his ex-wife felt the need to get out of here. How she could stand to look at the two of us I will never know. I was ashamed of myself for what I did to her.

Sam called and he knew instantly that something was wrong. I was all done trying to hide what I felt to avoid his reaction. I told him how I was feeling and that I felt badly about it, especially if he was being honest about how he had been working and what he wanted. After I told him what happened, he said, "So all this work we've been doing is for nothing?" It felt like a slap. I told him that if I couldn't tell him how I was feeling then maybe all the work really was for nothing.

I had to feel what I felt. I had to mourn the loss of trust and the loss of my relationship. If I ignored these feelings so that he wouldn't feel bad about what he had done, then we would have learned nothing. It would come out later and I wouldn't be able to work through it.

"It is what it is," I said, to which he replied, "And it's not what it's not." What was that supposed to mean? That my feelings were somehow not what they should be? What a shitty day. God, I hoped tomorrow was better.

Wednesday, May 14

I walked at the wildlife refuge. I wouldn't walk in The City by the Sea again; it was too painful. I saw Sam briefly and it felt awkward. I didn't know what to say or do. Once again, I was at a loss.

His reaction to me last night reinforced my fear that he was working for himself, but only to get me back. How true was that work? And what would happen if I could never get past his betrayal? Did his sense of accomplishment and self-esteem rest on me? That was a burden I didn't want to carry.

When I looked at him, I saw someone that I once loved beyond reason, a man who was kind and generous. I felt warmth and love but no sexual attraction. Was that normal? And I thought, how could I, after what he had done and where he had been? Did it get better? Did it come back or was it gone forever? I had no answers.

I was out walking, and I was thinking about sacrifice. I remembered when I once tried to sacrifice myself for the comfort of my siblings. *When I was four or five years old, someone turned the heat way up in the middle of the night. When my father casually asked who turned the heat up, it was met with a chorus of, "Not me!" That upset him more than the actual heat being up, and he called everyone in for a chat and a spanking. When it was my turn, I confessed to turning the heat up. "Did you really?" he asked. "No," I replied through my tears. "Then why did you say you did?" "I didn't want you to spank anyone else."* That had been my pattern. I'd spent my entire life making sacrifices, large and small, so that others could thrive and be happy. I couldn't do it anymore. And I was not willing to sacrifice myself for a relationship that was not rich and whole and complete and, above all, committed. Then I thought of Sam and wondered why he was willing to jump right back into a marriage that made him unhappy enough to seek comfort elsewhere? Was he that uncomfortable alone? I forced the separation. Would he be able to recognize and articulate it if he needed more time? Would I? Was part of the reason I was willing to work to put this relationship back together, because I was afraid of his reaction if I said no? I had felt that biting, mean side of him and it was devastating to me.

How could I make him understand that I saw him working, I appreciated how hard it was, how painful. I was proud of all he had done. All his hard work should not have made me obligated to jump back into a relationship with someone who had hurt me so badly. Someone I didn't trust. How did I say that and make him hear me without climbing on his defensive horse and lashing out?

I looked at the cans of paint that were in the middle of the living room floor. They had been there since the 27th of April. How long did I wait for him before I just did it myself? What had changed? We still didn't complete anything we started.

So, what was different? I bought the paint and I would end up painting the house, because I loved my family and wanted them to live in a space that was beautiful. I could do that on my own.

Thursday, May 15

Another shitty day. Sam and I went to see Dan and Caroline and it was a horror show. I told them what had happened on my walk through The City by the Sea and how it left me feeling. I told them that when I had talked to Sam about it, he responded with sarcasm that cut me down and pushed me away. Dan said that I was grieving the loss of my marriage, as I knew it, the same way I would grieve a death in the family. Both he and Caroline said they were glad it hit me because I had been plowing along like a bulldozer.

When they tried to get Sam's take on the situation, he started to get defensive. He said it was like we were working our way up a mountain together and suddenly, he turned to look, and I wasn't there. I was back at the bottom. He felt abandoned and rejected but instead of saying that to me, he chose to be sarcastic. So, there I was at the bottom of the mountain and instead of giving me a hand up, he kicked me down more or told me to hurry up.

The whole conversation just went downhill from there. He yelled at Dan and he was combative with Caroline. Then he was even more sarcastic, mimicking me, with his hand on his cheek, looking coyly over his raised shoulder, and saying in a simpering, high-pitched voice, "Well now, I don't know . . ." I thought for a minute that Caroline was going to come right out of her chair. As I was talking, he put both hands behind his head and leaned back in his chair as if to say, "This ought to be good."

I completely fell apart. I cried and gave voice to my fears and frustrations—and then he blew up. He really blew up.

I didn't know what to do. He did all this great outside work but I still felt like he was looking for ways to justify his choices and actions.

When we left, I tried to talk to him. I loved him and I wanted this to work. I didn't want him to leave the parking lot without making some kind of connection. I had tried to explain how he was coming across in the meeting. That really concerned me. If he continued to act that way, how could Dan and Caroline possibly advocate a return to the marriage? Anyway, when we left, things seemed a little more even.

Around seven p.m. I called the house. I knew the moment he picked up the phone with the terse "hello" that he was in a foul mood. He put Faye on the phone and she immediately began to cry. She said she was scared when Daddy yelled at Caleb and Caleb yelled back. I told her she needed to tell her dad how she felt. I told her she could call me anytime and could come and stay with me if she wanted to. She said she sleeps with me every night and she didn't want her daddy to feel bad she doesn't sleep with him. Great. Now my eight-year-old was mothering her father.

Then Caleb got on the phone and he was hysterical. He called Sam a monster and kept saying how much he hated his father. He said that Sam was taking out all of his anger on him. I knew that a big part of his angst was that he was thirteen. But I also knew that Sam had little to no tolerance for defiance or difficulty, particularly with Caleb. I tried to be supportive and encouraged Caleb to talk to Sam.

When Sam got back on the phone he was just as cold as before. When I asked if there was anything I could do, I got the sarcastic reply of "No, because you're there and I'm here." Honest to God, sometimes it would be easier if he just gave me a slap.

I couldn't be productive and do the work I was trying to do on me and my marriage if I was afraid that while I was away, my husband was taking out his anger on our kids. He could place his anger on me if he wanted, but certainly not on two innocent children who, not only were defenseless, but look to him for protection.

When I hung up, I decided to go for a walk with Sophie. I wished Sam had a friend like Sophie that he could talk to. Someone who wouldn't make him feel judged. Someone who could sit back, listen, and give him support. He only had me. And obviously that was not enough right now.

Friday, May 16

Tonight was the school variety show. Faye was wonderful and I was proud of her. I was also proud of myself for putting these girls together in five rehearsals. Sam came to the show. It felt as if we were completely disconnected.

Caleb was still in a foul mood. Now it was his turn to cycle. It was getting to the point where tough love was all he responded to. He was angry at both Sam and me. I was not sure what had caused this flare up right now. Maybe Sam really was using Caleb as the whipping post last night. Whatever it was, it made me feel like I needed to push Sam away in order to make peace with Caleb. Sometimes it felt like there was this bizarre competition between them. I used to say to Sam all the time, "Could you at least pretend to like him?" No wonder Caleb hated us.

I read the quote by Abraham Lincoln that Sam put on the wall at the apartment. "People are about as happy as they make up their minds to be." So, this morning I decided I was going to be happy. And for a while I was, sort of. I still felt lost and disengaged, but not miserable.

Then, on the way home tonight I began to think of yesterday in Dan's office. I thought of how Sam cruelly mimicked me and, when I brought it up outside, he said he never said or did that. How could he fix something that he couldn't or wouldn't see that he was doing?

It was interesting. We have had had these amazing talks and I think, wow, we're really getting there. And then we continue to slip into the old routine of hurt, lash out, stifle. Two steps forward, one step back.

Once again, I felt that Sam was distant and had changed his mind about us. I felt like a yo-yo. It was exhausting.

Saturday, May 17

Sam and I spent most of the morning talking on the phone. I spent several hours trying to defuse his anger at Caroline, his frustration with Dan, and his fears about me. How could you make someone understand? Someone who, for whatever reason, couldn't hear you? Not only did he not hear me, he also didn't hear Dan or Caroline.

Who was the real Sam? Which one? The Sam who was generous and loving, who did the little things to show he cared? The Sam who wanted to help others? Or was it the Sam who was sarcastic and mean? Someone once described him as caustic. Was that true? What good was self-preservation if you were left alone in the end? What had you really preserved?

I only hoped that Dan and Caroline didn't quit.

I spent the day working around the house. It felt good. We were planning on going to see the big Victorian house tomorrow but we were one hundred forty-one dollars overdrawn in our checking account. It was disheartening. When His mother died, we would be forced out of this house. Then what?

We were no closer to getting our debt under control. What was he waiting for? This was an indication to me that he still wanted to skate like he had always done. He closed the store four and a half months ago. What was he waiting for? If I had to do it all, I was going to be pissed. That would only show that nothing had really changed. He was saying everything he knew I wanted to hear, but he still wouldn't completely step up to the plate. Just do it! Be a man.

I had to stop writing, stop thinking. Sometimes it was just too confusing. I needed to focus on me again and how I was working, and then next on the kids. Sam needed to do his own work so that we could put this together.

Caleb had an awesome day. He was fun and funny and sweet. Faye was sound asleep. I went downstairs and saw Caleb on the futon, snuggled up to the dog, reading. So cute.

Sunday, May 18

We went to church together as a family. It was interesting to watch Caleb change when Sam came in. Men and their fathers. We took the kids to see "our" house. I wished there were some way to afford it, but we were so heavily in debt, I didn't see how it would ever happen. Oh well. It was good to dream.

Sam and I went on our date. I wanted to pack a picnic, but the weather was iffy. We hiked to a lookout over the beach. We talked and cried and talked some more. I tried to explain how I felt. I tried to get him to tell me what some of his frustrations were. He didn't.

I told him some of my needs and he asked me to write them down, so I did.

First, I needed to feel special. When I found out about all his affairs, I stopped feeling special. I felt like I was no longer the love of his life. I was just one more woman in a long line that just happened to be the mother of his children. I needed to be the most important person to somebody.

Second, I needed him to love me enough that he wanted me to be surrounded by beauty. Yes, I would have loved to have that beautiful Victorian house but that was not likely to happen. Paint the walls here. Help me keep it clean and beautiful in a way we could afford. Don't wait. Tomorrow might never come.

Third, I needed a partner. Someone who wanted to take care of me emotionally, physically, spiritually, and financially. I could certainly meet my own needs, especially if I were alone. But if I was going to share my life with and give my love to someone, then he should want to take care of me. Doesn't mean he had to.

We talked openly and so well that I really wished he could be this open and honest in Dan's office without all the hostile defensive crap he brought in. It was counterproductive and made people think he was an ass. I didn't want people to think badly of him, but I didn't know if he could understand or if he even cared that it happens.

More days like this. Healing days. No sarcasm. No fear. No regrets.

Monday, May 19

Are we finally working together? I met with the financial planner. Poor guy. He met to talk about investing. What he told me was that our ship was not just listing to one side, it was upside down. We were sinking fast. No kidding.

It really forced us to sit down and examine where we were going. I would try to get a job in the school system. Sam would work at my school. We were just going to have to suck it up. It felt like failure to me, but I just looked at the numbers. We were in a staggering shit load of debt. If we could get into a debt consolidation program, then maybe we could crawl out.

Talking about this was very emotional for me. It was hard not to feel like a failure. It was devastating to admit that I had put my children in the exact same place that I was growing up. A place I hated.

I didn't even know what he still owed vendors from the store.

The time for feeling upset or embarrassed was long over. We needed to get this under control now! Our ship was upside down and we needed to take drastic steps to right it before we all drowned.

Tuesday, May 20

It was an emotional day. I called my mother to tell her that we were not coming to my niece's party. I told her about our debt situation, doing everything I could not to cry. She got it. She had been there. I was sure she felt sick over the fact that I was right back where I started from. I know it made me sick. She called me later to see if she could take Faye for a bit this summer. They would have "Camp Grammie" so Faye wouldn't miss out. My mom could be so good. Sam made an appointment to meet with the attorney about bankruptcy. I sure hoped it was good news. I thought Sam finally got it. This was where all the hiding and lying and warped thinking and behavior had gotten us. When I first dragged him in to see Dan years ago, I could see this coming. I just couldn't make him understand or even care.

Sophie asked me if it brought up all the rage at his behavior. For right now, it really didn't matter. I wasn't sure why. Maybe it was because all of this came to a head after our great talk and great date on Sunday. If it had happened on Friday, who knows? Maybe I would be the one meeting with the lawyer and not for bankruptcy.

Tomorrow my plan would be made. I tried to get started on my cover letter and resume. I called some people for letters of recommendation. I did what I could do to help us get out of this terrible situation intact, with at least a shred of our dignity.

Wednesday, May 21

I would be relieved if my life would stop going from crisis to crisis. I sincerely hoped that I was not one of those people that thrived on chaos. I craved peace and contentment.

Sam and I seemed to be working together for the first time in years. This was his opportunity to prove to me that he was willing to take a chance, get out of his comfort zone, to provide for and take care of us. I tried to step back and let him step up to the plate. So far, he had done that. I prayed that it would continue.

I had been frightened for the last four years, knowing this was coming and feeling like I was facing it alone. Now that I didn't feel like I was alone, it somehow seemed a lot less scary. We would come through this, God, and Sam, willing.

Thursday, May 22

What a day. I was working all day to try to increase enrollment at school. I was feeling productive and really looking forward to the meeting with Dan and Caroline.

Just before I left for the meeting I was on the computer. I decided to check Sam's Gmail account, which I hadn't done in ages. I knew he wasn't using it, but I felt like I needed to reassure myself every now and then.

There it was. An email from Emily. I really couldn't even begin to describe the catastrophic effect it had on my body. I began to shake uncontrollably, and I was in danger of losing control of my bowels. I opened it up and it said, "Master, I miss you. Love, Lolita."

So now what? She was trying to contact him. What would he do? I went on MySpace and looked her up. She was very pretty, noticeably young, and she looked very brazen.

I went to my meeting. Still shaking, still sick to my stomach. Caroline knew immediately. I told her what a great weekend we had had, and how we worked together, and I was afraid of hitting him with this. Afraid of his reaction. She said this was a great way for him to help me. That we could work through it together. I couldn't stop shaking. She had me sit back and try to relax. She said," Props are not your friends." I was not to pick up the tea Dan made for me because my hands were shaking so badly.

Terrified, I told Sam about it, and he totally rose to the occasion. He was kind and loving and sincere. I could not have asked for more. It was completely opposite of our last session. At one point, Caroline told him he was behaving like an entirely different person. It was a huge relief. She praised him for how he handled things. I hoped he heard her.

Earlier in the meeting Dan told Sam how much he liked him, but he was so out of control last time that he was not likable. Dan said he should've stopped him last time, but he feared Sam would escalate. I felt good that he was calling Sam on it. I was afraid that I was the only one who was afraid of his reactions and temper. At least I knew that I had not been exaggerating in what I tried to explain to Sam.

So, the session was good and positive. I finally stopped shaking. Poor Caroline kept signaling me to breathe. I think she was afraid I would pass out or something. After the session I asked Sam to promise that if Emily called him, he would tell me. He did. Both he and Caroline gave me permission to respond to Emily's email so I did. It wasn't pretty, nor was it kind. But suddenly I was not powerless. I was not a doormat or some guy's bitchy wife who didn't understand him or give him what he wanted. I was an intelligent woman. I mattered. I was beautiful, articulate, and strong. And I was through being fucked over.

Sam called and left me a message saying that when he was driving home there was a beautiful bright rainbow. I felt like God was giving us all the signs that we were on the right path.

Friday, May 23

Today started off with what could've been a problem, but we were growing and changing. Sam picked up a shift at work, so he asked me to come to the house this morning. He said that he would have to leave for work directly after dropping Caleb off at the carpool.

On my way to the house, I saw high school kids waiting for the bus. I was thinking that riding the bus next year would be a panic point for Caleb but how God does provide. As I was pulling into the driveway, the boy next door was pulling out. I thought, *that's it*! Caleb could ride to school with him and give him some money for gas. When I got out of the car, my neighbor, the boy's mother, called to me and we stopped to talk. It seemed that her son just passed his driving test the day before.

While I was chatting with her, Caleb called me over and said that Sam was looking for me. When I went in the house and said good morning, I discovered that there seemed to be a misunderstanding. For some reason, Sam assumed I was going to drive Caleb. He told me that Caleb had been in a foul mood the night before and some of the mood was still lingering. When I called Sam later, I explained that I would have been more than happy to drive, but nobody asked me. He said something like, "Well, I don't remember what was said and what wasn't said." Although there was no malice in his voice, it really bothered me. It was a cop out he had used a lot to cover his mistakes. In a way, it was a form of lying, something we would need to watch so it didn't escalate.

He explained to me that Caleb had been upset last night because Sam took Faye for ice cream after Brownies. Then, when it was time to go to bed, Caleb wanted to sleep with him, but Sam told him that Faye had already asked.

How was it that a man who had such tremendous rejection and abandonment issues couldn't recognize those same fears in his own child? Poor Caleb. He must've felt completely rejected. He didn't have a way to deal with it, so he lashed out, which caused Sam to reject him more. Sam was doing exactly what his parents did to him and I told him that. I offered to take Faye for a girls' night so the boys could reconnect and have fun. I hoped they would be able to talk a little and that Sam could help Caleb. He was such a great kid. I had heard that from so many people. I wished Sam could see him as I was able to.

So, Faye and I had a girl's night. We ate leftover pizza, veggies and oranges in the dining room and watched a movie. She really was very sweet. I hoped she felt special being here with me. I felt special that she wanted to be here. I was hopeful that Sam had used this time with Caleb wisely.

Sophie and I walked this afternoon. She had a long, emotionally exhausting day, meeting her ex-husband's fiancé for the first time. I just let her talk. I tried to give back some small measure of support. She'd very nearly held me up more than once. She has grown tremendously in the last year. I hoped she could really process that.

I got into bed to snuggle with my baby. Our children really were remarkable. I prayed Sam and Caleb were having a good night.

There was no response from Emily. Poor thing. She probably thought I owned a gun. Who knew what kind of negative things

Sam told her about me? Who cares? I took a piece of my life and dignity back. Not that I was putting the blame solely on her. Sam was a big boy and made some disastrous choices. Now he was living with the consequences and so was she. We all were.

Saturday, May 24

I found porn in his bag. I tried to talk to him about it without being confrontational. He said we had an understanding that he would watch it occasionally, but I remembered no such understanding. I couldn't look back in my old journal tonight because I was at the apartment and only had my current book. I would look when I got home, but I didn't remember being okay with his watching porn.

Why did I have this issue with Sam and porn? Yes, we used to watch it together occasionally and that was fun. After Faye was born, he began to collect it. He was still in denial about that. It became a secret, and it took the place of him being involved in our relationship. The porn and the masturbation became so obsessive that I finally had to ask him to do it before he came to bed because I was tired of being woken up nightly by his masturbating. He now says the porn was not part of the addiction.

He collected it when we lived in The City by the Sea. He had at least thirty, maybe more, videos that I found hidden in the closet. He said they were given to him by a woman he used to work with who bought a video store. Lies, I was sure. I made him throw them out when we moved. He said he did. More lies? We were only in the house a year or two. Caleb was eight when I found a garbage bag full of them under the bed. Then I found a big box of them in his trunk. I found them under the couch, under the bed and in bags next to the bed. Never the same ones. He couldn't go six months without it. And now he said he was "borrowing" them from Frank, a client. That was so inappropriate! If his job were to find out about it, they would probably fire him. When we talked about this before, he said he told his boss about his addiction, and that he wasn't going to scan any more films for Frank. Did he really tell her?

The porn was connected to the secrets—the "don't ask, don't tell" life we were living before. It would lead to more acting out and more lying. I knew it had before. He said that he wouldn't get them anymore. Did I believe him? Now I felt like I had to check everything all over again.

So, I got very little sleep. I was up with his mother, while he went off to the apartment to watch porn and masturbate. It was wrong, unfair, and dishonest and it all felt incredibly dirty.

Sunday, May 25

I went to the graves of my grandparents to plant flowers and found myself wondering how their lives were reflected in mine. My mother and I had been putting flowers there since I could remember. I used to go alone to weed and water the flowers. Sometimes I would just sit and pray to understand why and how my father didn't want me.

On this day, I was there with my children, my mother and my aunt Bitsy. This was the first time I had ever been to my paternal grandfather's grave with a member of his family. My aunt Bitsy was to me what Aunt Nattie was to Sam. I wished Aunt Nattie was still alive. Maybe then Sam would feel that someone in his family loved him just because he was lovable. He certainly didn't have that with his mother or his sister.

When I got home, his mother was pissed because she thought I was coming home in the morning. I tried to calm her down and told her that I didn't understand what the problem was. She looked at me and said in the meanest, nastiest voice, "Maybe *you're* the problem." It just escalated from there.

I was done. I was tired of getting up in the night. It had been a long time since I'd had a full night's sleep here. I was tired of feeding her, washing her, and cleaning for her. I constantly had to turn down dinner invitations because I had to be home to take care of her. All the while, she was mean and nasty to me. I hated her for that. Sam was supportive and loving and I was trying to trust this was all sincere. The latest round of porn threw me, but I would get past it.

We went for a long walk after dinner. It felt good to just be together. I was trying to get the feeling back. I really was. Time would tell.

Monday, May 26—Memorial Day

It was a long and difficult day. I picked up Faye from a sleepover at ten in the morning. The mother informed me that the girls didn't go to sleep until 3 a.m. Faye started crying at about 10:30 and didn't stop all day. She eventually developed a fever.

Then there was Caleb. He was defiant and obnoxious and did nothing without a fight. I told him that what he was saying by his actions was that Sam and I were only here to pay his way to school and camp and that was it. After thinking about it, he apologized.

I was looking forward to getting the garden in, but Sam hadn't come by, so I called him only to find out that he was up all night. He had taken two sleep meds at 4:00 a.m. and didn't arrive until 11:00. After Sam came, Caleb was as difficult as he could possibly be. There was nothing likable about him at all. My niece called and asked if it would be okay to come down for the night. I was thrilled but at the same time the house was a disaster. Letting things slide was fine until you needed them to be clean. We decided to have her stay at the apartment.

When she and her boyfriend arrived, we had dinner and it was awful. Sam and Caleb both talked incessantly with their mouths full. Perhaps they felt they had to act happy or maybe they were just stressed out—whatever. I was so embarrassed.

After I delivered my niece and her boyfriend to the apartment, I took a drive around town. While I was gone, Caleb threw another one of his defiant tantrums. Sam was pissed and rightly so. When I tried to talk to Caleb, he was hostile and belligerent. His lack of respect was alarming, so it was time for tough love. The Xbox was taken away. I was sure there would be a massive scene tomorrow.

So, Sam was at the house and my niece and her boyfriend were at the apartment. I told Sam that it was okay to sleep in the bed with me. In some ways it felt normal but I knew I wouldn't sleep at all. It felt incredibly awkward.

Tuesday, May 27

It was such a long day. It felt like the last time I wrote was last week. Of course, I got very little sleep last night and Sam got even less. He was coughing and my shoulder wasn't comfortable. Faye got up this morning with a fever of 102.4. It responded to medication, so I didn't worry. She snuggled up on the couch and read all day and seemed better in the afternoon.

I had a meeting at Town Hall but had no sitter. I was assured we were one of the first ones on the docket, so I left Caleb in charge. It ran extremely late.

When I got home, Caleb was still up. He was so good. I praised him like crazy. Faye, on the other hand, had a fever of 102.8 and I had no medication left. Poor Sam. I called him to find out which pharmacy was open. He said he would go, but he had already taken nighttime meds. I assumed that when he got here he would spend the night, but he went back to the apartment to sleep.

I was grateful he seemed happy to go. The old Sam might have done it, but not without sighs of exasperation at the inconvenience. It was selfless and loving and kind. Maybe that wonderful man I fell in love with was truly making a comeback.

Wednesday, May 28

My days seemed to get busier and shorter. When I said my morning prayers, I thanked God for the wonderful gifts he had given me: life, health, Sam, the kids, and my school.

I had a fun dinner later with the kids and then got them both into bed early. Faye was a little sad to sleep in her own bed and asked if I would snuggle with her. We lay in her bed and laughed ourselves silly. It was one of those great fits of giggles that, just as it is slowing, spontaneously starts up again. At one point she reached toward my face in the dark. I asked what she was doing. She said she was checking to see if my nose wrinkled up like hers when she laughed. Such an incredibly beautiful and infectious laugh.

Caleb was also a lot of fun tonight. I must say that this separation from Sam has helped me to look at my children differently. They have brought me such joy. I only hoped I was returning the favor.

Sam seemed a little cool since his sleep over and I wasn't sure if it was his miserable cold or something more, so I asked and I'm glad I did. He assured me that there was nothing underlying and that his coolness was completely unintentional.

In order to move toward healing our marriage, we both needed to foster openness, communication, forgiveness, and love. I found myself wondering where sex fit in. How did I get the feeling back? I was still at a loss about that.

Thursday, May 29

The minute I got up, I was already feeling a little behind the eight ball. So much was going on! Sam was going to meet with the attorney for bankruptcy, and there were several items he needed to take with him. Caleb needed thirty dollars for field trips, but I only had five dollars and no checks. Thursday was my day to drive for the carpool, get Faye ready and off to school, his mother fed and myself packed for the apartment. It all had to be done by 8 a.m. I not only got it all done, but I was not stressed out and I even made muffins.

Sam came in to get the stuff for the lawyer. He looked great and he seemed positive and hopeful. After meeting with the attorney, he came back to fill me in. We sat on the floor of my classroom and it felt good. It was great when he walked in and the kids said, "Hi Sam!" That hadn't happened in years and it filled me with hope.

Dear God, you have already filled my life with so many blessings. Thank you so much. Please grant me the wherewithal to use what you have given me to the best of my ability. Amen.

After work, I arrived at the apartment with mixed feelings. I was sad not to be with Sam and the kids, but it actually felt good coming here. Sophie, her husband, and I went out for a walk and then we ended up going for dinner at the beach. It was a great, fun night.

When I called the kids to say good night, I felt a slight hesitation to tell Sam where I was. The old, sick Sam would've felt threatened and made me feel guilty. Tonight, he said, "Good for you. Have fun." I spoke with him later and tried to explain to him how nice and different it was. He brushed it off as my perception and fear of his reaction, not his actual behavior. Was he truly unaware of how he used to be or was this just him trying to move on? Dan said that he feared Sam's escalating. I feared that all the time. My fear and misperception or his actual reaction?

What was the pivotal turning point? Was it that awful session? Our talks afterwards? The next session? Doesn't matter. I was glad it happened.

Friday, May 30

Sam had a good meeting with Josh. It seemed like they were certainly making progress.

I spent a lot of time with Sam. He came by the school twice and it felt good. We did some very honest talking. In the evening, we went for a walk through The City by the Sea. We walked and talked for an hour and it felt very natural and open. We held hands the entire time. I loved the way his hands felt. His skin is so different from mine. He looked handsome and relaxed and I told him so.

It dawned on me that what happened yesterday was something Caroline told me to watch for. A couple of months ago, she said that when I was feeling happy, I needed to stop and take stock—try to recognize and name what had occurred just prior to the happiness, so that I could manufacture the feeling at a later time. She assured me that, after a while, the happiness would just begin to happen more and more spontaneously.

Yesterday was such a good day and when I came into the apartment, I was feeling so good that I was actually questioning what was going on. It took me a full day to realize that I felt happy. How pathetic was that? I spent so many years being okay, being fine, or not being fine, or being unhappy and just accepting that that was the way it would probably always be, that when real happiness showed up, it was almost unrecognizable. What triggered it? True hope. An actual light at the end of the tunnel. Sam's love. Sam's belief in me. My belief in myself. Sophie and her husband–good friends. Honesty—finally honesty.

When we finished our walk tonight, Sam and I stood in front of the apartment talking. I told him about my lack of sexual feelings and my fear they would never come back. All I could picture was him standing beside the bed, being exasperated with me and caught up in his own crap and saying, "Well I'm certainly not going to live in a sexless marriage." I just didn't know how to bring it back. Caroline said it would come back. Tonight, Sam said, "Be patient." Only time would tell.

Saturday, May 31

I felt connected to Sam last night. I slept well and got up early. By 8 a.m., I was returning to the apartment after an hour-long walk.

Sam and I went off to Home Depot to buy plants. When we got back, he headed to work, and Caleb and I planted the garden together. We worked quietly for three hours, side-by-side. It was comforting.

Later in the evening, I found that on Thursday, someone tried to get onto a porn site—two of them actually. It was time stamped at 4:45 p.m. I think Sam was picking up Faye, but I wasn't sure. I know it wasn't Caleb. Sam swore it wasn't him. Not good when I'm PMSing.

It was disheartening to feel like everything was going along just fine, making good progress, and then to find that. Wham! Slapped back down again. Once again, not enough. It angered me terribly. Not at Sam and not at Caleb. At the way, the world was becoming in general and for us.

Sunday, June 1

I put my wedding rings back on. Caroline said that when it was time, I would know. It felt right. I was scared to death. Sam said to "Let go and let God." I felt like that's what I did before, and God let me down. What was the alternative? To end my marriage? To close the door on the man I have loved for twenty-two years? The father of my children? I was so afraid that he would stop being honest, stop being faithful, and once again I would stop being special. I knew that if that happened, I would walk away and never look back.

I supposed one good thing that had come from all this was that I could cry now. For the longest time, I couldn't cry. I had no idea why. Perhaps I saw it as a sign of weakness when I had to be strong. Maybe I was afraid that if I started, I wouldn't be able to stop. I wasn't really sure, but now I could cry and let it out. Sometimes when I least expected it, my eyes would begin to leak.

Monday, June 2

I started my period and had miserable cramps. Although Sam was kind and loving, I was nervous about trusting and getting hurt again, but I was trying to let go.

Caleb was struggling terribly. He was incredibly moody— sometimes silly, sometimes sullen, but mostly obnoxious. I knew his hormones were running rampant. We measured him only to discover that he grew three inches in six months. I was beginning to fear that his moody personality change was substance related but I hoped not. I didn't know how to tell—what to look for. All I knew was that he was my heart, and he was going through some kind of crazy struggle and I felt powerless to help him.

Tuesday, June 3

How strange life seemed. Sam left for Rachel's graduation in New York. I was glad he was going. It would be good for him to see his girls—our girls. I wished his ex-wife wasn't going to be there. Not because she shouldn't be, but because she was mean, and he was vulnerable. And I felt left out.

So here I was at home. Caleb and I had a good productive talk. Sophie and the girls came for dinner and now I was snuggled up to my beautiful, almost nine-year-old baby girl. I began to wonder; would I forever mark time in her life by Sam's infidelity? How unfair to her. I hoped it was something that would fade as trust was built.

Sophie's mom told stories tonight of her own dad and the wonderful way they would play at night—the kids and the adults—games like tag, hide-and-seek, and sardines. That was what we were missing. Sam's parents were not the playful type, but mine were. When did it stop? When did we get so busy, so bent on survival, that we forgot how to play with our kids? And in doing so, preserve the kids inside us? It needed to be a priority. We couldn't wait. There might never be another chance.

Wednesday, June 4

My kindergarten class and I spent the day out on one of the islands. The family who invited us went overboard with the day and it was delightful, beautiful, peaceful, and serene. I found myself wishing that we could go over and spend a week as a family, simply enjoying each other. I wanted to be there, not with these children, but with my husband.

He was on his way home from New York. I wished he were already home. He had a good time and he was enormously proud of Rachel. I could hear it in his voice.

School had become incredibly stressful. I had gotten a major attitude since I was forced to make some HR changes. It had been emotionally draining and I would have to deal with it all next week. Right now, I needed some sleep.

Thursday, June 5

It was an intense, stressful day that turned into an equally shitty night. It was Caleb's last day of school and the graduation was in the evening. Sam picked him up at 11:30 and was greeted with an attitude. Caleb was acting like a complete ass. He was mean, combative, sullen, and sarcastic. It was draining, to say the very least.

He was pissed at me because he had outgrown his sport coat and, since I didn't have money for a new one, I made him wear a vest. At the graduation ceremony he was so difficult that I couldn't even take a picture. I finally told him that he was ruining the whole evening for me and I started to cry. Not only was my life precariously perched at the time, but my son was moving out of private school and on to public high school and was acting like a jerk. I felt like I was losing him.

After the ceremony he apologized. I told him that I accepted his apology but that he was acting like a jerk. Not only could he not see anything other than himself, but he was also pushing away anyone who was trying to get close or help.

We talked it out and he told me how scared he was to be moving on to high school and that the admissions director wouldn't give him a scholarship for next year. I told him again that when he pushed away the people who love him, he pushed away his support system.

We talked some of it out, but he refused to talk to Sam. Sam was irritated and angry at Caleb and I felt the wall go up between us. I tried to break it down, but he was distant and quiet.

Caleb was so angry with Sam. I was afraid that either he had found the letter Sam left on the computer or else he was just beginning to figure it all out. Sam had a good reason to be angry with Caleb. Caleb was acting like a shit but, for as long as he could remember, Sam was dissatisfied with him and sought to push him away. If Caleb had somehow figured out the truth, I wasn't sure if Sam would ever be able to mend it. I also didn't know if he could get past his own anger to try to save his son. Where did that leave me? And us?

Friday, June 6

Nine years ago, I was in labor and heading to the hospital. It was hard for me to comprehend, but this beautiful little girl sleeping beside me was born out of love into a marriage already tainted by infidelity.

It was after midnight and I was very tired. I made two things for Faye's birthday. First, the skirt I meant to make for Easter, but I was too sick to do it, and also a top. I hoped she wasn't disappointed with her gifts. We were on the budget plan.

Sam and I talked this morning about Caleb. I ran some of my theories by him. I was just trying to figure out why Caleb was so angry at Sam. Then Sam said something that stopped me in my tracks. He was angry about Caleb's belligerence and difficult behavior and said that he was not going to live like that. This put me in the middle, but I already knew what my decision would be. I loved Sam with all my heart, but Caleb was my child and my responsibility. Our responsibility.

We met with Caroline and Dan. They gave us some good insight and ways to help Caleb label his feelings. We shall see. I was very sleepy. Tomorrow was the big day; my baby was turning nine.

Saturday, June 7

What a sad, strange day Faye's birthday turned out to be. I made her a special breakfast and when Sam got home, she opened presents. She seemed genuinely delighted with everything. After she went off to rehearsal for her performance tonight, I spent several hours cleaning. Then she and I went to do the shopping while Sam went off to work and Caleb went to a friend's house.

I spent the rest of the day dealing with a personnel crisis at school. Did I really just fire someone?

Sunday, June 8

Faye's party was a huge amount of work but also a huge success. This was the first party that Sam was home for in a long time. It felt good to have him here and great to have his help.

I needed a good night's sleep, and all the strength and courage God could give me to get through school tomorrow.

Monday, June 9

What an emotionally exhausting day. I was losing staff because of the changes I needed to make to keep my school afloat. It was like losing family. By the time I got home, I was spent. Poor Sam was so good and supportive. I could barely remember my name, let alone recall all the goings on.

He had sent me a card from New York, and it came. It was very welcome, although I wish it had come on a day that I could actually focus on it.

Tuesday, June 10

The last day of school, thank God. It was so emotional and disappointing, with the drama surrounding my teachers, that I didn't even want to write about it.

I didn't get home until after 6:00 and I just wanted to go to bed, probably to hide as much as to sleep. Sophie brought Faye home from a birthday dinner with her daughter. Sophie and Sam made the evening enjoyable, silly, and fun and I forgot my troubles for a while.

Wednesday, June 11

I made it through my school graduation. I felt a sense of accomplishment as I graduated my first kindergarten class. What a year. Sam stayed with me. He was very supportive.

Afterwards I came home, and the house was still a wreck from the weekend. I threw in a load of laundry and took a nap—something I hadn't done in ages. The laundry was piled high, the lawn needed to be mowed and the painting had not been done. Had things changed? Sometimes it didn't seem like it.

The letter came from St. Andrews. They rejected our request for a scholarship for Caleb. He was heartbroken. He cried and I tried to comfort him. Sam still had not spoken to the guidance counselor at the public school. I asked him months ago to do it. Were we really moving forward or was he just doing enough to shut me up so we could go back to how things were?

I needed some sleep.

Thursday, June 12

I felt like I should pat myself on the back. It was the shittiest six months of my life, but I was still standing. Everything in my life had become a waiting game: waiting to hear from St. Andrews for Caleb; waiting for the intimate feelings to come back to me; waiting to see if Sam and I could actually put this marriage back together. Sometimes I felt completely stripped of power over my own life. When I felt that way, my tendency was to work harder to fix it. How did I find the middle ground and still provide for my family? How did we work harder together?

I bought a new T-shirt at a local discount store yesterday. As I put it on, the smell transported me back to my childhood. I wasn't sure if it was the T-shirt, the heat, the combination, or what. I thought about how, as a kid, I got new clothes when I went to visit my dad in the summer. It may have been only underwear and socks, but I was not allowed to wear them until I got there. I would open my suitcase, thrilled about being with my father, and be engulfed by the smell of new underwear and socks. It made me feel special and worth something. Pretty sad.

Friday, June 13

Friday the 13th. Tim Russert died. How sad.

I was sitting alone in my car at the mall, killing time waiting to pick Caleb up from the first party he'd been invited to in years. I prayed he had a great time.

This was my first full day off. I wanted to do some things before Faye's school BBQ and her writer's workshop at school. I had just begun to make my list for my sister's party when I heard his mother's walker thump and Caleb call to me. She had fallen on her backside and taken the walker with her. Thank God we were home. I called Sam at work because I wasn't sure if I should try to get her up and his sister was at work. He wanted me to take her to the hospital so off we went. Of course, she was utterly charming to everyone she came in contact with.

There was no place for me to sit so my back and legs began to ache. As the hours ticked by, I started to get very resentful about missing Faye's school function for his mother, who obviously wasn't hurt and who was acting like an entirely different person. At one point, the nurse asked if she was good about taking her medication. She said, "Oh, yes. My son makes sure I get it." I wanted to say, "Yeah, two days a week. The rest of it falls to me." It was petty I know, but I felt invisible.

I ended up missing Faye's BBQ and got to her writer's workshop late. She looked so grateful that I wanted to cry.

When Sam got home, I decided I would take Caleb to the party because, even though it was an hour away, I felt that it was important for him. I would do without any time for myself and any time with Sam. I was feeling stressed out, cranky and irritable. I called the landlady at our apartment about getting out of the lease by July 1st. That made me nervous. I really did want to spend more time with Sam, but I was also afraid. When I tried to tell him this, he shrugged and said, "Well then, keep the apartment." It was sarcastic and meant to hurt. And it did. I told him that if he was going to make flippant remarks when I expressed to him how I was feeling, then I'd stop telling him. I guess I just felt incredibly taken for granted.

Just before I left, he asked if there was anything in the oven. What happened to him cooking too? I know he worked all day, but I did that every day. I felt like I was back to cooking, cleaning, doing the laundry, and shouldering all the care of the family.

Was this my cycle and why was I feeling like he didn't care? I called him four times to try to connect. Fix it. Fix it. Fix it. Was it premature to get rid of the apartment? How could I know? I was scared all over again.

Saturday, June 14

I supposed that we seemed much more disconnected because we hadn't sat down and talked in quite some time. We had only been on two dates since we got the apartment. After our hike overlooking the beach, I told him that I wanted him to plan the next one. I waited a couple of weeks and then left the menu to a local bistro out. We had a gift certificate for it, so I asked him if he'd like to go there and then asked him to plan it. Nothing. Maybe he really didn't want to go out with me. He said he did. It was very confusing. That was a little like what I'd tried to tell him before. He asked me to be conscious of what I said and did, and I was trying very hard. I also tried not to constantly say, "you." But I felt if I voiced disappointment or resentment, whether it had to do with his words or actions or not, I was told to get a grip and move on. It was disheartening. I hoped he heard me.

I went to the Garden Party for church. I spent ninety-five

percent of the four hours we were there sitting by myself. I felt awkward and lonely but I did enjoy watching the kids have a great time. I couldn't wait for tomorrow. A new day. A new start.

Sunday, June 15—Father's Day

It was a good day. We went to church together and then Faye went off to a birthday party while Sam and I did the grocery shopping. There was an easy familiarity and it felt really comfortable. I'd been thinking about the ambivalent feelings I had been having over the last few days. As I looked at it now, I thought that anger over Sam's betrayal was just rearing its ugly head again. I was trying to feel it for what it was and not to push it aside or stifle it. In doing so, I was also trying extremely hard not to bring it up and punish him. And then I thought, why? Why not punish him? Why were his actions seemingly without consequence? But I realized that it would do no one any good, so I put those thoughts away and just didn't tell him. Now how much progress have we really made?

We watched The Notebook later. It was such a moving film. It was nice to be on the couch together. I would have loved to snuggle up, but he didn't seem interested. I kept putting my hand on his leg and he didn't respond. Oh well.

Monday, June 16

It was a day for progress. We went to drop a check off at the lawyer and sat in the car talking about Gabriel. I just couldn't seem to make Sam understand that he was my choice, not Gabriel. I remembered, when I was feeling badly about his ex-wife, Sam had said to me, "Look, she pushed me to the door and opened it up. It's not your fault that you were standing on the other side." That was how I felt. I felt like Sam pushed me to the door and opened it up. But I looked at Gabriel standing on the other side and closed the door.

I didn't know what else to say or do to make him hear me or understand. Was he still trying to justify his actions by my actions? Did he really think that some hot and heavy kissing in any way balanced out years of extramarital sex? Maybe I was wrong. Maybe this wasn't meant to be. I couldn't believe that God would lead me through all of this incredible pain, have me struggle with forgiveness, only to have my marriage end because Sam couldn't move beyond Gabriel. We would see. Time would tell.

I asked him to lie down with me on the couch. It seemed he wasn't going to initiate any kind of intimacy that I did not ask for directly. Where was the romance?

Tuesday, June 17

It was Faye's last day of school. Sam and I cleaned out the pantry closet. So much crap. It felt good to clean it out together. I knew he got overwhelmed with the enormity of even the simplest tasks. Maybe doing it together would be the only way he could face it. It was a beginning.

Later, we took Caleb to the public high school. Of course, Sam knew everybody and it was interesting to watch. He said that I saved my smiles and my energy for everyone but him. I never really considered if he did that until now. I watched him do a lot of talking, a lot of interacting with a lot of people, mostly women. He was outgoing, bubbly, fun, very chatty. This was the man I caught glimpses of occasionally.

The vice principal looked at Caleb and it was as if she could see right into his heart. She spoke of how St. Andrews was a tight-knit community and how he would miss it, and how he would love the public high school. She talked immediately about AP classes. She got him and I felt better after that.

At the moment, I was feeling wiped out. Time to sleep and stop thinking.

Wednesday, June 18

It was 10:30 and Faye and I had just finished watching *Princess Diaries* together and eating popcorn. She peeked around the corner and then came into my room, her hair around her face, her cheeks flushed. I was struck by how beautiful she was, not only on the outside but also on the inside. She was kind and good and loving.

I had the same revelation looking at Caleb yesterday. He was handsome but he was so much more. He was bright and articulate and loving and funny. He also had a tendency to get so excited about something that he had to stop and tell you right then and there, just like when he was little. All he wanted for us to do was listen. Maybe we were fixing things after all. Maybe they weren't really broken with him. Maybe we just weren't willing to listen.

Thursday, June 19

Sam and I had a good day. We went and got my bicycle, took Caleb to school and registered him, had a great dinner, and then went out on a date.

When Sam and Caleb went to the golf course, I looked in Sam's car. I guess I was checking for porn. I found his journal. I knew he had been reading mine, but I had not seen his in a couple of months. I didn't care if he read mine– maybe it would give him some insight—but it put me at a slight disadvantage. I didn't know whether reading it was helpful or not. One thing I was surprised about was just how much he wrote about Gabriel. It was on every other page and all I did was skim. At one point he said he was coming out for church and passed Gabriel going in the other direction. He wondered if Gabriel was coming from visiting me. He was bordering on obsession. Honestly, aside from the fact that I told him I didn't want to date anyone, and that Gabriel and I did NOT have an affair, it seemed as if he honestly believed I would have Gabriel over with his mother and my children in the house. The whole situation had become ludicrous and his obsession was very unhealthy, not only for him but for me and for us.

Sam and I went to the Tea and Coffee House with the express idea of working on "Emotional Infidelity." Right from the start we were in trouble at the first chapter. I thought we were going to work on some of the exercises in order to move forward. He'd highlighted a lot of the book and wanted to go from the beginning. He began to read to me, "All of us know that adultery—sex outside the marriage—is one of the gravest blows to a marriage as well as a painful rejection for one partner, but you don't have to have sex with someone else to be unfaithful. Emotional infidelity is just as—and at times more—destructive to your marriage." He put his hand on my leg, looked at me, and said, "Do we both agree on this?" I wanted to punch him. It was like he was poking me in the chest and saying, "See? What you did was more destructive than what I did! Says so right here!" I felt defensive and vulnerable and beaten up and I told him. This began a whole evening of what seemed like, "Let's point out all you've done wrong" talks. At one point I felt like telling him to forget it and just walking out the door but I didn't. He never came right out and asked me anything about Gabriel. Even though I told him. He continued to sneak it in the back door. I felt like no matter how many times I said I was sorry, or that what I did was wrong, he was intent on punishing me and justifying his own behavior.

He said that I was allowed to express my feelings, but when he expressed his, I got defensive. Was that true? I had to ask to make him express his feelings. He didn't express them on his own. His habit had been this roundabout dance that seemed judgmental and punishing. It was just like his mother.

We finally began to defuse the situation, but I wasn't sure how much was accomplished. His crazy obsession with Gabriel made him intent on playing the victim. There didn't seem to be anything that I could say or do that changed that. I wanted to pack up and leave and never look back.

We talked about sex and being sexual. He said that he had discovered with Josh the way he expressed love was not only with his words and actions but by making love. I tried to explain to him that for an awfully long time there were few words and almost no actions. How did you make somebody understand that you needed to hear more than "you look sexy"? I didn't want to look sexy going to work in a preschool. I wanted to look pretty and professional and stylish and slim, but sexy wasn't appropriate. He took that as "I'm not interested in him or in sex." He was so far from right.

I tried to explain that for years, the pattern had been for him to come home, pour a glass of wine, and sit down and watch the news while I started a load of laundry, started dinner, helped the kids with homework, got them to set the table, served dinner, finished the laundry, packed bags, picked out clothes for the next day, started more laundry, and got the kids to bed. Sam would do the dishes after dinner. There was little or no conversation. I'd finally sit down around 9 p.m. and he'd be upset and frustrated that I didn't initiate sex. In no way, shape or form was that showing love.

I knew things had been changing for the better, and I was trying very hard to adjust. If the changes had come without the affairs, then we would already be past this point. We could be celebrating these changes and rediscovering our love. Instead, we were distrustful of one another.

He said that when he would be fun and suggestive, I would act like all he ever thought about was sex. But if he was only ever feeding me with suggestive remarks, what else would I think?

I was confused once again and, as had been normal in the past few months, I felt like curling up in a little ball and crying. Would we ever be happy? And honest? And trusting?

Friday, June 20

We met with Dan and Caroline and it was good. Sam and I talked in the morning when I was walking. It was awkward at first but then more comfortable. I was trying to see his fears without being defensive, but when they were blown out of proportion, it was extremely difficult not to say so. I hoped that he could put the whole Gabriel issue away. It wouldn't bother me if I never saw

Gabriel again, not that he would believe that.

When we sat down with Dan and Caroline it was uplifting. I spent an awful lot of time talking. Sam didn't say a lot but did talk about his latest book. Sometimes it helped me to think out loud. I tried to give Sam a forum to air his grievances. He has been clear, on a number of occasions, that he has had many. He had nothing to say in that regard.

We all agreed to go on from this point without Dan and Caroline unless we needed them. They felt like we were doing so much work on our own, that unless we came up against a specific problem, they didn't have an awful lot to add. I felt good. And scared.

Maybe *After the Affair* was right. Perhaps we just needed to jump back into sex again and not wait until I felt like it. The kids would be gone for the next two weeks. Maybe we could try to spend some good time together. We would see.

Saturday, June 21

It was a day filled with activity—packing suitcases for the kids to go away, baking for coffee hour at church, paying bills—all things I wanted to do with Sam's help but he was at work all day. Somehow, I didn't get terribly overwhelmed and got most everything done. Sam left me the most beautiful card.

My Josie–

Let us love and laugh, and a kiss and hug, then laugh and love some more under the summer romance tree. And maybe, just maybe, the romance tree will bloom for all seasons.

Love you–

Your Sam

The love and romance that I have sought, begged for, pined for, and finally resigned myself to its nonexistence, was here. Could I open myself up enough to respond to it in kind? God, I hoped so.

Sunday, June 22

It was a busy day, full of tiny triumphs:

> I read well in church.
> Coffee hour was a success—People liked my food.
> We drove the kids to Maine. Sam and I together.
> We had a great talk on the way home.

On top of that, my body was finally starting to awaken. I actually felt horny. I knew it was in response to his love and attention. I was not dead inside after all.

Monday, June 23

It was a busy day. There wasn't even time to miss the kids, although now that the house was quiet, I missed them a lot. Sam did too.

The flat tire on the way to work was not the best way to start my day. The old me would've been completely stressed out but Sam came to help so it was fine. When I got to my school, I started camp for the kids. It was busy and fun, and I really enjoyed the work

Tuesday, June 24

Caleb went camp. He was off and running and I hoped he would have a magical time.

Sam finished painting his mother's bathroom. He did a great job. The color was beautiful, and I was sure she would like it if she could actually see it. I hoped he experienced a sense of pride and accomplishment in finishing something and doing it well.

That evening, Sam and I made dinner together and it was fun. Then we watched a movie that was silly and sexy. Afterwards we begin to make out. We were kissing and, for the first time in a very long time, my body began to respond. I didn't know if it was making dinner together or the fabulous kissing that triggered the feelings. Hell, it could even be because he finished the bathroom. Whatever it was, I didn't care. It was warm and loving and inti-mate. I wanted to ask him to make love, but I didn't quite dare. There were still times when he was kissing and touching me that I thought of him kissing and touching somebody else, but I tried to push that aside. I tried to concentrate on my husband, the man I loved. and I prayed he wasn't fantasizing that I was someone else.

Wednesday, June 25

I had a lot of time to think about last night and how good it felt. Oddly enough, we had less contact than we'd had in a while.

The contact we did have was loving and warm. He left a beautiful card on my seat. Very romantic.

As beautiful as last night was, I had doubts and fears that kept cropping up. For instance, the panic I felt waiting for him to say, "Tell me about fucking someone." Then what? Would that I could try to enjoy each moment as it came.

I put his mother's bathroom back together. Sam did such a beautiful job with it. He had put an old bottle of cologne on his mother's bureau, so I put it back on his bureau. It was then I noticed that a small blue bottle of cologne that had been there before was gone. I asked him a few months ago where it came from. He said Faye got it at the Elves Room at school and gave it to him for Christmas. Not true. I told him I didn't remember that. Now the bottle was gone. A gift from Emily?

I was tired of feeling vulnerable.

Friday, June 27

Well, it seems that three orgasms help you to sleep like a baby. Last night after dinner we walked around window shopping. We bought ridiculously expensive ice cream cones and sat and watched the sunset. It was very romantic. Afterwards Sam wanted to go parking. It was an immediate turn off. The old me would've done it anyway, fearful of the backlash. If I had said no in the past, the old Sam would've been sarcastic and mean. I said no. He was disappointed but respectful. We went home, where we had a repeat of the other night. Slow kissing, touching and for me, orgasms. He was so loving and so encouraging. I couldn't help thinking that he if he had behaved this way, being romantic and loving, the sex would have naturally followed after Faye's birth. Instead, focus was on the sex and I felt completely unloved and misunderstood.

Also, the weight he lost and the fact that he was taking care of his body was incredibly attractive and sexy. Maybe because I was not a product of the sixties, I had a difficult time feeling sexy with someone who was un-showered and smelly.

Whatever. I really didn't want to leave the house. Actually, I wanted both of us to leave the house and spend the night in the apartment. Privacy was such an issue for us, and we were never without his mother or the kids. But he sent me home. I drove back to the apartment feeling completely intoxicated. I was happy and peaceful, and I slept like a log.

I think I figured out why Sam was so much sexier and appealing. He was happy and he liked himself. Consequently, he carried himself differently, related to people on a different level, more equally, and looked younger.

Saturday, June 28

I was at the beach by myself for the first time in about twenty years. Sam and I made love last night for the first time in six months and twenty-five days. It was intimate and loving and afterwards we slept. When we woke up, we made love again. In some ways I felt closer to him than ever before. In other ways I felt a barrier that I needed to keep there for self-preservation. Last night after we made love, I started to say I love you and I was so completely overcome with emotion that I sobbed. Poor guy, I think I scared him half to death.

So now that we were on our way, I was as afraid as ever. What if the work stopped? What if he shut down? He told me how beautiful and sexy and intelligent I was. Why was it different? Couldn't he see that before?

We talked a little about my wanting to take Caroline's suggestions to write this whole experience all down to share it. He didn't shoot me down, which was something. I had never been a writer, but I knew that what I was looking for was a story of hope when there wasn't any in my life. I wanted to give that to others.

I went for a long walk down the beach and I felt refreshed with a clear head. Enough being afraid. I was where I was because of the decisions I had made– and so was Sam. I chose him. For now, he chose me. That was all I could ask for.

I needed to get my shit together. I would sink or swim based on my own decisions.

Monday, June 30

Yesterday Sam and I spent the entire day together, from waking to sleeping. It was so good. We went to church, had lunch, walked, ran errands, made dinner, and made love. It was never tense or difficult. It was loving, open and comforting. I walked the exact same path that we walked yesterday. I really did enjoy walking alone. It was always when I had my best mental dialogs. I could think clearly and rationally.

Sometimes I felt as if God was saying to me, "Okay, I gave you these gifts. Now what were you planning to do with them?" And then I looked around at the staggering beauty surrounding me and I was filled with a sense of gratitude.

But as I walked, I began to miss Sam. It had been sort of a

honeymoon period for us with the kids gone (although his mother was there). It had been healing to be together without the worry of the kids and protecting them. I prayed that this lasted, that the loving and nurturing man who had come back into my life was there for good.

Tuesday, July 1

A new month. A new beginning.

We went together to get the apartment ready to show. We cleaned quickly and quietly together. There was a sense of camaraderie and teamwork that I had been trying to recover since just after Faye was born.

On our way to get a tire for his car, we passed the parochial school. I knew it was where not only Gabriel's daughter went but also Emily. I said as much and wondered if they knew each other; they were only two years apart. It wasn't that I wanted to punish him. He'd punished himself, I think. But how would he have felt if Becca, at the age of eighteen or even now for that matter, had sex in the store of a sixty-year-old man? If it were Faye, I would have hunted him down. Did he understand how lecherous that made him appear?

Tonight, for some reason I was thinking of his MySpace account. He listed himself as forty-nine and single. It wasn't that I was having doubts. I wanted my marriage to work. I just felt like I needed to keep in the back of my mind the horror I felt at what he had done. Was that how we ensured it never happened again?

Right now, the sex was beautiful and loving and satisfying. What happened when he needed more? Last night, while we were making love, he started to talk about someone else. I felt myself jump inside. I didn't want that. I wouldn't get caught up again where there could be any mistake between fantasy and reality. Would that be enough? No, would *I* be enough? Time would tell.

Wednesday, July 2

I didn't feel well tonight. I started my period and I felt sick. His mother had the ball game on so loud that it made my head ache.

Sam was working tonight, and I felt very lonely, stuck in this house without my children, my only companion, a miserable, self-centered old woman. When I was alone, I doubted and feared. I hated that. I felt unsure all the way around—my family, my business, myself. I needed to stop feeling sorry for myself. That was the only way to move ahead.

Saturday, July 5

The last few days had been very full.

I woke up yesterday morning at 5:30 and my heart was racing. I had dreamed of Emily. She came back and she wanted him. She was tall and thin, with beautiful eyes and long straight dark hair. She was dressed provocatively in leather and leopard and she looked me right in the eye, licked her lips and said, "I win." He came up behind her and wrapped his arms around her waist. They began to move off and right behind them were Caleb and Faye, looking imploringly at me, suitcases by their sides. I begin to panic. What would I do? Where would I go? I had just given up the apartment—my safety net. Now where would I take my children to protect them? I woke up in a cold sweat, my heart racing, terrified.

I drove to Maine and when I got there, I couldn't hug Faye enough. We spent the day packing the truck to go camping. Then we headed to the beach to watch the fireworks. We sat on the beach with a particularly good band playing behind us on a hotel patio. We were right in front of what used to be Merriman's, my first business venture, a small restaurant—a lifetime ago. *When I was in college, I rented a small restaurant one summer. It had twenty-eight seats in the dining room and a take-out window on the beach. It was my first taste of being my own boss. I was hooked.*

The fireworks were spectacular. The band struck up the national anthem when they were over. We all sang and it felt magical and childlike.

In the morning we finished packing up the car and headed north to Bar Harbor. I hadn't been here since high school. The one-act play festival had sent me to the New England festival—to G, my future professor—to RWC—to the theater company and finally to Sam. How fitting that he would join us tomorrow. Serendipity? I couldn't write that word without thinking about Sam's email to Emily. Stop it!!!

I found myself eager to see him. Eager for him to see Faye and experience what we always did without him each summer. I hoped it was fun and restful.

One year, when my children were two and seven, my dad gave me a tent for Christmas. My sister Thea and I took the kids, along with their friends, camping each summer together. Sam had never once come with us.

I was sitting at our campfire at Acadia in Maine. It had been a long drive, but it was peaceful and beautiful. Thea and Faye were playing cards, the fire was crackling, and the sky was darkening. All seemed good. I thought about the call from Shawn while I was on my way to Maine. He told me that our friend and colleague at The Theatre was killed in a plane crash. Her husband was the pilot. Life was too short.

The mother of one of Caleb's friends called me too. They had been in Boothbay looking at a boat for her husband, and they were so close to where Caleb was at camp, that they stopped to visit him. I was thrilled to hear that he was a "happy camper." I wanted him to relax and have fun. He had been through so much.

Sam was coming tomorrow with my mother. I hoped she was kind to him. He thought she was great. I wished she knew that and could see what a good man he was.

Tuesday, July 8

Sam was here and had gone back to work for a day. Unfortunately, when he arrived, he brought a new level of stress, along with my mother. Faye picked up on the negativity. It was sad and disturbing to watch.

Interestingly enough, Sam began to rub my back and my mother started to get all weird. "None of that. None of that." To which Sam replied, "Yes, more of that." I felt caught in the middle. How could a woman who lived life so fully in the seventies have become so prudish thirty years later? She saw any kind of compromise as me being a doormat, which I tended to be, even with or especially with Sam. He saw her reaction and pushed harder. He seemed to be aware of this, though, and was trying not to bite at the bait she set.

It all left me exhausted, torn, and frustrated. Although I was glad that he had been here sharing this with us, I also felt weird. We were close and intimate and yet I felt a little bit disconnected, as if there was a part of me I couldn't allow him to have access to anymore. And I supposed it wasn't just him. It would be anyone. In the name of self-preservation, I needed to keep my distance a little bit. The fear of abandonment rippled just under the surface. I was afraid that I would never love as completely and as fully as I once loved him. Time would tell.

Wednesday, July 9

We were at Echo Lake for about fifteen minutes and Faye had already made a friend. I marveled at her ability to connect so quickly. It happened everywhere we went. My mother and Thea opted to stay behind. I wished Sam were here. The lake was clear, the mountains rising all around, and there were three ducks that were paddling in the water. Even with other people nearby, I felt close to God up there in Acadia.

Saturday, July 12

As we headed home, I wished we had another week here. Faye, Caleb, Sam, and me. I would have liked to do more hiking, more resting and more enjoying each other's company. It was a good week where everybody behaved pretty well, but the stress level was high, and the threat of eruption was always just under the surface.

Thea and I walked around Jordan Pond on Thursday. It was a stunningly spectacular 3.6-mile hike. As usual, I did my best thinking when I was walking. My mother and my sisters all had their own stories to tell, and then there was me. I was molested at ten by the fourteen-year-old babysitter. My mother told me he was just being a boy. When I was sexually assaulted again in college, she said, "How could you trust him?" When my uncle, her brother, solicited oral sex with me, she responded by telling me "That's just him." Then I had an affair with a married man fifteen years my senior, married him after his divorce, and now I was working on taking him back after he had a ten-year string of affairs. What did that say about me?

I was still desperately trying to figure out my ambivalence. On one hand I loved him with everything I had. When he was focused and present, he was kind and giving, humble and open. When he wasn't focused, he was opinionated, often bordering on rude, self-centered, demanding. and difficult to like.

I wanted to put my family back together but what did that tell him about the consequences of his actions? That he was allowed to do what he wanted, wait a bit, and then just pick up where we left off?

He had stopped going to Josh, stopped going to SA and he was drinking more than I was comfortable with. In the first two and a half days he was camping with us, he drank an entire big bottle of wine.

Where were we headed? Time would tell. I would not stay in a relationship in which I was not happy, genuinely happy, not just okay.

Sunday, July 13

I came home alone last night. Faye stayed in Maine to visit with my dad. I suddenly felt my stress level rise, although I was trying hard to hold onto the peace and serenity I had found in the forest.

Why did I marry into a family like this? Nastiness and underlying insults, double meanings. It made me feel sick.

I wanted to be a normal family with my husband and my children. I wanted to run away and be just us. Maybe then we would have a chance.

Tuesday, July 15

I was missing Caleb terribly. I was so proud of him, his compassion and his zest for life. I was sitting on the couch with music playing softly. Sam was working, Faye was spending the night with friends. His mother was in bed. I was attempting to create some "me" time, like I had at the apartment. It felt good.

Tomorrow I was headed back to work. I was trying not to be frustrated by finances, both my school's and my family's. I felt utterly defeated, kicked down, and under tremendous pressure to fix it all. Sam was working full time and finally making a steady paycheck. He wasn't making much, but at least it was steady. As it had been for the past ten years, if it was going to change, it was going to be up to me. At times like this, I felt like I was drowning. God, I sounded pathetic.

Wednesday, July 16

I sat in the classroom, rubbing the backs of hot and sticky children. There were three little girls that were three, four, and five years old. They were good friends and snuggled together on one pillow. As I sat with them, I watched them bring their heads together very close. They touched each other lovingly, rubbing backs and tenderly touching hair and faces. They were loving and nurturing. It made me long for a time when my friends and I could hold hands and nurture one another, without fear of being a "space invader" or being thought gay. Innocence was a wonderful thing. I hoped I could help my children hang onto it as long as possible. I hoped that by developing close friendships with women again, I could regain some of that natural bonding process.

I was just sitting down after a long hot day I spent cleaning. It was disgusting how filthy this house had become. I knew Sam thought I should just sit down and relax and I agreed. However, the sad reality was that otherwise it wouldn't get done so then I gave up whatever free time I had to do it. I ached and I hadn't had a decent night's sleep all week. I was stressed out about school and finances. I was trying hard to keep it contained and not take it out on anybody, so I took it out on my house.

Two nights ago, Sam and I were having sex. At one point he was lying back, masturbating. He was talking, not to me, just talking. It was so raw and so vulgar that I was immediately taken out of the moment. Listening to him, I was completely turned off. I thought, this is what it must've been like for him. There was no connection, no communication, just Sam and the steady stream of sex talk. Afterwards I tried to explain but I don't think I did a very good job. Part of me felt like we were back to sex or nothing. He was already not showing interest in intimacy without sex. My whole life seemed so fucking scary sometimes.

Tuesday, July 22

I really missed writing each day. It was a way to unburden my heart so that I could have as clear a head as possible. Now that we were together, there seemed to be little or no time to write. It was important to me and something I needed to keep up.

Sophie came tonight for dinner with the girls and her mom and dad. Although my first connection was with her dad, I was so grateful for Sophie. *Sophie's dad came to teach at the university when I was a freshman. In essence, we arrived together. He was a brilliant teacher and a wonderful man. And he loved me like I was his own.* I felt like Sophie was my first real girlfriend in many years. If it wasn't for her, I probably wouldn't have been lying in this bed right now and certainly wouldn't have been waiting for Sam to come home.

As we talked tonight, I realized how far she and I had come— she in the last two years—me in the last six months. It was staggering to think of the journey. I also saw how far we had to go.

I would have loved for Sam to have offered to just hold me or just snuggle up without any sexual overtones at all.

The other night we were making love and I had a flash of "49 and single." I felt sick and sad. I struggled each day with his betrayal while he seemed to have just moved on. So how did I deal with my feelings openly and honestly without punishing him? I struggled silently.

Wednesday, July 23

I was working at school alone. Sam had come in when he could, and my assistant was there for part of yesterday. Although it was a pretty easy bunch of kids, it was grueling to not let down your guard for six hours. I had to go to the bathroom so badly and I couldn't. I waited and waited for Sam to come. I finally called him, and he came a little while later. I nearly didn't make it. When I got home, I found an empty wine glass in the dishwasher. It was hard not to be resentful. He knew I was alone and yet he took the time to come home and have a glass of wine. I was doing my best to hold my school together. I was tired and afraid, and he was home drinking.

Saturday, July 26

I made it through the week and the "circus" with my assistant and Sam's help. I never would've been able to pull it off without them. My stress level was so high that I was afraid of having a heart attack.

Sophie and I cleaned out the garage. We organized the stuff from Sam's store for a sale and got rid of a lot of crap we inherited with this house. *When Sam closed his store, he just threw everything in boxes and put it in our garage.* I was really nervous going through it. I was afraid of finding some piece of Sam's old life—his secret life. I tried to explain to him how I felt. How I seemed to be struggling right now while he had moved on. He seemed irritated and a little annoyed but then he kept calling to see how it was going. Sophie said he must be really worried about me. After the third phone call I told him I was all right, and he stopped calling.

The work was hot and difficult. Everything was dusty and dirty and sometimes it was hard to breathe. Sophie got light-headed. In the end, we made tremendous progress, something I never would've been able to do on my own and something Sam would not or could not have brought himself to do with me.

I picked out some things for our home—things I liked. Sophie was encouraging. She said that it was time to stop being a guest in my home and start making it mine. She was right. It was time to clean out and start fresh, in all aspects of our lives. Would he help me? Time would tell.

Tuesday, July 29

I rode my bike to and from work. God, did I feel old. When I got home, I just wanted to sit for a while and relax. I told his mother that, to which she replied, "Well, are you going to use the sofa?" as she was coming out of her room. So, what I wanted didn't matter. I had to go and help her down the stairs and then hide in my room for a little solitude. My anxiety level was through the roof again and I wasn't sure why.

Becca took us to the restaurant that was across the wharf from Sam's store last night—his old stomping ground. When I tried to talk to him before we left, he sighed, stuck his tongue out of the side of his mouth and rolled his eyes. If I couldn't tell him how I was feeling without his clear message that I should get over it, then we had no honesty—no relationship. I didn't want to go back to my old life of "smooth it over." I was trying to deal with my fears and anxieties without punishing him, and when he acted like that, I wanted to yell, "You fuck! You created this!" I wanted to work on the book. I wanted to make a plan. We had already begun to slide away from touch points during the day.

Yesterday I woke up with thoughts of Emily in my mind. All I could think of was she was eighteen when they began. I lay awake with my thoughts rather than wake him up because I knew rather than get reassurance and love, I would have gotten annoyance and exasperation. We wouldn't survive like this. Love was not enough. I wanted more. I wanted trust and caring and understanding. I deserved that.

Last night at dinner I felt like people were looking at me. Entirely paranoid, I knew. I looked around and I thought, "How many of them knew?" I told him that. Annoyed, he said no one knew. Was he really that naïve? Women talked more than men, and an eighteen-year-old would have never kept her mouth shut. They probably all thought I was some kind of moron. I wondered if he complained to them about how misunderstood he was.

Listen to me. I haven't felt this frightened and resentful in months. Caroline said you learn to live with the fear. When? How?

He knew I was anxious last night, and I knew he was trying to help. He kept holding my hand. It was reassuring, but why couldn't we have talked about it? And why was it always me? Was he really so self-absorbed that he couldn't in any way feel my struggle and help me address it? Did he care? I spent the evening trying to figure out why I was afraid. I knew I was stressed about work, but what was it about my marriage that made me afraid?

I was afraid of falling back into the role of fixer, breadwinner, homemaker, etc, etc.

I was afraid that if I trusted him, he would hurt me terribly again, and I would never recover.

I was afraid that I wouldn't know when he was lying.

I was afraid that my kids would never recover and develop

healthy relationships.

I was afraid that he would do just enough to keep himself in the house but not enough to recover from his addiction.

No Josh

No SA

No "Emotional Infidelity"

No writing

Wednesday, July 30

Tonight, I went to the apartment to move out. Sam had gone over earlier to begin bringing our things home. Interestingly enough, we moved out separately. Same way we moved in. So now it was done. We made a decision and what we did with it was up to us. We had to keep talking. That was the most important thing. I knew he thought that the sex was the most important thing, but it wasn't. It was honesty, intimacy—making love with our clothes on.

Saturday, August 2

Yesterday was a whopper! Sam and I were trying to figure out the bills. I wanted him to take over paying them, yet I didn't trust him to do it. So, I pulled them out and added them up. The total came to around fifteen hundred dollars and we only had a thousand. I decided that going to Maine for the family reunion was something that I just couldn't afford.

When I called my mother to tell her, there wasn't even a touch of empathy. Not "Gee that's too bad" or "I wish there were something I could do to help" or "are you okay?" What I got was a snide remark that Sam shouldn't have made two trips up when we were camping. I told her that I wanted him there and then I told her I resented her attitude. She said that maybe I ought to look back over the weeks, months, and years. I hung up on her.

I called both Hannah and Thea to tell them I wasn't coming if I didn't get an apology. I wasn't going up for the Olympics either. *Each year Thea organizes a family Olympics. For three days, we all camp in the backyard in "Olympic Village," we have Opening Ceremonies complete with a torch, play outdoor games and we end the weekend with a big cookout and medals ceremony. It's magical, especially for all the kids and their cousins.* I felt terrible about Thea's birthday but if my mother was going to force me to make a choice, I would choose Sam. God, I hoped that was the right choice.

Work was frustrating because I felt so trapped. I canceled my plans to see a movie with Sophie because of the money. Then Sam called to say he had made two hundred dollars more than he expected, so we both went to the movies.

What a day. Thank God the movie was fun and mindless. I wondered how much of it I missed.

Before we went to sleep, Sam and I made out. Just kissing. It was the best gift he could've given me.

I spent hours cleaning the house. Literally, all day. If I was going to be out straight, then I needed my house to be in order. It felt good to work hard and get so much done. I would pick up Faye tomorrow and Caleb in a week. I couldn't wait. I was so looking forward to having my family altogether. I had missed Caleb so much.

Sunday, August 3

I drove to New Hampshire to meet my dad to pick up Faye. The ride was quiet, like when I go walking so I was able to begin thinking clearly. I thought that the reason I was having such a hard time right now was because I still felt like a victim. Only now it wasn't just in my marriage, but in my professional life as well. I hadn't had any control over where my business was going and, as my staff left me one by one, I felt victimized each time. Clean slate– take control–move with confidence. Confidence. That was what I needed. My confidence was badly shaken. I would run ads, hire new staff, and move forward with a positive attitude. Those girls were not my school. I was my school.

Then there was my marriage. It was time for me to start writing my book. It would give me a sense of control and would go far to rebuild my confidence at home. Confidence that was still shattered. Sam didn't want to talk about me writing the book. He changed the subject or laughed. He either didn't think I was capable or that I had anything worthwhile to say, or else he was afraid of the story being told. More looking in the mirror, probably both. But if I could heal me, empower myself, build my confidence and self-esteem back up as a wife and mother—without being the fixer—and if I could touch even one person in the process, it would be worth it. It was for me, and if he didn't want to support it, that was his choice. But I was going to write it. I was going to take control of my life. Live a full life, full of love, the way God intended.

Saturday, August 9

It was a busy week. I started my book. Good for me. I began my interviews for school and things were looking up there. Yesterday I got back from the beach with the kids and there was a letter from the attorney my former teacher had hired. What a mess. She needed to just walk away. So now she was threatening to sue me—over what? Take my business? Please!

The vestry took their vote, and my second school location was tabled for six months. That was a good thing. It felt too shaky. I realized this week that Sam was not going to be reliable enough for me to lean on. There was this whole scenario—played to the hilt by my mother—and it involved Sam and comments he made to my niece when she was here which she found insulting and belittling. When I tried to talk to him about it, he basically threw up his hands and said, "That's my sense of humor." I couldn't even believe it. How many times had I heard those exact words come out of his mother's mouth? That was her standard line to avoid taking responsibility for her inappropriate behavior and comments. And now it was Sam's too. Nope! Not accepting that. I put my shoes on and walked out.

I walked to church. I wished it was open. I sat on the steps and prayed and thought. I knew I could be sarcastic. It came from my mother's example and I was trying hard to curb it. I believed it was just a bad habit and, if I could pause before speaking, I could break the habit and be kinder and more authentic. Sam, on the other hand, was so sarcastic that it was cutting. The problem was that he couldn't see that in himself. He said so at a therapy session, to which Caroline replied, "You are *very* sarcastic." It was his nastiness and sarcasm that made her come out with "I don't care whether you two stay married or not." He was pissed, but did he see the truth, or did he really believe it was just his sense of humor? When I came home, he asked me if I was angry. I told him yes. I had been trying hard to maintain and improve what little relationship he had left with my family and he wouldn't even take responsibility for his own actions. He apologized. We would see. We needed so much more work. Was he willing? I knew I was.

Even my dreams were filled with stress and anxiety over my marriage as well as my job. The next morning, I came to the realization that I could only control myself and tried to explain it to him. I said it was not my job to tell him the kind of person he needed to be. It was very tempting, but ultimately it was not up to me but to him. What I needed to figure out was whether the person he chose to be fit into my life or not. I didn't know if he understood. Time would tell.

Friday, August 22

I felt somewhat at peace. After an incredibly stressful weekend at my mother's, we were up at my dad's camp for nearly a week. My stress level dropped (my weight increased) and I felt like, for the first time in a long time, I was beginning to make some sound decisions for my life.

I hired my staff. I was determined that this fresh start would be good for my school. I would build my relationships with my husband and my children. We celebrated fifteen years on Wednesday. Where we were going from here was up to us.

Most importantly, I decided (we decided) that when his

mother was gone, we would spend at least a year in England. I wanted to teach. Maybe I'd even open my own nursery school there. Sam could find employment in the direct support work that he loved so much. The kids could go to school. I needed to talk with his sister and my friends over there and maybe plan to go over in February to figure things out.

So finally, we were acting and not reacting. What a change. It was refreshing. I certainly hoped we could keep it up.

Tuesday, September 9

It had been so long since I'd written, and I felt like my head was about to explode. I came back from camp and three days later was diagnosed with pneumonia again. I wanted to crawl into bed but there was just no time. I had to get my school ready, have my open house, which went well, and move right into Rachel's wedding party. It turned out beautifully, despite how I felt. Then, life went right into opening the school year. Would it ever let up?

While we were away, we never worked on the book or talked about our relationship. I left him a couple of cards over the past couple of months. He left me nothing. He was even slowing down on the laundry. I had the distinct feeling that he changed his mind about our relationship. When I asked him about it, he said, "Not yet." It felt like a kick.

The other day I couldn't reach him on the phone and I began to get panicky. When I finally got hold of him and told him what was going on with me, I could feel him bristle. He said he didn't want to feel like he was on a leash, but he would try to deal with it.

Why shouldn't he deal with it? If he could be trusted, he wouldn't be on a leash.

I was home and he rushed off in the morning to meet with friends for coffee. I was not invited. I was not sure what was going on. The night before we were making love and he began to touch me very differently than he had in twenty-two years. It was very pleasant, but it set off immediate warning bells. Afterwards, when I asked him about it, he lied. I know he did. All of his telltale lying behaviors were there. And he knew I knew.

Now what? He continued to drink during the day, before work, and got defensive and denied a problem when I asked about it. The laundry had fallen by the wayside. We hadn't been on a date, although I asked him to plan one. I had to harp to get him back to SA.

I was not going to enable him and I was not going to give him any more chances. He wanted this marriage and family or he didn't.

I came home after a full day of work and the laundry was just where I left it yesterday. I was feeling resentful and angry and foolish. He started again. Why the lies last night? Why did he get up and go out into the other room after sex at 11:00? Did he discover that I was not enough?

And he began to ride Caleb again. The poor kid did little to nothing right in his eyes. He was destroying the precious little time he had left with his son, and he would not listen to reason.

So resentful. I needed to stop now.

Thursday, September 11

My frustration level was mounting, and I didn't know what to do. I'd spent the past couple of days thinking that I was too harsh and critical. I felt guilty and uncharitable, so when he came home from his uncle's funeral, I told him how nice he looked. He really did. He looked put together, like he had taken the time and care. It made him look very handsome.

I still felt an underlying tension after sex the other night. He had lied to me. I was not sure what about but, I knew that for some reason, he was not being honest. That forced me to shut down for self-preservation.

At dinner, he and Caleb began their ridiculous competition dance, and I was tired from nursing a sick Faye and getting up with his mother twice in the middle of the night. I had just burned my hand and it got too painful to wear my wedding rings. My sense of humor was sorely lacking and I was crabby. Sam started to get pissy, and the kids were both obnoxious.

After dinner, I tried to explain how disgusting it was when he chewed with his mouth open. He jumped all over me. All I ever did was criticize, he couldn't do anything right and on and on. So that meant if I had something to say, I needed to just keep my mouth shut. If I felt he was lying or if I thought he was drinking too much, shut up. If he chewed with his mouth open or if there was anything else I needed to say, shut up.

Our lack of communication began once more and we became disconnected. I asked him to plan a date this week again. We would see. Last month he said he wanted to use my gift certificate to have a nice anniversary dinner. It wasn't mentioned again.

I would not make excuses. He was who he was and that was his choice. My choice was whether I wanted to spend the rest of my life with the person he decided to be.

Tuesday, September 23

Up and down, back and forth, until my head was spinning. Last week I tried to talk to Sam about the distance I was starting to feel. He got defensive and told me that I was demanding and controlling, not asking. Trying to give him the benefit of the doubt, I agreed that maybe we both needed to rephrase and be clearer. I was disappointed that we had not had any time to ourselves, something that hadn't seemed to bother him.

Then I found porn in his car again. I felt sick. When he came home from his meeting that I insisted he go to, he lied to me about it. Now we were back at square one again. He was lying to me and I couldn't trust him. Caroline was right. I needed to trust my instincts. I knew something was wrong.

He began to immediately complain of being controlled and manipulated and that I did not initiate sex enough. Three months and we were right back where we started.

I was angry. He couldn't see the difference between sex and intimacy. If the intimacy was there, the sex would come.

Wednesday, September 24

Caleb pointed out that it would be two months until he was fourteen and only three months until Christmas.

I was afraid my marriage was over. I was trying to get Sam to talk but he barely did. I was sleeping on the couch which meant not sleeping. I told him that if he lied to me again, I would leave him. I knew I had already said that. Was it an empty threat? I would not be an enabler.

I told him that I felt he had already decided that I, and our marriage, was not what he wanted. There was no argument, no denial, no professions of love, or promises to change. No notes of apology or explanation.

I would not ask him again to see Josh or go to SA. I would stay until I had enough money to leave.

Thursday, September 25

I talked with Sophie last night. If I didn't have her, I probably would have been sedated long before now.

I think we moved way too fast. Sam was not, like the rest of us, inspired to change until he became uncomfortable. Three or four months of work with Josh and a dozen SA meetings were not enough to undo the years of damage. Although there was a part of him that was forced to face his addiction, the comfortable part of him was denying what was actually going on. As long as that was the case, nothing would ever change. That was completely unacceptable to me. We were sexual but losing ground with the intimacy battle daily. His relationship with Caleb was still in the shit hole. They butted heads on everything, and Sam refused to look at it from any angle but his own.

At no point did he express that he was sorry for my discomfort over his lies. He never suggested that he knew or understood how I felt and, as a result, offer to sleep on the couch. Instead, he gave me a self-righteous attitude about sleeping on the couch where he said he doesn't fit. I just didn't want the kids to know. Not now.

I was worried about more than the emotional aspect of getting through each day. I had no idea how I was going to pull off Christmas.

There was more to this than his lies over the porn. I knew there was. Something else had happened but I just wasn't sure what. Did he act out? Did he have sex? He said no, but he denied the porn too.

What the fuck was I doing here? How did my life become such a mass of lies and garbage? I needed a new journal. I had believed this would be my last one. Now I didn't even have enough money to buy another.

Friday, September 26

Sam came into school before he left for work. He was all lightness and smiles, bearing coffee. He acted like there was absolutely nothing wrong, like the last three days of silence never happened and I felt like a fucking psycho!

I tried to talk with him about it, but it became the usual, all I do is complain, control, and manipulate. Sex was already routine and obligatory. There was no explanation for his pulling away, his picking up porn, or his lies. I felt as if he had destroyed what fragile trust had begun to grow. Sophie asked if he changed his mind about us, what would he be going to? I told her I didn't even care. If this was going to happen over and over, I wanted out.

BOOK FOUR

Saturday, September 27

I found this new journal at the grocery store. It was sixty-two cents, just about all I could afford.

It had been a really bad week and Sam acted like nothing even happened. I made an appointment to see Caroline on Wednesday and I couldn't wait.

The other night when Sam and I were talking, I tried to express my frustration over our lack of work on our relationship. Of course, he denied it and made excuses. I asked him to bring "Emotional Infidelity" up to camp so that we could work. He did but we didn't. Maybe it was naïve of me, but I didn't think I should have to lead him by the nose. A few nights ago, he came in and I was reading it. He asked me about it, and I explained that I wanted to get back to work on it. He agreed and that was the end of it. Same with the romance book. I took it out. It was sitting on his bureau, covered with crap. I was all done doing all the work for this marriage. If he wanted it, he would have to work too.

We were sitting on the couch the other night and I took a good long look at him. I asked, without any animosity at all, if he was capable of honesty. He said, after really thinking it over, that he thought he was capable of it, he just didn't practice it. My jaw dropped. What did that say for our future? Then, I asked him if he had a sex addiction. He got all pissed off.

"Jesus Christ," he said, "I don't know. You seem to think I do."

I said, "What about Josh?"

He said that Josh had never said so.

I went back and re-read his confession, which I think he should do occasionally, so he couldn't minimize it in his own mind. I forgave him and agreed to work on our marriage based on his self-portrayal of sexual addiction. If he didn't have this illness, then he was just a philandering womanizer—and he talked smack about Gabriel. Did he get me to agree to work on this marriage based on more deceit and manipulation?

Last night he wanted to have sex. I couldn't believe it. Was he really that self-centered and insensitive? He broke our agreement and got porn. He lied to me. He didn't speak to me for three days. He was irritated that I asked him to go back to SA and to see Josh. He said that I was controlling and manipulative and then acted like nothing ever happened. Apparently, I was supposed to just jump into bed with him because he made dinner (that I asked him to make). Either there was something very, very wrong here, or I was so out of touch with the basic laws of truth and decency that I was being completely unrealistic. I needed to see Caroline.

One of the guys that Sam worked with died. I couldn't even imagine how hard that must have been.

Sunday, September 28

I was sad at church. I felt like I did before all this sex crap came out. Like I didn't matter to anyone enough to put me first or close to it. I tried to explain to Sam how I felt, like a promise was broken, trust was violated, and I was angry and hurt. How could I tell if he heard me?

After church we (I) added up the bills to be paid and compared to the money on hand. We had twenty-five hundred dollars in bills and only thirteen hundred in cash. So here we were, talking about how we were going to make ends meet and he went out and bought a fucking bottle of wine. Oh no, no alcoholism there! I would be extremely interested to see if he ended up going to that meeting tomorrow. I was not asking.

The situation had become more unbearable with each passing day. Caleb was nasty and belligerent all week. I told Sophie earlier in the week that I was afraid he had heard our conversation on Monday, but he hadn't said anything. Tonight, he was out of control. He was rude to Sam, who behaved like a juvenile right back. It wasn't effective at all, but Sam was too busy needing to be in control to think clearly or change his approach.

After Caleb was sent to his room and lost his new phone for the week, I went downstairs to try and talk to him calmly. He told me that he overheard Sam and me talking. He heard about Emily, and he knew Sam had been having an affair. He was so angry and hurt. I tried to comfort him, but I thought it was important that he talk to Sam. After all, Sam's actions were the source of his anger and Sam had such a great conversation with him in the spring. What a mistake! Sam was defensive and irritated, as he had been with everything and everybody lately. Caleb was even more withdrawn, and I was furious with Sam. He was angry with Caleb about his behavior, which was understandable, but he couldn't bring himself to offer any comfort to the wounded child. His child—his wound. I blasted him. I was cruel and to the point. I hated to do it, but he needed a verbal slap to get over himself and start undoing his damage.

Tonight, he didn't want me around and I didn't want to be near him. He pushed us all to the edge of the cliff and I felt like he'd throw anybody over to keep from going over himself. Now Caleb was blaming himself for the argument that Sam and I had. How much more?

Monday, September 29

Another shitty fucking night. I had so much turmoil about what was going on in my home that I was having diarrhea again.

Before Sam came home, I made another search. I found that there was a condom missing from the box. I dreaded asking him for two reasons. First, I didn't want him to feel like every time he went out, I found something to bitch about. Plus, what would I do when he lied to me again and turned it all around on me? Of course, that was exactly what happened. It felt like I couldn't do anything right. He said I didn't talk to him correctly, I was too uptight, I controlled and manipulated—although when I asked him to explain that, he changed the subject. The corker was that he started out the conversation trying to pin all this anxiety on my relationship with my father. Talk about not taking ownership.

I had coffee with Sophie. Thank God for Sophie. She's the one who should be writing the book. She really was the voice of clarity in all of this since the beginning. I told her about what had been going on all week, particularly about last night and what happened with Caleb. Her reaction was, "What, are you fucking kidding me?"

It seemed ironic—there I was on the futon, but he was the liar; he was the manipulator; he was the one who was unfaithful and put us all at risk in so many ways. And to top that off, he was so good at what he did that I was left lying there feeling like the bad guy. Fuck that.

Tuesday, September 30

With the clarity that a bad night's sleep can sometimes bring, I was beginning to understand my frustration. My argument for a month now was that we were not working to build a relationship or strengthen our marriage. I could only suggest and ask. I would not force. He needed to want it too. When he didn't respond or responded with irritation, I began to feel pushed aside and it started to stir up anxiety that this marriage was not actually what he wanted, but he was only here because it was comfortable. Add to that the porn, the lies and Caleb's devastation, and all the old wounds were reopened. He was angry and I felt lost. I truly didn't know what to do.

We were at an impasse. I wrote him a note thinking that, since we had been having such a hard time talking, maybe putting it on paper might help defuse the situation. Because he's a writer, and it had happened before, I expected at least a note when I got home. Nothing. The notebook with the note was put on my nightstand. So, I waited anxiously all day for that. He did bring me coffee to school before he left for work. I was already gone from school, running errands. He then called me and said, "I got your note." Nothing more.

Yesterday he left for his meeting. Before he went, we had dinner and he didn't have wine, but he drank water. When I checked the bottle after he left it was half-full. He always bought the big, 1.5-liter bottle. He opened it Sunday night at dinner and by Monday afternoon it was half gone. When I came home at 2:30, the bottle was gone and a new one was in its place. Ten dollars per bottle. So yesterday he drove with the kids after drinking and then he went to work after drinking, again. He could get fired or worse. When I asked him about the wine, he told me that I was mistaken, just like everything else.

There was also absolutely no movement on the bankruptcy issue. Maybe divorce was his way out. I wasn't sure about anything. He told me he couldn't afford to give the attorney three hundred dollars. Of course, if he bought a bottle of wine every two days, that added up to one hundred fifty dollars per month. Coffee out was two dollars. Even if he only got it three times a week that was another twenty-four dollars per month. In just a couple months, he would've had the three hundred dollars.

I was thinking of us as a puzzle. We were trying to put the pieces back together. If he was a sex addict and was not receiving proper treatment, then he was dry, not sober, and his puzzle piece was broken because he was still thinking and behaving like an addict. If he was not an addict but was just unfaithful and was not addressing the issues deep down, then his puzzle piece was broken and would stay broken, because he would continue to be deceitful and unfaithful. Either way, his puzzle piece was broken, and the puzzle couldn't be put back together. My own puzzle piece was, at the very least, bent, and wrinkled, if not broken as well, but at least I was trying to get help.

I decided I would ask him to go back to Dan and Caroline.

Wednesday, October 1

I met with Caroline and I was so glad I did. I told her all about the past few months: our lack of work, my struggles to communicate, the porn, the lie, Caleb's disclosure, the condom, the seesaw and my feelings of anxiety, helplessness, and fear of unrealistic expectations.

We talked about Sam's inability, more than unwillingness, to talk, change and face what was going on. She assured me that neither was I crazy, nor was I having unrealistic expectations when it came to commitment and truth. She said that Sam had learned some very slick coping skills and one thing he was extremely good at was making me feel like it was all my fault. He turned it all around on me.

The difficulty was that as he cycled, he went completely back to the beginning, to the precontemplation stage. There was no problem—denial. However, I knew better. Now it involved Caleb as a key player when he wasn't before, and Faye's anger was also beginning to show. I couldn't risk that for my kids.

I was also not willing to be the one to cut Sam off completely, to force him to do the work he needed to do. It put me in a position of power that I had no desire to have. I was not willing to live in a relationship where I needed to keep begging and threatening to have an emotional partner. I was not willing to have someone who loved me, turn everything I said against me, no matter how terrified he was to look within himself.

Last spring, when it was a do or die situation for me, I completely cut him off. I couldn't even look at him without my whole world reeling. In his panic, he rose to the occasion. He worked hard to convince me that this marriage was worth fighting for. While I had one foot in the door, he was still working. Caroline said I needed to make him cry. Not so easy. He didn't even cry when he tore my world apart or when I was throwing him out. He was in that same place again.

My decision became, do I give him another chance to be honest, faithful and grown-up or do I walk? I think I made my mind up the night he lied to me about the porn. It would never be any different and now I needed to create a healthy, honest environment for Caleb and Faye and for me. An environment that didn't include deceit or patronizing or manipulation and control. Funny, he used those terms to describe me when that was precisely what he was doing.

I needed to think very carefully now that Caleb was so vulnerable. If and when I left, it would be over. I couldn't let my son become a yo-yo.

I told Caroline that I really needed to think about it. I was not feeling emotional at all. It was odd, but all my emotions were spent in the spring. She said that my decision would be the right one for me and for the kids. She also said that I had been completely right all along. She commented that often when she counsels one spouse without knowing the other, when they do finally meet, as she did with Sam in Dan's office, she sees major discrepancies in what she's been told compared to what she sees. She said that was not the case with me. What I told her about Sam, the ugly side as well as the good, intelligent loving side, was completely right. She said when he started to turn it around on me and make me feel like I was crazy, to walk away and have the understanding that the craziness does not live within me. Something deep inside of him was broken. I couldn't fix it and it wasn't my responsibility to do so.

Thursday, October 2

It was the end of a long day and I was tired. I barely even knew what to write. Thankfully, there was little tension in the house, apart from Sam acting like a wounded puppy at times. It wouldn't work. I had closed the door on manipulation. He knew exactly how to play me, and I had let him do it. Not anymore.

One good thing was that he seemed to be taking some steps to reconnect with the kids. It had been going on for a few days and I hoped he could keep it up. He was also being nice to me. Yesterday he brought me coffee again and encouraged me to take a nap. It was nice. It didn't do anything to fix the problems, but I certainly appreciated his kindness.

Friday, October 3

Caroline called me. She was trying to set up our appointment with Dan for the four of us. Because of conflicts, we wouldn't all be able to come together until the nineteenth. Two weeks. I was disappointed and so was she. I asked if she thought it would be good for Sam to have some time with Dan prior to the meeting so that when we all came together, he wouldn't feel so alone. She thought that was a great idea. She said that last time was difficult and scary for him and she was sure he felt ganged up on. Neither of us wanted him to feel that way again. When I told him about her phone call and our idea that he talk to Dan, he dismissed it. I asked a second time, making sure that it was phrased as a request and not a demand. He dismissed it again with, "We'll see what happens." I wouldn't ask again. He was done. Everything he did told me he was done. Could we get through this and still keep our friendship intact?

Last night I was checking the history on the computer and I found a weird site. It was a gay T-shirt site. There were also lots of club.com, stripclub.com, clubbingthecitybythesea.com. I didn't even ask. Sam or Caleb? The T-shirt site was odd though. Was he gay? Was that the turmoil within him? Maybe that was why, when I thought sex was warm and loving, he thought it was routine and obligatory. I just didn't know. If we could maintain the level of peace we had, then the future apart didn't look so grim. He had been my best friend for so long. That was the part I hoped he chose to fight for if nothing else.

Saturday, October 4

I did some measuring. I wanted to make sure I was not over-reacting. I accused Sam of drinking too much and it was something that he flatly denied. Was that an alcoholic denial or was I being a nag? He went through a bottle of wine in two and a half to three days. He opened one on Sunday night and by Tuesday afternoon it was gone. He opened one on Thursday night and this morning it was two thirds gone. It was his usual 1.5-liter bottle. If a serving of wine was four ounces, then there were twelve and a half servings per bottle. Four glasses a day? I would characterize that as a drinking problem.

I spoke to Sam a couple of times on the phone. He was gone when I got up and I would probably be in bed by the time he got home. He picked up another shift for tomorrow. He did call and ask me, and I said it was fine. We needed the money. Maybe it was easier for him if he didn't have to see us. He was fine on the phone. He didn't say "I love you" or "I miss you." There wasn't any attempt at connection other than to pass along necessary information and to say hi. I resigned myself to the fact that he just wasn't willing to fight for me. The demons he faced must have either been too overwhelming for him, or else he just didn't want me. Either way, it was painful.

Sunday, October 5

I was closing the garage door and the cat ran under. For some reason, he didn't set off the sensor. He ran out again and I couldn't find him. I felt sick at the thought of him out in the rain, possibly in pain, and there was nothing I could do.

We were low on food and out of money, but we would make it through the week. I would just have to be creative. I was more than irritated that Sam spent twenty dollars on wine and who knows how much on coffee out last week.

I was putting ribbon back in the front closet after wrapping a birthday gift and I found an old wallet of Sam's father. There was a picture of his sister inside—how typical. I checked behind it thinking that maybe, just maybe, there was also a photo of Sam. Of course, there wasn't. There was, however, a twenty-dollar bill. I went to the market and bought eggs, chicken, and potatoes. We would be fine, but what a shit my father-in-law was for carrying just a photo of his daughter and not his son. No wonder Sam was so fucked up. No wonder he couldn't deal with Caleb in a healthy way but was so good with the girls. Did he truly not know who he was as a man? Was that why he didn't relate to men?

I spoke to Shawn. The other day when I called him, he told me that he and his partner had bought a house and they were moving on December first. I called to ask him about his apartment. It was not rented yet. It was three bedrooms, everything included— washer, dryer, and cable—for twelve hundred dollars a month. Could I afford that? Sophie is selling her house. A beautiful little fisherman's cottage. I would love to buy it, but I knew I couldn't afford it.

Another night of our polite friendship. It was as if a truce had been called and we were both following the rules. There was polite conversation, some laughter, but nothing of substance. Nothing any deeper than how was your day? He made it clear that he was not interested in talking about more. To keep the peace and respect his decision, I complied. His silence said so much to me. Maybe we were just destined to be friends and parents. Nothing more.

Both kids asked me why I was sleeping downstairs in the playroom. I said, "Because I want to." Faye was okay with that but Caleb, not so much. He blamed himself. He said that if he had not come upstairs to say goodnight, he never would have heard or reacted to anything. Then Sam and I would not have fought, and I would not be on the futon. I felt sick over it. I assured him that my decision to sleep out of my bed happened before he told me what he had heard. I hated to give the kids too much information, but I didn't want him to blame himself, ever. I told him that it was between just his dad and me. We were doing our best and he seemed comforted. I told him no matter what, he would never be put in a position where he had to choose one over the other.

I saw an old friend that I haven't seen in months. She said that she was sorry because the last time she saw me, she had no idea what was going on. She asked me where I was living, and I told her I was living at home. I was a little confused and she was a little tipsy, I think. It was hard to tell with her sometimes. Then she asked me if the divorce was final. My mouth must've been hanging open. I hadn't told anyone about my decision.

I hoped it didn't show.

I hoped Sam changed his mind.

I hoped I could hold it together.

I hoped I could be strong for my kids.

I hoped...

Monday, October 6

Sam came to school to help clean out the gardens. He put the air conditioners away and actually fixed the toilet. It was nice and thoughtful and kind. It was also empty. This was his manipulation. He did some loving, giving things on the surface, and underneath refused to do any solid, hard work that built him as a person and us as a couple. So, when I got frustrated, he could turn it around on me and say, "I do so much that you never acknowledge." I was careful to thank him and told him how much I appreciated his work. He asked if I wanted to go to a movie Friday night. I said yes. He did not volunteer what happened at his meeting tonight, and I did not ask. We didn't talk of anything deeper than the moment— the here and now. Maybe he just wanted me to go through life pretending that nothing ever happened. I looked through his copy of Emotional Infidelity. It was interesting to see all the passages he had underlined and starred. I wished he'd go back and read it. I was very tired and sick inside over what had and had not happened in my marriage. I needed some sleep.

Tuesday, October 7

There needed to be an end to this craziness I felt. I was hoping that Friday night, maybe after the movie, would give us a chance to talk, really talk, about where we were and where we were going. I knew he did not want to talk and I couldn't change that. All I could do was talk myself. I was not going to make excuses for him. If he chose to pretend that what happened wasn't all that bad, that was his choice, but it wasn't one I could live with. I told Sophie that he asked me to go to a movie on Friday. If he had done that a month ago, we probably wouldn't even be here, but who knows? She said it was probably going to be a rollercoaster ride with him, and I needed to decide if I could stand the ride. If he was doing the work, getting help, and working on the twelve steps, then I could stand the ride. I would have liked to sit him down and have him read his letter of confession again, so he might step back up to the plate, stop self-medicating, and start his journey again.

I felt like I was marking time until we went to see Caroline and Dan. I tried to look at this from all angles to check and see if my wants and needs were overly demanding. I needed their support. He had called me a nagging bitch but he listened to them. So far as I knew, he had not made an appointment with Dan, so he would go in feeling outnumbered. His choice. He finished the bottle of wine before work. I hoped he didn't get fired.

Wednesday, October 8

This whole situation that we had been calling our marriage became more and more of a joke.

It was a bad day. There was just enough opposition to a class-room move at school to make the day miserable. One mother, in particular, was very nasty. I called Sam for support and he was great. He said he was leaving The Creamery when I called and that he was headed over to take the vacuum cleaner to be fixed.

At 1:15 or so he came to my classroom with two coffees from The Coffee House. He finished his coffee, leaving the cup in my trash. After being so supportive, I didn't want to remind him that he told me last weekend not to spend any money because we didn't have anything extra.

When I got home, I took Caleb to swim practice and then ran home to make dinner before heading off to a Girl Scout leader's meeting. By the time I got home around 8:30, I had to make Caleb something to eat, get Faye to bed, deal with his mother and get the kitchen cleaned up. There was a take-out coffee cup from The Coffee House on the counter. I thought maybe Sam had come home after bringing me my coffee, but I knew he went off to work. He told me he had been leaving The Creamery earlier. Was he lying? Why?

He called to say goodnight to the kids. They were acting silly and fun. When I got on the phone, I asked him about the cup. He said that he had gone to The Coffee House after taking the vacuum in. I said, "So you went to The Creamery for coffee, left there and went to take the vacuum, got coffee at The Coffee House, came home and then went again to get coffee for me?"

I could feel him bristle. "Yeah, so what?"

"Well," I said, "that's a lot of coffee and we can't afford all that coffee out."

Between The Creamery and The Coffee House, he had spent easily nearly ten dollars for coffee. He was the one who said we had no money. Then it escalated with all the tension that had been just below the surface, bubbling up into an explosion that was very ugly. I said we couldn't talk about anything that wasn't entirely superficial. He said that I don't talk, I just accuse and bitch. He said it more than once. Nice way to talk to the mother of your children. I told him that he was pushing me out the door. He was sarcastic and mean. I said if that was what he wanted it was fine, but at least have the common decency to admit it. I told him I was not going to allow him to drag me or the kids under again. I asked him to go back to Dan or Josh. I was asking him, and he had the right to say no. He told me he wasn't going to say anything while he was so angry.

I called Sophie. I was shaking and I couldn't stop. I didn't want the kids to see me, but Caleb heard. Once again, Caleb heard everything between me and Sam.

Sophie and I were on the phone for over an hour. She was dumbfounded at his inability to own even a tiny piece of what had brought us here, his denial over all things emotional and financial, and his inability to look inside himself and see how his behavior, both past and present, affected his wife and children.

I was so tired I couldn't even think straight. I was thrilled last night because I felt like I had found the right gift for his birthday. I planned a party for him. Now I wanted to call Rachel, and my dad, and everyone else and say forget it. Party was off. Why should I kill myself to throw a party for a man who said such horrible things to me? It was not enough that he broke my world into a million pieces. It was like he wouldn't be happy until my soul was broken too.

Shame on me.

Thursday, October 9

Another day, another fucking argument. I was angry and resentful and sad and sick. After such a horrible argument last night, Sam called me this morning like nothing had ever happened. "Hi. I'm just calling to make sure everyone got off all right." I never knew how he would be, so I found myself just shutting down so he couldn't suck me into his insanity.

After work and another stress filled day, I took Faye to Barnes & Noble to get the dictionary she wanted to get him. I found myself stalling so I wouldn't have to go home because I knew when I did, it would be another blow up. Sure enough, master manipulator that he was, he turned it around on me.

Since the middle of August or before, I had been trying to get him to get back to work on our relationship. Now he said, "Things were good all summer until you went back to work." No matter what I said, he twisted it around. I commented that he had a tremendous amount of work to do that I couldn't help with. He had work to do, I had work to do, and we had work to do together. That came back to me, laced with sarcasm, that I said (repeatedly pounding the table) "*He* (slam) had work to do." "*He* (slam) had work to do." "*He* (slam) had work to do." Oh yeah, and we had some work to do together. And then, as an afterthought, and I might have some work to do too.

I reminded him that things had been terrible since I found the porn and then he lied about it. He responded that maybe it was my reaction, not the porn or the lie that was bad. When I asked him what he wanted, he was finally able to tell me. He wanted a relationship that was loving, warm, open, fun, without any resentment and anxiety. The list went on. Nowhere in that speech did he mention me. He wanted the relationship, not me. As things were escalating, I told him if he wanted to divorce, then fine. Let's just get divorced. Now it was said, and he could still play the victim in his own mind and say, "See? I knew she'd leave me."

The fight raged on and began to escalate again. I just stopped. I looked at him and said quietly, "Look at us. This is crazy."

I left. I went and sat at the beach and cried. I had such high hopes and so much love. I thought that if anyone could conquer this, it would have been us, but I couldn't do it alone. I deserved a life too. I deserved love and happiness and trust and intimacy. I wanted it to be with him.

I picked up Faye and we went to watch Caleb swim. As I was driving to swim practice, Sam called and wanted to know where I was. I told him we were going to watch Caleb swim and that I was taking the kids out for something to eat. He immediately got pissy and said, "So we're going to fend for ourselves? Thanks for letting me know." Sarcasm, sarcasm, sarcasm.

I didn't want to go home. I wanted to be anywhere he wasn't. The kids and I got some dinner with the grocery money his mother gave me. There wasn't enough for me, so they ate and shared a little with me. I couldn't remember the last time I sat in a restaurant with my children.

What, are you kidding me? Was he really expecting me to come home and cook for him? Yes. Just the way he expected me to get into his bed at night, no matter what he did and how he treated me. Nothing had changed. Nothing was different. Except that now I knew.

Saturday, October 11—Sam's 60th birthday

We went to a movie last night. It almost felt normal. It was as if our fight of the night before didn't exist. Or as if he felt, "Oh good. That's over. Let's move on."

It was strange and more than a little unstable. I was thinking about what Sam said he wanted. He went on and on about his expectations for our relationship. What he didn't say, and I failed to ask, is what he planned to do to make those things happen.

He wanted to work on this relationship, but not with me downstairs. He was clear about his resentment over me abandoning "the marriage bed." Why would I want to come back? Had he built trust or love or kindness? Had he been affectionate or respectful? Or truthful?

There were so many things that he just couldn't connect. Infidelity aside, finances and what it would take to get our house in order seemed to be beyond him. He didn't understand that if there was not enough money to pay bills or buy food then you couldn't spend money on extras like coffee or wine. Because of his adamant refusal to see this, it reinforced the concept that he was alcoholic. If I mentioned it again, he was going to go through the roof again.

We talked about this idea pretty openly when we first began to talk. Why the backslide? The denial? Why couldn't we just be honest?

The anniversary card and the one hundred dollars his mother gave us was gone. It had been in Sam's top drawer. It was there when I found the porn and last week when I counted the condoms again and one was missing. Now nothing was there. The money was gone. The card was gone. He had cards on his bureau from the last few years. Why get rid of this card? Was he that angry? What did he do with the money? I called him and asked him. He said he took the money out a month ago to pay a bill. He said he didn't know what happened to the card. Couldn't remember what bill. More lies. Lies. Lies. Lies.

This was not what I wanted. I wanted to be happy. I was not happy and eventually I would become bitter and angry. I was worth more.

Monday, October 13

We just got back from a visit to the local farm. It was pleasant and for a little while there was peace.

Yesterday we went to church. Sam and I never touched. I told him that contact was important to me, as I knew it was to him. I supposed that if I felt the way he did, that he was totally in the right, I might not have reached out either. In fact, I didn't reach for him because I felt like I did the majority of reaching out. I did at the farm. I reached for his arm and he never reached back.

We had his birthday dinner last night and Rachel came. He was pleased to see her and happy about the party, I think. He certainly seemed present and connected, quite different from how he had been. Not sure whether that was due to the audience or genuine pleasure. It didn't matter. For a few hours there was a truce. Before Sam knew there was to be a dinner, he snapped at Rachel over peeling an eggplant. She was surprised and a little taken aback. I told her about what had been going on and that I was afraid we weren't going to last. She told me that she was surprised that I was even willing to try at all. She asked how his therapy was going. When I told her he wasn't going, she let out a shocked, "What??" She was supportive and understanding without being disloyal to her father.

I told her that the night before (Sam's actual birthday), I had gotten some daisies and put them on his nightstand. When we had had dinner on our first date, he had taken the daisy off the table for me. We planted some this summer. The symbolism could not possibly have been lost on him. The next morning, he said nothing, but when I went into the bedroom, he had moved them to my nightstand. That said to me, "Take your flowers and shove them." She agreed.

I didn't know if he heard any of this or not, but shortly afterward he came out and said, "Oh the flowers are really pretty. Are they for me?" It was his birthday and I put flowers on his nightstand. Who else would they have been for?

The evening went on and Sam was relaxed and a lot of fun. It felt good and I was glad I made the effort. Rachel went back to Brooklyn and this morning we went to get pumpkins. As we were checking out, I saw the man and woman behind Sam asking him to move ahead so he wouldn't hold up the line any longer. I had to turn away because it was embarrassing and it stressed me out.

I knew my reaction would have been, "Oh I am so sorry," and I would have moved. However, I didn't want to judge Sam for a reaction that was not like mine and one that I didn't even see. But I know him and, "Oh I'm sorry," is never the first thing out of his mouth. I was determined not to judge him because we differ.

Tonight, Caleb had a meltdown. He had asked Sam to pay him the ten dollars we owe him for mowing the lawn and take him to Barnes and Nobles to buy an AC/DC CD. I'm not an AC/DC fan but he did mow the lawn and we owed him the money. Sam wouldn't take him so I told Caleb that I would. I didn't think that it was fair to promise him the money and then not pay him promptly but expect him to jump to do his chores. Sam argued about Caleb's choice of music and when that didn't work, he pointed out that we had decided Caleb would have to save half of all of his money. That being the case, he didn't have enough money to buy the CD. Caleb was furious and rightly so. I felt caught in the middle. Sam insisted that I support him with Caleb, and I had, even if I thought he was wrong. But when it came to supporting me, he could tell me how wrong I was. Not only that, if I didn't agree with him then I was not being supportive. It was a no-win for me. Caleb lost it. He was angry and mouthy, and I finally got him to go to his room. I stood in the kitchen, chopping vegetables, reeling from the conversation I just had with my son in which he told me he wanted me to die. I let him calm down a little bit and went down to talk to him.

It turned out that a friend's boyfriend told him to keep his fat ass away from her. He was heartbroken and embarrassed and angry. Rather than talk about it, he let it fester until it came out in an entirely inappropriate manner. Sounded familiar. After I talked with Caleb, he came upstairs to apologize to Sam. Before Caleb could say anything, Sam said to him, "Don't come in here looking around for your Xbox." It was snotty and juvenile. Caleb left without saying anything.

Dinner was tense. I said to Sam before dinner that Caleb had been on his way to say sorry. Sam said, "Well, I didn't know that." Never "I'm sorry," and especially not to Caleb.

Was that judging him based on the fact that he didn't respond like I would have or was it the preservation of my child?

Tuesday, October 14

Sam was calmer when he came home from his meeting. I told him about the comments from Caleb's friend's boyfriend. He said, "Poor kid." I wanted to say, "Yeah and the crap you're putting him through everyday isn't helping."

He was still barely speaking to me but at least when he did, it wasn't laced with venom.

I waited until today to make an appointment with Dan and Caroline. I wanted to give him time to go to therapy on his own. He didn't and it had been two weeks since I saw Caroline last. I felt like we were going into this meeting to begin to plan our divorce. Somehow, as sad as that was for me, as much as I never wanted it, it was a big relief. I had to be practical. I had to do what was best for me, for Caleb and for Faye. I had to trust that Sam would do what he needed to do to become healthy and whole.

I couldn't cry. If I started, I might never stop. My marriage failed and I was starting again. I felt sick to my stomach all the time.

Thursday, October 16

What a day. I didn't write last night. By the time Girl Scouts was over and I picked up Caleb, I was too tired to think straight. It was a crazy day at work. The kids were wild and I felt tense all the time. The girls at school all got together and gave me a laundry basket full of baking supplies for Boss's Day. I thought, "I may need all of this to start again in my own apartment."

I told Sam that I was prepared to go in and see Dan and Caroline to start planning our divorce. He agreed. Neither one of us wanted to be anywhere near the other. It was very painful but true.

Although we didn't resolve anything, we were at least able to talk a little. I was very worried about Caleb. We took the kids out to dinner to celebrate Faye winning the reading T-shirt design. We were all so proud of her. Caleb was a nightmare—obnoxious, rude, and all directed at Sam. He was so angry. And he wasn't like that when Sam wasn't there. He was still hurting terribly from his discovery about his father, but he couldn't talk about it. We needed to protect him, before it was too late.

Friday. October 17

Steps forward, steps back. It was a long day at school. Like last spring, I felt like I was only partly there. It was as if I were sleep walking through my day. It felt hit or miss with Sam. I called him to tell him that my former business partner was looking for a theater teacher for the middle school and that I recommended him. We talked some about Caleb. I was afraid that Caleb would begin to exhibit signs of sexual addiction. I told Sam that I was not willing to sacrifice Caleb so that his father wouldn't feel controlled on the computer. Although we had both been saying some things that were difficult to hear, we were at least being honest for the first time in a long time, if ever.

After work I took Caleb to the arcade. I gave him five dollars to spend. It could've been one hundred. He was cheerful and fun and a joy to be with. I was sad that Sam rarely, if ever, got to see that side of his son.

When I got home, I made pizza and we had a movie night. I sat between Sam and Faye. He never touched me. At 9:30, he said, "I don't know about you, but I'm going to bed." Off he went, before me or the kids. That was a first.

Saturday, October 18

Sam was gone when I got up. I had a great day with the kids. I took Caleb over to Saint Andrews for homecoming weekend. Caleb was so happy to go back and see his friends. He had such a good day. Faye was a love. We finally painted her magic eight ball she made for a reading project. She discovered that Sam had bought ice cream for us yesterday. It was a nice gesture and I thanked him for it.

I talked more with Shawn about his apartment. Moving the kids was such a big decision. It was one I didn't want to make lightly, but I didn't think they were best served by this sham of a marriage, particularly Caleb, who could do nothing right in Sam's eyes.

I was also concerned that Shawn's apartment was in The City by the Sea. If I tried to keep them in school, and his sister were feeling vindictive, she could report us. I couldn't put a change of schools, on top of a change of home, on the kids.

I went online and started to look. At first, I found nothing under fifteen hundred a month. Then, as I was about to give up, I found a cottage on five acres in our town. Maybe it could be a haven for us, a place to start again. I was going to make an appointment to see the cottage.

I was not sure what to expect for the meeting with Dan and Caroline next week. Maybe they would tell me to shut up and get over it. Maybe they would look at him and say, "What are you doing?" I guess that was what I was hoping for. Some validation. As far as I knew, he didn't call Josh yesterday. Whatever.

I was exhausted and I had miserable cramps.

Sunday, October 19

The days we spent together seemed to crawl by. We didn't speak or play. There was no joy. I couldn't even write this without crying. I felt sick. My marriage was over and he was going to just let us go without a fight. I was trying hard to be strong, but I was beginning to fall apart. I couldn't watch him be mean to Caleb anymore. Faye cried when I was putting her to bed. This was so unhealthy for all of us.

I made an appointment to see the cottage on Wednesday. It was twelve hundred fifty plus utilities. I didn't think that I could afford that. Shawn's was only twelve hundred including everything. How could they stay in school?

The thought of living with someone else's furniture bothered me. If it was just me, fine, but for the kids, it just wouldn't feel like home. They needed their stuff. Then, as I thought about dividing up our belongings, I felt completely overwhelmed.

I turned off NetNanny. I was so tired of hearing him whine and complain about not getting onto sites. There was never a thought of Caleb's safety or well-being. He was acting like a complete narcissist. All he thought about was himself and how controlled he was. So, I let him manipulate me and I shut it down. Another nail in the coffin. There was no "thank you" or "I appreciate it" and there certainly wasn't, "I'm done now, you can put the block back on."

I wouldn't last through Christmas. I was hoping to stay through the holidays to make it easier on the kids, but I wouldn't last that long walking on eggshells. He quite clearly acted as if Caleb and I could have fallen off a cliff and he wouldn't care.

God, I was so sad and hurt and angry and scared, and now I couldn't go to sleep because I was crying, and my eyes would be all swollen in the morning.

Monday, October 20

I was having mixed feelings about starting over in someone else's space with their furnishings, but now I was kind of excited. Like being excited over surgery. You just couldn't wait to end the pain and discomfort.

I checked the wine bottle this morning. Sam opened it Friday night and had a glass or two. He worked all day and all night Saturday and was home on Sunday. This morning there were fewer than two inches in the bottle. If I mentioned it, he would blow up, so I didn't mention it.

Yesterday he told me he was going to mow the lawn. He was signed up to read to Faye's class at 10:00 a.m. but then didn't have to take her to dance until 3:30. I called him this morning to see if he had an appointment to see the lawyer. He was at The Creamery getting ready to go read to the fourth grade. Sophie and I were going to meet for coffee at The Coffee House at 11:00, but just as I was pulling in, she called me to say Sam was there. I didn't want it to be awkward, so we went for a drive and I drove her past the cottage. She loved it. I wondered if he was using sitting at The Coffee House as a way to meet lonely women. I got home and the lawn was not mowed. If I mentioned it, he would have blown up. I didn't mention it. So here we were. Put up and shut up. No, not anymore.

This morning as I was leaving, I asked if he wanted a hug. He said, "Sure," but he wouldn't return it.

I hadn't heard of an appointment made with Josh. It seemed like such a no-brainer. On one hand, you work with your therapist, work with your wife, and you get to live with your wife and children. On the other hand, you don't. How could he possibly choose not? But that was what he was doing.

I felt sick and fuzzy all the time. I woke up with my mind racing, and I couldn't go back to sleep.

Faye was already writing to Santa. I prayed for strength. And money.

Sam came home from his meeting tonight. We sat on the couch and I asked him about it. It was like pulling teeth.

"Were there a lot of people there tonight?"

"No. About a dozen and a couple came in late." It was the same thing he told me last week.

Silence.

"Was it a good meeting?"

"It was all right."

Silence.

"Was it a step meeting or did you have a speaker?"

"It was just a meeting where people talked about whatever they wanted to. Did I tell you I ran into the woman who runs your competition school?"

I didn't believe he went to the meeting. Sophie asked me if he was actually going. At the time, I was certain he was. Tonight, I was just as certain he was lying. All his tells were there.

When I found the porn in his car, he lied to me, not once but repeatedly. He only confessed when I told him I already had it. I didn't believe that he was being honest. Ever. I couldn't trust him.

Tuesday, October 21

There were times when I felt crazy. The last thing I ever wanted was a divorce. The last thing I ever thought was that Sam was a liar and a cheater. He could be so kind and loving and angry and dishonest.

Sophie told me that first night that he needed to be uncomfortable. It was then, when he was living at his uncle's, that he really did some work. He looked at his family and what he risked losing and made up his mind that he would do the work and make the changes. He skimmed rock bottom. Now he was comfortable again and all the work stopped. He needed to be uncomfortable to read, write, pray, reflect, go to therapy and look to the future? That was fine. I was going to see our new home tomorrow. The problem now was that the kids were aware. Caleb was angry and resentful of Sam.

Faye had been crying spontaneously. So now the kids needed to be protected and didn't our kids deserve parents that were happy? Didn't they deserve to live in a house without tension that they could feel? And didn't Sam and I deserve to be happy?

This whole situation made me feel so sick.

Wednesday, October 22

Such an up-and-down day. This morning, Sam was his usual cool self. I asked if he had anything planned. He said he had to work and deal with his mother. He asked about my day. I told him I was working all day, but I decided that honesty would begin with me. I said I was going to see a cottage. He said, "For what?"

I told him, "For me and the kids."

"How much is it?"

"Twelve hundred a month"

"You'll never be able to afford it."

I asked him what he expected. How long did he want me to wait? I asked if he had called Josh and he said not yet.

I said, "You're sixty years old. What are you waiting for?"

I told him there was nothing here for me. No love. No companionship. No conversation. No support. It was starting to affect the kids. Caleb was seething with anger he couldn't express, and Faye had begun to cry for no reason. Then he said, "So it's all my fault?" God, he was such a martyr.

I said no, that it was *our* fault. Then another comment about me being able to afford an apartment. He couldn't even talk to me. Then his mother came out and he began to deal with her. I said something about him not even looking at me. He spat, "I'm trying to deal with her. What do you want me to do? Split my head in half?"

"No," I said, "I want you to grow up and be a man."

I left and went to work.

At 11:00 I went to the cottage. It was beautiful, bright, sunny and beautifully furnished. I thought, "This is someplace I could make a home for my children. Someplace we could all be happy."

The owner told me there had been a lot of interest in it. I said I would let him know ASAP. What was I waiting for? Not once did Sam say, "Wait, let's think this through," or "Give me a chance." Sophie said I should give the landlord a hundred dollars and ask him to hold it for twenty-four hours to see what Sam did at the session. I wanted to go home first. I was certain that I would get home and there would be a note there, professing love, offering an apology—something. There wasn't one. I was disappointed. I called the landlord, but the cottage was gone. It took everything I had to hold it together. I felt trapped.

That afternoon I said to Caleb, "Honey, how would it be if you, Faye and I lived away from dad for a while?" He said after a moment, "I would really like that."

God, please open a window.

Thursday, October 23

I felt sick. Sam was really going to just let us go. We met with Dan and Caroline and it was like a war zone. He was angry and I couldn't stop crying. Sadly enough, he didn't even seem to care. Dan was able to impress upon him that Caleb and Faye were the number one priority. It was one of the most painful days of my life. My husband didn't want me or our children enough to take responsibility for his actions and work to solve problems. They said we needed to talk to the kids tonight.

After the meeting, I went to get Caleb and take him swimming. It was pretty obvious that I had been crying a lot. He asked so I told him that we had been to see Dan and Caroline. He began to talk and said that his father was a control freak who had controlled me for too long. Now that his dad couldn't control me anymore, he was taking his anger out on him. Caleb said he hoped Faye wised up to her father soon. I just let him talk. I wanted him to get it out without me saying, "Oh honey, that's not true." I wanted him talking.

We talked with the kids together later and Sam did most of the talking. It was the least he could do. Caleb said nothing. Faye cried. Sam said almost verbatim what Dan told him to say, that we were having problems and that we were trying to work on it but that no matter what happened, they were both loved very much by both parents. It was painful. Caleb got up and walked out without saying a word. After a few moments he came back and told Sam what was really on his mind. He said, "I hate you. You are a control freak and you have controlled her for too long. I'm sick of you taking your anger out on me, so get out of my life and leave me alone." Faye cried harder. My heart was tearing in two.

Friday, October 24

I made it through another day. I was exhausted and so congested I couldn't breathe. I knew it was from crying all night and my eyes were very swollen when I got up. I was exhausted all day at work. I played phone tag with Caroline and never got to talk to her. Faith stopped by this morning. Thank God. I really have felt so alone. I was having a hard time writing anything at all without my eyes prickling with tears. After work, I came home, and Sam had made dinner. I wasn't hungry. Caleb couldn't even bear the sight of Sam and I knew Sam blamed me. I took Caleb and Faye off to the homecoming game. Sam didn't want to go. Caleb was singing the national anthem with the chorus and it was great. For a little while, I forgot what a fucking train wreck my home life was and just enjoyed my children. There needed to be more of that fun and joy. There hadn't been any in this house for far too long. We were off to New Hampshire tomorrow. There was a part of me that would like to just keep driving and never look back.

Saturday, October 25

I took the kids to New Hampshire to visit with my sisters and their kids. We went swimming and out to dinner. It was fun being with them away from all the stress of home. I talked with my sister Thea a little bit and shared some of my frustration over Sam just giving us up. She said it wasn't like I didn't try. That was true. For years I had done everything I could to hold it together. Now I needed to help my kids before it was too late for them.

Sunday, October 26

It was a long, sleepless night. Faye and I slept on an air mattress, which was losing air. It was painful. After a month of sleeping on the futon in the playroom, which was like sleeping on the floor, I was looking forward to a night in a real bed. A full night's sleep when I didn't have to be listening for anybody. It just wasn't meant to be. I ached all over.

My mother was nasty to me. I found it interesting that the two people who had manipulated and controlled me for most of my life, Sam and my mother, should both become so nasty when I say enough! Nasty and mean. Odd that they have been the two I have loved most in this world. Now I had my kids and they needed me. Faye cried on the way home. Once again, she was sad and she didn't know why. I was able to talk her through it. Caleb on the other hand, was still simmering with anger. He talked with Hannah and told her that he was afraid that he was like Sam. That was something that, if he could recognize, he could change. When we got home and saw Sam, Caleb immediately shut down. It irritated Sam and Caleb reacted, culminating in Sam pushing Caleb and Caleb threatening to have Sam arrested. We really needed to get out of there. I would call the attorney in the morning.

I found myself lying on the futon, staring at all the familiar things around me in the playroom and wondering which things would stay and which things would go with us.

Monday, October 27

Another fucking lovely day. I talked with Caroline. Once again, very emotional. I told her I was sorry for the way I acted at the session. She told me she was proud of how I acted, that I stood up for myself. I told her what had been going on between Sam and Caleb and how it was affecting Faye. We talked about how unhealthy it had become. I told her I needed to do something, but if I brought it up to Sam, he would just explode at me. She said to try and talk to him about what the next step was. I called him and said I wanted to talk about the next step. I told him I would like to preserve what little relationship we had left for the sake of our kids.

Sam came home and we sat down to talk. It seemed that his idea of the next step meant I got the bed and he would take the futon. We couldn't afford anything else. I told him there was no "we." It was "I." He said I had to fulfill my obligations to the house and pay half of the loan, the utilities, etc. Then he said something about his share of my school. I told him I would pay my portion of the loan but that he had no ties to the school. He started spouting legal shit at me. He said he gave unconditional financial support as well as time and sweat equity and more bullshit. Fine, if he wanted the school, he could have it. I would figure a way to get out. I would save money, make a budget, pack up, and the moment I had enough, I would leave.

He seemed to think that we were going to go on for an infinite period of time here. He said that having two houses didn't say anything to the kids about relationships and how people behave in them. He said he thought that it would be no more detrimental to the kids for us to live together and actually more harmful to them if we were to live apart. Control. Control. Control. I hated myself. I hated him.

Tuesday, October 28

I was crying all day. I kept hoping I'd wake up and my husband, my real husband, would roll over and smile at me and say, "Good morning. I love you."

The words of our conversation last night kept ringing in my ears. I told Sam I didn't condone Caleb's disrespectful behavior, but at least he was talking, that was the goal, to which he replied, "Who's goal?"

I was genuinely confused. "What?"

"That may be your goal, but it isn't mine. Don't lump us together."

That earned him, "What an asshole!" from Sophie, who never speaks that way about him.

Then I said to him at the end of our frustrating, controlling conversation, "So we're just supposed to live here together while you watch your porn and search for your girls."

And he jumped in with, "And you can do anything you want."

Not "I wouldn't do that," but "you can do anything you want." There was no respect for me as a human being, let alone his life partner for twenty-two years and the mother of his children.

I was not going to live like that. I would find a way out.

Now it was out in the open.

My former business partner came over to drop off a Halloween costume for Faye. She said to me, "Listen, we have been friends for a long time and just because we're not business partners anymore doesn't mean we're not friends. If you ever need to talk, you just call me."

I said, "How did you know?"

"Someone told me," she said. I cried and she did too.

Jasper came up to me at swimming. I said, "How are you doing?"

He said, "Fine, but I hear you've been better." Of course, he would know. Faith has my stuff, all the stuff I printed from my computer scans and Sam's online exploits, in her safe deposit box.

I picked up Faye from Sophie's parents' house. Her dad came around the table, took me in his arms and I fell apart.

I went to the library to get a book for Faye. I got *Conscious Divorce*[8] for me. Sophie gave me a copy earlier in the year and I sent it to a friend because I didn't think I needed it. I couldn't even get through the introduction.

I was so scared and sick. I was ashamed of my failure as a wife and as a mother for my inability to protect my children. I sat in the library crying, wondering how Sam could not look around him and say, "Oh God. Look what I have done."

Wednesday, October 29

I was given a gift. I had a great talk with Caroline. She reinforced my decision to move out. I told her that Sam said the kids wouldn't be any more harmed living together than living apart. She said that's not true. She said it's proven that children have a clearer, healthier picture of a relationship if they're not living in an unhealthy one. She said that the right place would come along and I would make it. She was thrilled that Caleb was going to see Dan. She praised me for the way I have been talking to him.

Then I called our landlady from the old apartment about a letter of reference as a landlord. She told me how sorry she was that things didn't work out. Then she asked what I was looking for and I told her simply a safe place for me and the kids. She said she had a place in my old building that she just finished renovating.

---

[8] Susan Allison, *Conscious Divorce: Ending a Marriage with Integrity*, (Three Rivers Press, 2001)

I went over to see it on my break. It was clean and bright and it only seven hundred seventy-five dollars per month, with heat and water included. I could swing that. I went over the numbers and over them again. It would work.

I picked Faye up from school early and she had a tummy ache.

I talked with my attorney who told me what my obligations and rights were. He said if Sam was not talking about child support, I shouldn't be talking about loan payments.

Then Sophie and I talked. I told her that the only one I was really worried about was Faye and moving her out. We talked about Sam taking the apartment, but he couldn't afford it. It wasn't exactly like he and I could talk rationally. I just couldn't understand what happened to him. Sophie said that maybe the fighting was God's way of making the separation easier.

Caroline said to keep in mind the lines from the movie *Shakespeare in Love*:

"It will all turn out well in the end."
"How will it?"
"I don't know. It's a mystery."

Thursday, October 30

I called Sam last night at work. I wanted to tell him about the apartment. He was defensive at first but after a while that dissipated a little. He even offered to take the apartment so I wouldn't have to move the kids. I broke down and told him how I was truly feeling. I asked if there was any concept of "Oh God, look what I have done?" He said there was. I hadn't seen it until now.

I needed to think. I needed to sleep.

Saturday, November 1

By the time I got into bed last night, I was too exhausted to write. Halloween. Sam got up in the morning and it was as if a switch had flipped. He was warm and affectionate. He told me that he had a call in to Josh. I told him I thought that was wonderful and I truly did. The healthier Sam and I could be, the better our children would fare. He told me I had said two things that really hit home, and he wanted to talk to the kids and me before we made any decisions. I thought about it most of the day. I was concerned that he would sit the kids down and say something about how much he wanted to work things out, even though I wanted to divorce, putting pressure on me to give in. I needed to get away from the craziness and I told him that last night. We had a long talk and he really was expecting me to give in because he had all of a sudden woken up. Oddly enough, even when he pointed to the work I needed to do, I didn't feel anger or irritation or even frustration. I felt sad for him. He had become someone I never expected him to be. I told him that I would support him through his work, but that I could not take the roller coaster ride anymore. He seemed to hear me. I hoped this was Sam being real and not just more manipulation. I couldn't even tell anymore. I did know that as he was doing all this lovely talking, he was still going through wine at a good clip and hiding porn in his trunk. New porn. I knew I had made the right decision.

Caleb went to see Dan. In spite of himself, he seemed to warm to Dan. Of course, with pizza and soda, Dan was speaking his language. I would call him on Monday to make another appointment.

Sam and I needed to sit down and talk about apartment versus house. And he needed to talk with his sister about us staying here if he was moving. I would let him do that alone. If she was going to explode, I didn't want to hear it and she should have every right to say no without worrying how I might feel.

Sunday, November 2

It was hard to believe that in twenty-two days, my son would be fourteen years old. I thought the talk with Dan had really helped to alleviate a lot of his anxiety, but he was still angry and nasty to Sam. Oh well.

Sam and I had a talk after church. I felt like a high school kid. My boyfriend didn't want me, but he didn't want anyone else to have me either.

I was beginning to wonder if Sam actually had two distinct personalities. He had tried to be so loving and kind in the past twenty-four hours, as if it would make up for the last six weeks. He didn't want to separate. All of a sudden, he was willing to talk and do the work he needed to do. He had made a complete 180° turn and although it was nice, it was making me crazy. I wished he would just pick a personality and stick with it, so I knew what to expect. I told him he was saying all the things he said to me in the spring, making all the same promises, and yet he had porn in his trunk. New porn.

He stopped for a minute, looked at me like he was seeing me for the first time in a long while, and he said, "We should separate." Was that because he suddenly saw things from my perspective and comprehended how much work he really had to do? Or was it because he was tired of me looking through his stuff? God knows I was certainly tired of it.

We seemed to come to an understanding that he would take the apartment. He needed to talk to his sister and his mother this week to make sure they would allow me and the kids to stay in the house without him.

He kept pushing me with the fact that he didn't want to separate. Either he wouldn't admit or else he had no concept of how mean he was. I couldn't go through it again. Finally, I just got so frustrated that I began to sob. I couldn't take it anymore. I was tired of crying every night. I was tired of finding things to do because I didn't want to come home. I didn't want to be near him.

I was so fucking tired.

Monday, November 3

Another long day. I asked Sam this morning to talk to his mother and sister so that we could let the landlady know. I thought we had decided last night that he was going to take the apartment. This morning he hit me with, "I don't think we should separate." I lost it. Last night it was decided and now he was running me through the ringer again. He kept hammering with, "I don't think it's a good idea."

I came back with, "Well I didn't think it was a good idea to stick your cock in that whore, but you did it anyway!"

I should be ashamed of myself. I left for work crying yet again. I should have just taken the kids and left.

I came home on my break to pack an overnight bag for Faye.

To help me out, Sophie took Faye to stay with her girls every Monday night. It gave me one-on-one time with Caleb and lightened my load a bit. It was a tradition that would last for years. Sam and I talked a little more. I said it was so great that he loved me, until he stopped talking to me again. Then I would struggle and hurt until he realized that something was wrong, and he would love me again until he stopped speaking to me again, and on and on. He finally seemed to get it.

He didn't go to his meeting tonight. He went to Walmart to price coffee makers. I didn't know if that was good or bad. One thing I did know, and Caroline talked to me about it, was that it now had to stop being about him and his behavior because it was completely unreliable. It had to be about me and what I wanted, and how I was going to gather information to make the decision to stay or go.

Caleb was thrown out of the pool tonight for being a wise guy with two other kids. He spent his afternoon on the web surfing for porn. Now what?

Tuesday, November 4

I have spent the day trying to shift focus from what Sam was and had been doing to me, to what I wanted and needed.

Sam talked to his mother and his sister last night about moving into the apartment. I don't know what was said or how it was reacted to. He didn't share that with me. He only told me that he talked to them because I asked. Did I give him the money to get the apartment or not?

I talked with Rachel tonight. She was so disgusted with her

father. She didn't even want to talk to him. She was sick about his lack of relationship with Caleb. She and Becca had decided they needed to intervene with Sam. Becca was in therapy. How much of that was due to what Sam had been doing? She didn't believe that this had started only ten years ago. She was sure that it went on in Sam's marriage to her mother. I was not so sure. She was as furious with Sam as Caleb was. She invited me down to New York for Thanksgiving with just the kids. She didn't want her father there. I felt sick over what he had done to the people who had loved him the most.

So, where did that leave me? Would I ever have a relationship that was honest and faithful? And how did I teach my children that it was not only normal but also desirable? It seemed I would spend the next year gathering information about what Sam and I had left in our marriage, and how that would or wouldn't fit with what I wanted and needed.

Wednesday, November 5

I had an interesting phone call. A former parent wanted to meet with me the next day about a joint project between her agency and my school. They would be taking over a large building in town. There was already a childcare center built into the building. We were going to get together and discuss the options for a merger or joint project. Could this be it? I was afraid to even hope. The first thing I did was call Sam. There was a part of me that missed him so much—the warm loving him—and with the exception of the last five days, that was someone I hadn't seen in a while.

He was reluctant to set a date to move out. I thought he was thinking that the longer he waited, the better the chance of losing the apartment. But what he didn't realize, or maybe he did, was that by completely disregarding my needs and wants in regard to this separation—the separation that his actions made necessary—he was reinforcing the idea that my needs were secondary to his and that they mattered little, if at all.

And to top that off, the dog got out and was at the shelter again. Caleb was back on the porn sites again, my panic was rising, and Sam's cousin told me that she might have thyroid cancer.

We were all twisted around and upside down. Let go and let God.

Thursday, November 6

Over the last few days, I had been worried that I was making the wrong choice. Tonight left no doubt in my mind that my choice to split was entirely the right one.

My mother came tonight. She and my sister Thea were leaving from here to drive back to Arizona. A few days ago, I told her that Sam and I were separating. The tension would have been obvious. I was still sleeping downstairs in the playroom and Caleb was still not speaking to his father. Caleb had a good session with Dan and was in particularly good spirits when I picked him up from swimming. When we got home my mother was already there. Thea hadn't arrived yet. Sam was a little tense and Caleb picked right up on it. He started acting like the proverbial obnoxious teenager, too loud and a smart aleck. Although Sam had really been giving him his space, tonight he couldn't. The situation began to escalate quickly and threatened to blow up.

I finally got Sam in the living room, where I could try to calm him down privately, when Caleb exploded. He began screaming profanity and hurling insults and threats at Sam, who responded by, "Tell him to shut his mouth or I'll come in there and beat the shit out of him." And then it happened. Caleb began screaming about Sam's infidelity in front of my mother and Faye.

Faye was crying, I was holding the kitchen door shut with my mother and my children on the other side. Caleb was pushing on it from one side. Sam was trying to push me out of the way to get to Caleb. All this in front of my mother. I wanted to throw up. Caleb was shaking. We tried to get Faye calmed down and then Sam's mother came out of her bedroom, scared to death by the sound of what had been going on. I told her that it wasn't Caleb's fault. He was angry at his father because Sam made some bad choices. She kept pushing, blaming it all on Caleb, so I told her Sam had been unfaithful. I couldn't let her blame Caleb. It was not his fault. Now his poor mother was sick over what Sam had done.

And now the whole damn world knows what I didn't want anyone to know. And once again, Sam was pissed at me. I was sleeping on the couch. He closed the doors to the dining room.

I felt sick to my stomach.

Friday, November 7

I didn't sleep last night. I was afraid that Sam would come out and stab me while I slept. I knew it was unreasonable, but then I never thought my husband would cross the line to getting physical. I had to literally step in to protect him and Caleb from each other.

I went to see Caroline. After telling her the entire horrific story of last night, she looked as if she wanted to cry. I told her that I needed a plan to get through the next week until Sam moved out. She said the first order of business was to send Sam a thank you card. If last night did not happen then he would have been able to drag this out for weeks. By threatening Caleb, he forced the decision out of the husband/wife decision and into the mother/caretaker decision. He was in the position of father/caretaker and he was striving to make things right with his son. Somewhere along the line he stepped out of that position and chose not to care if things were right with Caleb or not.

She said that now that everything was out in the open, it was encouraging to see how much support I had from people who only had a splinter of the truth. Imagine what would happen if they knew the whole story.

We came up with some answers to his siren song. She said I really needed to take a page out of Caleb's book. I needed to stop worrying about Sam emotionally and financially. He would figure it out. He had before. I needed to concentrate on moving forward for me and the kids, making a new life, one that would be happy and healthy.

I would work out a plan for the kids and his mother. I knew Sam needed to be at the house during the day, but I didn't want him there until after I left in the morning. I also wanted him out before I got home. I told Caroline I was so frustrated with Sam that I told him to pack his bags. She said, "Good for you!" Tonight when I came home, he was standing around with his wounded-animal face. I told him I was picking up his lease tomorrow. He said, "My lease? It's not in your name?"

Another bravo from Caroline. I told him no.

He said, "Well, if that's what you want."

More 'oh poor me'? I was not falling for it anymore.

I asked Caroline if she knew last winter that we would end up this way. She said that first of all, we hadn't ended up yet, but it was not until she met Sam that she knew. She said that there was a certain arrogance about him that said he was going to do just enough work to pacify me and no more. Dan asked her this summer if she had heard from either of us. She said no. He said he hadn't either but sometimes clients go and do the work and he never hears from them again. She told Dan that they would hear from me.

I told her I was so numb that I was back to not being able to put an outfit together or grocery shop. She said on Maslow's Hierarchy of Needs, I was still on the basics of food, clothing, and shelter. Putting outfits together and grocery shopping were much higher up.

Saturday, November 8

It was a good day. I didn't get much done, but Sam was gone all day, the kids were really good and fun, and I made some progress. I actually went to the grocery store and got almost everything on my list. I took Caroline's advice and wrote it all down. It worked and I was able to be a little productive rather than wander aimlessly through the aisles or cry in the produce section.

I picked up the lease from the landlady. She was so warm and kind. I hoped Sam would come to appreciate that. I paid the money to get him in, but after that he was on his own. I told him he was welcome to take anything in the house. So far, he had not indicated a single thing he wanted or started to pack at all. Sophie's husband said he would help him with the move. I made that offer.

They came for dinner tonight and it was fun. It felt so good to have friends I could rely on. Sophie's husband took Caleb off to the Boys and Girls Club to go hear a ninety-three-year-old guitarist. Since Sam had given up on Caleb, I needed to try to surround him with positive male role models. This was a good beginning. A good day, low on stress. We would see what tomorrow would bring.

Sunday, November 9

I went to church by myself. It was sad but that was my new reality. After church I went home and Sam was gone. When he got back, he didn't share where he'd been. Conversation was awkward at best. I asked him if he would like to set down some sort of routine for the kids. He said he couldn't do that now. I asked if he was planning on having Faye come over and stay with him. He said he didn't know. He could be so self-absorbed it was sickening. All he could do was 'oh, poor me'. There seemed to be no thought to the pain of the innocent bystanders. And of course, as usual, I was the bad guy. All this kind of behavior did was reinforce the decision to separate was the right one.

I told him Sophie's husband was willing to help him move. So far, all that Sam had indicated he wanted was a bureau and the futon. I would have to make him a list. I was really hoping he could get a handle on this and rise to the occasion, but it was just not going to be. I would have to figure out the finances too. A small price to pay for an end to the lies and betrayal.

He disappeared again this afternoon. I was out at the wildlife refuge walking and when I came home, he was gone. He just left Faye there playing outside and told her to go next door if she needed anything. Of course, he didn't ask anyone next door if that was okay. This was yet another example of his needs came first and screw the rest of us. What if our neighbors had needed to go somewhere? Would Faye have been left outside to fend for herself? I told him where I was going for a walk. He could have called me. When I asked him when he'd be home, he was vague. I had to go to a Girl Scouts meeting, I couldn't give his mother an answer and I didn't know how to plan dinner. Who knew if he was having coffee or sex?

If I asked questions, I got terse, one-word answers. If he asked questions I was expected to answer fully. Tonight, I went down to get into bed with Faye, who was sad and crying over a movie, and I got an exasperated, "Tch!" I couldn't wait for this shit to be over. He just wouldn't take responsibility for anything.

Faith called me. She had left me a message during church reminding me of her son's first birthday dinner at Gabriel's house the next evening. Of course, this was news to me, but the kids love to go over there, and they really love Faith's kids. So, she called to tell me what time. Caleb would be psyched. Interestingly, I had not seen Gabriel since May. I had no desire to see him or call him except to give him an apology for treating him so coldly when I told him I couldn't talk with him anymore. It was necessary to try and repair my marriage and restore Sam's confidence, something he was unwilling to do for me. Gabriel had been a good friend and I didn't have to be rude. I should probably say sorry for that.

I was thinking that if this new project fell through, I would seriously begin to look into England. In church, the blessing the priest gave was the same blessing that was said at our wedding.

Monday, November 10

I made a list for Sam. He was frozen. I wanted him to be able to make himself a home where he could be peaceful and happy, but he didn't seem capable of doing that. I would start packing for him the next day. I didn't know when we were going to talk to the kids. Again, he didn't seem capable right now. Things were already bad with Caleb. I didn't want to have to talk to Faye on my own.

Caleb had a meeting with Dan, and he was so happy and loving afterwards. I didn't know what Dan was saying, but it seemed to be helping. Caleb told Dan about the other night and how shocked he was by his own use of profanity. He said he came barging in to protect me because he could hear Sam yelling, but he couldn't hear me saying anything. He was angry at me because he felt I let Sam walk all over me. He was not the first one to say that. Caroline said I needed to take a page from Caleb's book.

We went to the birthday party and it was very relaxing and fun. Faith and Jasper and their kids, Gabriel and his wife and their kids, and us. The kids were raucous and loud, and they had a great time. No one ever told them to quiet down or be good. Caleb asked me if he could sleep over with Gabriel's son and my first reaction was, "No, not tonight." Faith said, "Why not?" I couldn't give her an answer. It would take some time for me to get used to saying "yes" to my children. They deserved it. So, when Faye asked if she could sleep with me, I said yes. Even though I didn't sleep well when she slept with me, one day she would stop asking and I would have missed my turn to say yes.

Tuesday, November 11

I was not exactly sure what to do. I was in pain every day. My shoulders and arms hurt so much that I had a really hard time rolling over at night. I knew it was stress, and I was not sure how much more I could take. I ached so badly that sometimes I just cried.

Sophie and I took the girls to the mall. Caleb spent the night at Gabriel's. They all had a great time. I loved to see my kids relaxed and having fun. That's what being a kid should be all about, but it hadn't worked that way in my house. I was determined to change that.

Sam had not signed the lease. He said he would. He also hadn't packed a single thing. I didn't know what to do. I would start packing for him. How sad. I hoped that someday he would be able to function completely and wholly in a healthy way.

Thursday, November 13

I was finding it increasingly difficult to communicate with Sam. This morning I was trying to talk to him about things he needed for the apartment. I really wanted him to see beyond himself and how it would affect Faye at least, if not Caleb. Actually, Caleb would probably be paying very close attention to how Sam handled this. Sam said he was going to at least take the futon and a bureau. I said, "What about a table and chairs? TV?" He said he didn't want a TV because he didn't want a cable bill. He would either take the TV/DVD in the bedroom or else the laptop. What the fuck? He couldn't function enough to put an apartment together, but he'd make sure the only thing he took with him would enable him to continue his porn addiction. I felt sick and

I was pissed that he was still trying to play me. The old me would have kept my mouth shut, let it fester and let the resentment build, to avoid making him angry and feeling the backlash of that anger. I couldn't do that. I tried to voice my frustration. I was tired of him playing the "poor me" card. We were where we were because of the choices we made. He chose to be dishonest and unfaithful. I chose to leave.

So, I would pack him up. He wanted to move over time. Drag it out. Nope. I would not come home each day to find something different gone and have to rearrange things again. Drag it out. Drag it out. I needed peace. The kids needed peace. Sam needed peace. We all needed to know what to expect.

We told Faye tonight. It was true what Caroline said, the kids have already been through the worst. This part would be easier.

Sam came by school to pick up a shower head I had bought for his mother's bathroom. I told him I thought he should take the red antique desk he gave me as a wedding present. He had been using it as a nightstand. He said he planned to take it. I asked him about the red antique chairs. He also planned to take those. He was unwilling to tell me what he was planning up to this point, only that he was moving Friday or Saturday. Very frustrating.

I had a meeting tonight in the city that I thought was next week. I knew Sam had picked up a shift tonight because he told me a couple of days ago, but I didn't know exactly when he was working. I had asked him to put his shifts on the calendar so I would know his schedule, but he didn't. I called and asked what time he had to go to work. His response was, "I don't know. Why? What do you need?" We played round and round until he finally told me

10:00 p.m., but only after I told him what I needed. It brought me back to when he used to pay the bills. I earned the paycheck, but he did all the banking. When I would say to him, how much money do we have in the bank? His answer was nearly always, "I don't know. Why? What do you need?" Was it his knee-jerk answer or his way to manipulate and keep me in the dark?

He gave me a little muscle massager as we were getting back together but it was gone tonight. Faye asked about it. Interesting that he took that with him. Choices. Choices.

I decided that since he wouldn't talk to me about any kind of schedule regarding the kids, I would just have to do it myself. I knew I would be accused of controlling and manipulating him, but I wouldn't have the kids guessing and waiting for him to show up or suddenly having to cancel plans because he miraculously had time to spend with them.

Friday, November 14

Sam was leaving tomorrow. I was filled with relief but also a sense of incredible sadness. It was such a no-brainer to me. Family or sex addiction? Choices. Choices. His words said, "Let's work on it." His actions and lies said, "Screw you."

I came home from taking Caleb to swimming and the bedroom rug was gone. He took all the pictures off the bedroom wall that I hung up for him. I nearly started to cry. I felt like I put all, or at least most, of the effort into making this house our home, and it was unraveling before my eyes. Well, my life had been unraveling, unbeknownst to me, for years. Now it was my turn to pick myself and my children up and make a home for us as best I could.

I was feeling sick and couldn't write anymore. I was trying hard not to cry in front of my kids.

Saturday, November 15

Was it the beginning or the end? I was glad I could get out of the house with the kids. I couldn't hold it together any longer. Sam was sad and I was falling apart. Could he really not see me asking, begging, and pleading with him to talk? To work? To get back to therapy? So here we were. We went to Faith and Jasper's for breakfast before Caleb's swim meet and I completely fell apart. I have worked hard to make this house a home. I would just have to do it again.

Caleb swam beautifully at the meet. I was so proud of him. I felt numb and would just randomly tear up. My children were my gift, and I would do everything I could to bring them up in love and grace and make them healthy, productive people who could love fully and honestly.

I came home dreading what I would find. I don't know what I was expecting. Sam took some things, not much. He cleaned up by vacuuming where he moved furniture. I cleaned up the kitchen, did some laundry, and completely stripped my bed. I put Faye's old quilt on it. I wanted to feel like it was a fresh start for me too.

As we were driving to the meet, it was raining on and off. At one point, Jasper said, "Rainbow!" I couldn't see it. Neither could the kids. We came around a group of trees and there it was. It was so faint it almost seemed like it wasn't really there. As I stared it got brighter. Was that a sign? A new beginning like God gave to Noah? A promise that I would never be destroyed like this again?

On the way home, a car pulled in front of us with a license plate that read "WITHIN." That was where my work lay, and I would work as hard as I could for as long as I needed.

Sophie's mom brought over the most beautiful flowers. Thank God for Sophie and her family.

Sunday, November 16

I woke up just before 6:00 a.m. I could hear his mother, in a little girl voice, talking very quietly. As it got louder, I realized she was calling for me, but she couldn't remember my name, so she was calling purse or nurse.

As I turned my light off last night, I thought of Sam going home to the apartment alone, making up his bed, if he bothered to, and going to sleep. I knew he was sad and scared, and I hated that. I hoped he would come to peace in time and grow and change.

I sat alone in the quiet this morning and tried to absorb the peace of the moment. Then I started. I cleaned my room. I cleaned out. It looked bright and simple and Caroline was right. It was like a weight had been lifted. Yes, I was sad. At times I felt like my heart was breaking, but it felt good to be in a position where I could just do whatever. I didn't need to ask permission or wait to do it together, only to be disappointed and do it myself anyway.

I worried about Sam, but he called me in the afternoon. He seemed to be holding it together. When I went to pick up Faye from rehearsal I drove by his apartment. In the front window there was a lamp and that vase from his store that was square with a guy's face in pop art. The face was looking out the window. It was cute and I was glad he took that vase. I didn't like it and I remembered that when he brought it home, I told him it was ugly. He told me it was some famous guy and that he was surprised Shawn didn't buy it because the guy was well-known to be gay. So why was Sam prominently displaying it in his front window? Is that what he was trying to say? That he was gay? Is that why that website with the gay T-shirts was on the computer? And why not trust me? If that's what was going on, I couldn't imagine how conflicted he must have felt inside.

Monday, November 17

I was beyond exhausted. I picked Thea up at the airport last night. We didn't get back to the house until after 12:30 a.m. Then his mother was up at four and my alarm went off at six. Mondays were difficult days for me. Maybe I needed a better system. I would have to put that on my list.

Added to that, I was on my period and had horrible cramps. I felt sick and I just wanted to curl up and go to sleep. I had to wait until 10:00 p.m.

I didn't shed any tears. Was that odd? I had a long talk with Sophie about the possibility that Sam had been questioning his sexuality. That certainly would have explained a lot. I was too tired to think straight now. I'd try again tomorrow.

Tuesday, November 18

Good day? I felt really good about how I was coping and I was proud of myself. The tears were not coming, and I suppose that concerned me a bit. Dan said that I already did my grieving. More would come, but not right now. Right now, I was simply happy to have an end to the drama. So were the kids. They had been fun and cooperative. Faye missed Sam and Caleb was still angry but there was a palpable sense of relief. Tonight, the kids were doing the dishes and they were singing at the top of their lungs and I didn't need to shush them. It felt wonderful and fun and free.

Faye, Caleb, and I all had a part in moving the bookcase from the dining room into the living room. In it was Sam's old planner from several years ago and I looked through it. In it was the first time we went to Arizona and the last time we went to England. He also made some interesting marks on the calendar each month. He was keeping track of something. I'm not sure what.

In the address section under E was E. T. Bond. Emily Ty (bondage)? Her number was in his phone as ET. In January, he said they had been together for about two years. That would have been three years after this planner. Also, in November she was twenty years old. That would have made her sixteen when he had this planner. Sixteen? I felt sick to my stomach. I wished I had some answers, and I knew I probably never would. Letting go was so hard.

Wednesday, November 19

I was a mess all day. In the afternoon, Sophie called the number from ET Bond. It was Emily, from the planner, sixteen years old at the time. I felt so numb that I was really not functioning well. In fact, I was not sure I could lie here next to my beautiful little girl and write. Caleb picked up on my energy tonight of course. He was so intuitive. So many questions, so few answers.

Thursday, November 20

I was learning to let go. I talked with Dan. I was hoping he could ask Josh if Faye was in any danger going to Sam's house overnight. We really didn't know all the facts about Sam's sexual exploits. We now knew that it began when Emily was sixteen. Did Sam have a thing for young girls or was it just this one? Dan said wait. Faye had not asked to go to Sam's house, and he had not asked to have her. If and when that happened, explain that I knew about Emily's age and that before there was a sleepover, I needed to talk to Josh. I needed his professional opinion on whether or not I would be putting Faye in danger. I didn't think so, but if anything ever happened and I knew I had had the power to prevent it, I wouldn't have been able to live with myself. Then again, I never would have dreamed that my fifty-six-year-old husband would sleep with a sixteen-year-old girl either.

My assistant, her husband, and her boys came over. So did Sophie and the girls. It was loud and fun. It was difficult to stop myself from shushing the kids. Now everyone was happy and sleeping. I ached very badly and was ready to close my eyes. I prayed each day for peace. For all of us.

Saturday, November 22

Caleb's first home meet. I hoped he would do well. He really needed this. His confidence was in the toilet and he did such negative self-talk. I was trying to help him break this habit, but it didn't seem to be working.

On the way to the meet this morning I asked Caleb if he would like to have a little birthday celebration tomorrow because I had to work all day Monday, his actual birthday, and then he had swimming. He said, "Okay Mom, but just family okay? Just Sophie and your assistant and stuff." Interesting who he considered family. I suppose "family members" are those that love and hold you up when all else seemed to be falling apart.

I asked Sophie and she was thrilled. We talked a little bit about Caleb's venom with Sam and how he seemed to derive pleasure from hurting his father. Sophie thought that indicated just how long and deep Caleb's hurt went. It was more than I imagined or could have guessed. Dan said he'd be fine. He just hated his father and it was nothing I could fix. I could encourage, certainly, but not fix. Sam and Caleb would have to do that. I told Sam yesterday that it would take all the perseverance he could muster. Could he hang in there and continually be told to "go to hell" until it didn't happen anymore, or would he give up and abandon Caleb? Time would tell.

Sunday, November 23

I just paid my first set of bills alone. I was very afraid of running out of money and I was trying to be extra careful. I really wanted this Christmas to be special for the kids. I did a little Christmas/birthday shopping yesterday. It was lonely and I wandered a lot, but I was actually able to make some decisions on my own and that was good. I had been on the verge of tears for the last two days. I was sad and angry that we had ended up here. I felt abandoned. I knew that I had really been abandoned long ago, but at least he was still pretending. I was angry that he would just let us go and I was scared that no one would want me again. I would be forty-five years old soon. I was not young, slim, and beautiful and I was terrified of growing old alone. I was afraid Caleb would hate Sam forever. I was sad for Sam but angry at him for putting Caleb in this position through years of emotional abandonment.

The end of the day had come and we celebrated Caleb's birthday. My baby boy would be fourteen tomorrow. I would've never have believed fourteen years ago that we would be in this situation. There was just so much I didn't understand.

Sam was off. The entire day went by without him making contact with Faye. Finally, at 8:30, I told her to call to say good night. She told me she didn't want her friends to know. She also spoke about the night my mother was here and how angry everyone was and how frightened she was. Did he not want her?

Monday, November 24

Another lovely fucking day. All day I was feeling very sentimental about the day Caleb was born. I worked a long day and talked with Sam a couple of times. He was also feeling emotional. Caleb seemed very chipper and said he had a good day. He got calls from England, and then Becca and Rachel after swimming, which he said went well. After he hung up around 9:30 p.m., he asked if he could stay up to watch a TV show at 10:00. I said no because it was a school night. He badgered and moaned. I kept saying no but he wouldn't let it go. I started to get irritated and angry and I told him that. The whole thing stretched out into a long argument in which he said that it was the worst day of his life. Apparently, gone were the days of "happy birthday" from well-wishers. Now there was a punch in the arm for each year old. His right arm was bruised so I knew it was real, but he never said anything negative about his day until he didn't get what he wanted from me. Controlling manipulation all over again. I would be so glad when this year was over. Next year couldn't possibly be worse.

Tuesday, November 25

It was an incredibly long day. I woke up this morning to pouring rain. I left the house before 7:00, after getting Sam's mother fed and medicated. I took Caleb to the carpool, dropped Faye at the dentist, took my car in to be serviced, where they gave me a loaner, picked Faye up and got her to school, then headed to school myself. All of that by 8:30 a.m.! And it really had not stopped. It was 11:40 p.m. and I was just now sitting down for a few minutes.

I had been thinking a lot about something Rachel said last night. Love the sinner, hate the sin. That was very mature, and I was proud of her. She was not withholding her love from Sam, even though she was sickened by his poor decisions. In many ways, I felt like that. I loved the person he was inside, beneath all the mean, deceitful behavior. But loving somebody does not mean you let them trash you and your children whenever they have a dip in their self-esteem meter. Sometimes, loving someone means being able to stand up and say, "Stop!"

We were headed to my sister Hannah's tomorrow for Thanksgiving. What was I thankful for? I thanked God every day for Caleb and Faye and the joy they brought to me and others. I would be very thankful tonight to get into bed.

It was midnight and I had to work a full day tomorrow before running Girl Scouts and then heading off to Hannah's. I waited up to bake the banana bread for Thanksgiving. We didn't get home from the Nutcracker dress rehearsal until close to 10:00 p.m. The bread pan started to slip as I was taking it out of the oven, and I dropped it on the floor. It shattered. The floor downstairs was soaked from the rain because the gutters needed to be cleaned out. I was out of coffee, and I felt like I just couldn't catch a fucking break.

Thursday, November 27

Thanksgiving Day. It was an awesome day. I was at Hannah's and we had a fun day making dinner and eating together. None of the elegance that we have always had at Sam's sister's. None of the tension either. I talked with Sam this morning and it was weird. He seemed perfectly fine. The kids seemed fine. Part of me was fine. When we hung up, I started to cry. I felt so stressed out that my entire body ached. I knew my marriage was over. I also knew that it really was over a long time ago. I did so much grieving throughout the spring, I wondered if my tears were all dried up, and then I had waves of terrible, all-consuming sadness. I felt very disconnected from my family, my children, my job, and sometimes myself. It was an emotional day and I was tired. I was also very tired of feeling tired and achy.

Friday, November 28

Faye opened in Nutcracker. She was nervous but she looked absolutely adorable. When she got home, she was exhausted and thrilled. On Wednesday or Thursday, Sam had said he wanted to be sure to get her an apple for opening night. *Sam was big into traditions. The Barrymore family gave apples for opening nights of performances and Sam's family did too.* Of course, he didn't. He didn't even call her. She had been acting out a little lately. How much of that was her age, and how much was her feelings that she had been abandoned by her father? Once again, here I was, sitting here saying, I just didn't understand. I needed to sleep. I hoped I could tonight.

Saturday, November 29

A good night's sleep. Thank God for nighttime sleep meds. After getting his mother fed, I decided to go to Home Depot to get stuff for the gutters. I didn't have my Home Depot card, so I called Sam to see if he had it. He did and we met at the local big box store so I could pick it up. We went in to pick up a rip stick for Caleb for Christmas. It was awkward and painful. We started to talk a little. I was feeling angry, scared, and resentful and tried to tell him. He listened, I think.

Afterwards, I drove to Home Depot in tears. I got what was needed for the gutters and went home. As I began cleaning them out, my neighbor came over to help me. It was such a blessing. After we finished up, I went inside to wash up. As I was running my hands under the water, I realized a diamond was missing from my engagement ring. I felt sick. Over? It seemed as though God was saying so.

I got Faye ready for the show. Again, he didn't call her. When I arrived at the theater, I thought I'd check on the floor to see if maybe my diamond had fallen out there and sure enough, another mom found it on the floor.

Sunday, November 30

I ended my day yesterday cleaning Sam's mother after yet another bowel movement accident. I didn't have the strength for this. She was getting more and more forgetful and that made everyone cranky. Sam's sister could not come to bathe her yesterday, so I gave her the message and then a little while later, Caleb repeated it. She told Sam's sister that we never gave her the messages and I think his sister actually believed her. It made me angry and frustrated.

Tonight, while I was at Nutcracker with Faye, Sam put groceries in my car. It was all the stuff the kids love. He also left me a note and all of us an Advent calendar. I had Faye call to say thank you and goodnight. Then my son, my beautiful angry son, who was trying so hard to make sense of it all, got on the phone and thanked his father. Afterwards, he asked me for the book that Sam had given him for his birthday. I was incredibly proud of Caleb. He has been such a blessing.

Now, as Caleb was in bed reading, I would snuggle into bed with my Faye and hopefully we would all get the rest we needed.

Tuesday, December 2

It was a fairly good day. Having Caleb and Sam at least able to communicate had lifted a great burden and I really felt it. Each day was still difficult, single-handedly taking care of his mother and the kids, but knowing I could at least ask Sam for help was tremendous.

I was trying to acknowledge my feelings as they arose and then doing my best to put them away and move on. I seemed to be functioning a little better. The fact that this was not just a temporary glitch continued to take me by surprise and surround me with sadness, anger, and hurt occasionally. I would have to trust that God was going to get us all through this unspeakably painful time. I had a headache and I was tired. I needed to sleep.

Wednesday, December 3

Tonight, I went to see Faye dance in Nutcracker. Sophie and her mom got me a ticket. The costumer, who I helped in exchange for Faye's performance fees, finagled one for Caleb. *Because of my lack of funds, the ballet company allowed me to work on costumes in exchange for Faye's dance classes. What I do doesn't come close to covering the cost. They are extremely generous.* I was immensely proud, not only of Faye, but of Caleb too. She danced beautifully. She was cute and very mouse-like. He was handsome and well behaved. All the girls came out to say hello to him. During the intermission I went downstairs to braid hair. When I returned, Caleb was having a conversation with the governor, who happened to be in the audience. He was such an amazing kid. He also said several times how much he missed performing and that he'd like to play the Mouse King. He wanted to take some dance classes. We would see.

Thursday, December 4

It was another incredibly long, unbelievably exhausting day. I let the kids sleep in a little this morning and then it was off to work. I heard back from the woman with the new school project. She was still excited about the new childcare center. I was trying to be optimistic but, at the same time, not get my hopes up too much. Faye, as exhausted as she was, was such a trooper. We raced from her Nutcracker performance to Caleb's Christmas concert. He was wonderful. The music was beautiful and very well-done.

Before the concert Sam and I sat together for a while. It was awkward and stressful. I was sad for the loss of what could have been, and I was angry at his choices that were major factors in our ending up here. But tonight, as I looked at him and talked with him, I found myself completely devoid of pity. I kept thinking, *you have looked me in the eyes for ten years and lied to me and betrayed me. Any trust in you has been shredded.*

By the time I got home my shoulders were so tense that my arms hurt.

Feel it, examine it, and let it go.

Saturday, December 6

Dishonorable. That is the word that Becca's godmother gave me. I had been thinking a lot about the time when her son was little and in my class. She came into my school one morning devastated and in tears. Her husband had had an affair and she was a wreck. I never knew any details but somehow, they worked it out. Now, seventeen years later, they are still together. She told me last night of his raging alcoholism and his affair, of her attempt to put it behind her as he got well, and her decision to make a new life, with or without him. She talked of how it was important and necessary to teach her son that she should not be treated that way and that he had no right to treat others that way, or for others to treat him disrespectfully. Then she said the word that just seemed to click for me, that her husband had acted dishonorably.

Dishonorable–without honor.

Funny how that word resonated deep within me.

Sunday, December 7

Peace. The Word of the season. People say it all the time without really thinking about its meaning. This morning, at this moment, I was at peace. Of course, the one day I could sleep in, I was up at 6:00 a.m. His mother had to use the bathroom and I was already awake. It was snowing. We put up our Christmas tree yesterday. That was probably something that should have triggered anxiety and sadness, but we went with Sophie and her husband to a Christmas tree farm to cut it down. This morning I realized that, for the most part, I have done it with the kids by myself for years now, with Sam only helping peripherally.

I got up on this beautifully snowy morning, plugged in the tree, lit a fire, and sat for a long time with my coffee, listening to Christmas music playing softly. And I thanked God for all the incredible blessings in my life:

For my children

For my health

For the shelter of my home, however messy it may be

For the love that surrounds me from family, friends, and pets

For easing my anxiety, right at this moment, about our futures

For all the beautiful memories I created with Sam

For the desire and ability to act honorably

Peace

Tuesday, December 9

I have been too exhausted to write for the past couple of days and Caleb was a little sick. I felt somewhat like I did last spring, like I just wanted to come home and go to bed.

Sunday night, we finished decorating the tree. The kids picked out ornaments for our tree and some to go to Sam. I think Caleb struggled—we all did a little. Caleb was starting to feel sorry for his father since he went for a visit at Sam's house. He was upset that Sam had only two forks, two knives and two spoons. I started to explain that this had been Sam's choice but then decided it was too much information for Caleb. I suggested that for Christmas Caleb get his father a set of silverware. That seemed to help.

Later the kids called Sam to say good night. Caleb asked if he could sleep at Sam's on Monday night and Sam said sure. I said maybe not on a school night. I told Caleb I would talk to Sam to straighten it out. When I got on the phone with Sam, I reminded him that he really had not made a place for the kids to sleep. I could feel his irritation. He said he had barely made a place for himself and that he didn't have money to make a place for the kids. I didn't remind him that my sister Hannah had offered bunk beds and they were just waiting. Why should I have to remind him? He was their father.

I told him that I wasn't comfortable with Caleb sleeping with him on a school night. He was fine with that. Then I told him before the kids sleep over, I wanted to talk with Josh to be assured that they were safe. When I told him about finding Emily's phone number and his old datebook he responded with, "What kind of a monster do you think I am?" I told him I had no problem with him seeing the kids but I needed to make sure they were safe. He said the phone number was from years ago and that he kept that book of addresses. He very well may have, but I'd have been an idiot to believe him. He was pissed at me. I told him that any other woman would be screaming from the top of the hills what he had done. Any other woman would have already called a lawyer and would have smeared him all over court by now. He said he knew that. He said he was doing some really good work with Josh that was incredibly painful. I told him that I was really happy for him to be working so hard. I reminded him that knowing the work would be so painful, I had offered to go through it with him. He chose to do it alone.

I also said I found it difficult every day to undo some of the tremendous damage he had done to me on a daily basis with, "You're a bitch," "You don't initiate sex enough," "You don't make me feel desirable," and on and on. Being the target of that kind of talk for years had done such a number on me. It made me sad and angry just to think about it.

Wednesday, December 10

I got my paycheck. I gave Sam money for the loan and then paid the bills I had tried to pay two weeks ago. When all was said and done, I had two hundred and thirteen dollars left to get me through the next two weeks. Caleb's swim money was due this week as well as his chorus trip money. I completely broke down with my assistant. I felt useless. I hadn't even been truly present at work—I was just a warm body. I wasn't going to make it financially. I didn't know what to do so I called Sam.

He had made no move to give me any money. Sure, he bought a few groceries, but he didn't tell me he was getting anything, so we bought the same things on the same days. I ended up dumping half of the milk. Then he did it again. I told him I appreciated the thought, but the cash in hand would have been far better for me.

He, of course, started to get pissed off, and his voice immediately began to rise. He blamed me for throwing him out. I was paying far more in bills than he, plus caring for his mother, the kids and all the animals, as well as the house. I had had no time off because he was not interested in any kind of set visitation schedule. I couldn't count on him for any money because he wouldn't commit to giving me anything. All he did was buy a few groceries here and there. Maybe he didn't trust me to spend it wisely or on the kids. Who knew? The attorney said I shouldn't even consider a loan payment until he committed to some kind of child support.

Sam said he loves me and the kids. What kind of love is it that acts selfishly without thoughtful consideration of consequences or collateral damage?

The conversation left me a wreck. I was frustrated, angry and frightened. What was going to happen to us? I would not go back to him for financial reasons. For God's sake, I had carried us all financially for years anyway. I had to look at this in a different way. The solution would come to me.

Friday, December 12
A better day.

I was trying to take each day as it comes, not letting the worries of yesterday or the uncertainties of tomorrow overwhelm me.

Sam came over tonight and I showed him the presents I got for the kids for Christmas. I needed to start wrapping but I wanted to show him first. He seemed relaxed and easy and at times tearful. It was nice to have him there because it was easy and familiar. It was also nice to have another adult in the house to talk to. Beyond that, there was nothing. I wasn't sad when he left and I didn't fall to pieces. It really was over for me and I knew that. I could never again feel the same for him as I used to, and I didn't think he could for me either. Right now, he thinks he could, but I would never be sure, and neither would he.

I needed clarity and simplification in my life and also something good, just one good thing for me each day. I was a good person and I was worthy of love, kindness, and honesty.

Monday, December 15

One month on my own.

His mother was in the hospital and I was so emotionally spent that writing seemed out of the question. On Saturday, I was baking something for the bake sale at church. She had seemed very weak and tired. We were joking around and all of a sudden, I looked down at her and she looked vacant. I called out to her, "Are you all right?"

"Sure," she slurred back.

Because this had happened four times already, it was upsetting, but not as much as it could have been. That was until she stopped breathing. I called 9-1-1 and then his sister. I sent Caleb downstairs to tell Faye's friend to call her mother to come get both girls. By the time the friend's father got there, Sam's mother was breathing again and coming around. Fire trucks were there and so was the ambulance and police.

I called Sam. He insisted that his sister, not I, go to the hospital and that his mother be admitted. The friend's father took all of the kids home and Sam's sister and his mother left with all the rescue workers.

Faye's friend's mom came over and told me to take time to do what I needed to do, that she would feed the kids. I took my bread out of the oven and drew a bath. Then I sat in the tub, in the dark and sobbed like I never remember crying before. It was as if my soul was shattering into a million pieces. I made sounds that I never made before and I could not stop. It was the first time that I had been alone since Sam and I got back together. It was like opening the floodgates. Good, but scary.

I was thinking about a talk I had with Sam a while back. I told him I thought maybe he had decided he didn't want to be married anymore a long time ago. Rather than hurt me by coming out and saying so, he began to act out until he couldn't stop. He said he thought that I had decided the same thing, that I didn't want to be married anymore. I told him he was right but not at first. At first, I kept trying to get through to him. I had dragged him off to therapy how many times? After years of that, I began to give up. As devastating as this was, it was also such a relief.

Friday, December 19

A snow day. I think the last snow day we had, when school was closed, was the day my entire world came crashing down around me.

His mother was in a nursing home and it was a huge relief in so many ways.

Caleb was failing biology. He was terribly upset and, like Sam, seemed to freeze in a state of panic. I determined to help him get his feet on the ground and develop a plan. I wished I could send him back to St. Andrews. I knew he missed it, but there was nothing I could do.

On Thursday morning, I went to my car to take Caleb to school. In the car was a card labeled: to Josie Allen from: S Claus. Inside was a Christmas card that read, "You've been good this year. Take care of yourself. Love, Santa." There was also two hundred dollars in cash. I was so overcome by the love and generosity that I began to sob. I decided I would take it to the bank the next day and start a savings account. It would be money for a home. This morning, I was looking through a box of pictures and came across an old card from a dear friend. Inside there was forty dollars in cash. I felt like God was looking out for me.

Sophie took me out to lunch to celebrate my birthday. We went to the local pub and then walked around downtown and shopped in the snow. When she invited me, she asked if I would feel uncomfortable downtown. I thanked her for her thoughtfulness.

When Sam and I were down there for our anniversary in the summer, I told him that I was uncomfortable, always thinking that others knew about his secret life. He became impatient and short with me. I knew he wanted to put our relationship back together but I wondered why. When he had it, he didn't want it. Even when we gave it a second chance, he couldn't commit. It was over. I was worth more. I couldn't even write without my throat hurting and my eyes stinging with tears.

In an hour and a half, it would be my forty-fifth birthday. I had spent a lovely day with my best friend and all day I had been fighting the urge to say, "We need to go home." I needed to reprogram myself. I would never be perfect and that was okay. I was human and I was worthy of love and honesty and commitment.

When I got into bed, I saw Faye had put a note on my pillow.

"The world is yours to keep
–Faye
P. S. Please share it with me.
P. S. S. You are the most important person in your life.
P. S. S. S. I love you!"

I loved my kids so much.

Saturday, December 20

My forty-fifth birthday.

A year ago, I was excited for Sam to close the store. Excited for us to get our family back on track. What a year it had been.

We had the most beautiful snowstorm last night. I got up this morning and shoveled the driveway. The dog stayed outside with me. I really needed to give the dog more attention.

I used a gift certificate I had for a massage and it was just what I needed. When I came home, Sam and the kids had made a little party for me. I opened gifts and the kids were cute and excited. Sam, however, got more and more emotional. Then, as I blew out the candles on the cake, Sam abruptly decided to leave. He was obviously upset. After he left, both kids started to cry. I tried to cheer them up, starting to panic about what might happen on Christmas Day. Then we sat at the table and ate the cake with forks. No plates—just us and the cake.

We had a lovely dinner at Sophie's house tonight. When I got home, there was a book under my pillow, *The Spirituality of Imperfection*[9].

My mother never called.

Monday, December 22

My mother called me yesterday morning. I told her, without bitterness, that she was a day late. She said she had gotten the dates wrong. Of all years to forget, this was not the one. She asked if I was mad and I told her the truth, that I felt forgotten and abandoned. She never called me, even just to see how I was doing. She said that she didn't know what to say, and she thought I would call her if I needed her. I replied, "You're the mother." She began calling more often after that.

Caleb and I argued tonight. When he was overwhelmed, he froze—he received an F in biology. When he was angry or disagreeing, his volume automatically went up. It was difficult to have that happening and not think "Sam." That was my challenge—to help Caleb work through those crippling habits.

Sam put new tires on my car. What a lovely Christmas present. I said so to Caleb, who rested his head on my shoulder and said, "You know he really loves you, Mom." I tried to explain that it was never Sam's love that I questioned, only his behavior. Unacceptable and unforgivable. He asked me if I would ever be able to trust Sam again. I said I didn't know but probably not. Why should I?

---

[9] Ernest Kurtz and Katherine Ketcham, *The Spirituality of Imperfection: Storytelling and the Search for Meaning*, (Bantam Books 2002)

He had never given me any occasion to trust, not even when he knew that it was all on the line.

Trust him? Not as far as I could throw him. Every time I called him and he didn't answer the phone, my mind automatically jumped to the conclusion that he was in someone's bed.

At least the fighting had stopped. Thank God.

Wednesday, December 24

It was six minutes to Christmas. The stockings were stuffed and the tree was full of gifts. Santa had come. I felt a tremendous sense of accomplishment as well as a profound feeling of sadness. What would the morning bring? Joy for my children, I hoped.

Thursday, December 25

A Merry Little Christmas

I invited Sam to spend the night so he could be there when the kids woke up. He declined but came over early. I felt good about how the day went. The kids were wonderful, and Sam and I were emotional but muddled through. As the last gift, he gave me an autographed picture of Laurence Olivier. I vaguely remembered him buying it the last time we were in London, five years ago. I asked about it and he said that he couldn't find it once we arrived back home. As each Christmas came and went, it was nowhere to be found. After the current festivities were over, I told him that it seemed very symbolic of what had been going on in our life together. He told me that he loved me. I never doubted that. That was what made his choices impossible for me to understand.

He said something interesting then. He said that he thought

giving up the sex would be more difficult. He had thought that in the last year, he would reach out for someone for comfort—someone to hold onto. However, he said that except for a brief time last summer, he had been entirely faithful. A brief time last summer? We were only together for a brief time last summer. Was it possible that the urge to sleep around only came when he was with me?

Why did he make such a big deal over it? I had known something was wrong but when I tried to be an adult and talk to him about it, he put all his energy into denial, making me feel like a crazy person. He almost succeeded.

Part of me wanted to call him up and ask who it was. There was a bigger part of me that was just done and would hope for the best for him. I would pray for him, but I would never trust him again. I would never hand him my power again. I couldn't afford to. It was pure self-preservation.

I guess I would look at this revelation as a Christmas gift. One of the most important that I've ever received.

His sister wanted to have a heart-to-heart talk. How much would I tell her? How much did she know? Would she be supportive or ask me to make other living arrangements? It made me extremely nervous.

Friday, December 26

I wasn't exactly sure how Lincoln did it, reading by candlelight. I was trying to write by firelight, and I was certain I wouldn't be able to read a thing. That was all right though. It was the writing, not the reading. that mattered to me.

I woke much earlier than planned and was sitting in a quiet

house. Caleb was asleep on the couch and Faye had slept in Sam's mother's room again. I was sitting by the fire enjoying a sense of peace. I felt good about yesterday. I think my kids had a happy Christmas. I really felt a tremendous sense of accomplishment and for right now, right this minute, I felt like we were going to be fine.

Monday, December 29

Three days at my mother's house—fun, busy, exhausting, and full of all kinds of tension. I really loved going to my father's house because there was no pressure to perform. We could just relax and enjoy each moment. Maybe there was just as much tension going on but I was simply not tuned in to it. I was okay with that.

I found myself still struggling with Sam's revelations about more unfaithfulness last summer. Revelations dropped on Christmas Day. The hurt and anger and feelings of abandonment were all dredged up again. I was furious with his self-centered, self-serving behavior, and I was sad at his inability to remain faithful, become honest, and care for his family. Mostly, I just felt like a lost little girl, not quite knowing what to do or where to turn next.

Tuesday, December 30

The year was drawing to a close. It felt like a new beginning was right around the corner for me.

We spent a calm relaxed day going together to the mall this afternoon. I got a little financial advice from my dad about the money Sam's mother gave the kids for Christmas.

I spoke with Sam tonight about what he said on Christmas

about the summer, and how I was struggling to deal with it. He told me that it was not what he meant to say, that he had not been unfaithful at all. He was only talking about the brief time we were together. Honest mistake or more backpedaling? I had no idea. I only knew that my psyche had taken a beating in the hands of his low self-esteem and his struggle to cover his lies and bad behavior. Would I ever trust or love again? Time would tell.

Wednesday, December 31

New Year's Eve

I had never been so relieved to see a year go. I prayed to God that this new year would be better for all of us, emotionally, spiritually, and financially. I prayed that the end of this year would bring about the end of some of the pain I had dealt with over its course. It was ironic that I ended the year at my father's house, the last place where I had been ignorant of Sam's actions. Now I was trying to be hopeful for our recovery. All of us—Sam's, mine and the kids.

The kids called him tonight to say good night and wish him a happy new year but he didn't answer. They had spoken to him three times in the past week. They called him all three times. He didn't call them or ask to see them. Did they realize? Did they feel abandoned? I didn't dare ask, in case they hadn't noticed, I didn't want to call attention to it.

I hoped the lottery ticket Caleb got for Christmas would win. It would be nice to have some choices. We needed to stop at my sister's on the way home. I would rather go straight home, but I didn't want to hurt her feelings.

Happy New Year

Sunday, January 4

Home again, finally. I was glad we went but also relieved to be home. I had a bit of a meltdown last night. I guess I was feeling sorry for myself. I really couldn't afford to do that. It was catchy. We had all been winding down around 11:00 p.m. after gifts and food and wine and much laughter. Faye began to cry. She was really overtired and upset because she wanted to watch Mama Mia with her auntie. She quickly became inconsolable. We got into bed and she cried about how homesick she was feeling and how much she missed her daddy, her pets, her friends, and school. I snuggled her and tried to talk soothingly to her. Then she hugged me around the neck and said, "Please don't leave me mommy! I don't want you to leave me. I love you so much." She was sobbing and clinging, and my heart was breaking as I held her. Writing it down, I was again brought to tears.

When we got home, I got settled and Caleb called Sam, practically begging for some time with him. Couldn't Sam see how much the kids needed him? Why were they never a priority? It made me incredibly sad for them.

It was 3:20 a.m. and I was still awake. Rather than lying in the dark with my head spinning, I decided to try to write out and work through where my brain was. Again, I was having panic about running out of money. I would get paid on Wednesday and half of it would go off to the electric company. Sam wanted another loan payment. Where did that leave me? He wanted to sit down and talk. Would we talk of emotions or practicality? He bought bread and milk. I bought bread and milk. He paid one hundred eighty dollars on my credit card and I paid one hundred fifty on the same card. Wasted money. More control.

Wednesday, January 7

It would be a year next week. A year since I found the vibrator. One year since my entire world, everything I believed I knew, turned completely upside down. I thought of where I was a year ago and the absolute terror I experienced. I was sick with grief for the person I used to be, but I was proud of the person I had become. It may not have been perfect or anywhere near, it was not what I hoped and planned for, or what I dreamed of, but I was managing. I was coping and surviving as best I could. I thanked God for my beautiful children and for getting me through the last year intact. Now I was ready to wipe away my tears and snuggle into bed with my kiddos doing the all-night battle for the covers. I survived. I was not dead. I was broken but mending. I was proud of how far I had come on a journey I was completely unprepared to take.

A Few Last Thoughts

There is so much more to the story. Sam and I did get divorced. Money continued to be an issue. I eventually sold my business and went to work in a private school. After the divorce, Sam went wild and began to indiscriminately hook up with men and women, causing us to end up back in court, where he was labeled by the court appointed advocate as "extremely manipulative."

Faye was stalked by a guy in a van at the school bus stop. The police were clear that they thought it was somehow connected to Sam's lifestyle.

Caleb continued to struggle. Five years after our divorce, in his freshman year of college, he tried to commit suicide. Now, eleven years after I first found out about Sam's secret life, as I am finishing this book, Caleb is still struggling to get his feet under him.

I left The City by the Sea last summer and moved to a big city in the southwest. Both of my children love it here. Faye, a sophomore in college, is a dancer. She is beautiful and driven. I wonder at her intellect and ability. Caleb is a musician. He is a gifted guitarist with an amazing heart. And me? I am happy.